That Curious Fellow:
Captain Basil Hall, R.N.

James McCarthy

Whittles Publishing

Published by
Whittles Publishing Ltd.,
Dunbeath,
Caithness, KW6 6EG,
Scotland, UK

www.whittlespublishing.com

ISBN 978-184995-033-6

Printed by

By the same author

Scotland: The Land and its Uses, Chambers Harrap, 1993

Scotland, Land and People: An Inhabited Solitude, Luath Press, 1998

Wild Scotland, Luath Press, 1998, revised 2006

Journey into Africa: The Life and Death of Keith Johnston, Scottish Cartographer and Explorer (1844–79), Whittles Publishing, 2004

The Road to Tanganyika: The Diaries of Donald Munro and William McEwan, Kachere Series, 2006

Selim Aga: A Slave's Odyssey, Luath Press, 2007

Monkey Puzzle Man: Archibald Menzies, Plant Hunter, Whittles Publishing and Royal Botanic Garden Edinburgh, 2008

Patrick Stewart: A Galloway Hero, G.C Books, Wigtown (in press)

For Cormac, Ewan and Rona

*That curious fellow, who takes charge of everyone's
business without neglecting his own.*

— Sir Walter Scott

The only known frontal portrait of Basil Hall – in his late twenties – was painted by Raeburn, but no current catalogues of his works include this. Its present whereabouts are unknown, but it was apparently sold to Newhouse Gallery, New York in the 1920s or 1930s for £2,500.

Contents

Foreword vii

Acknowledgements ix

Introduction xi

1   'Inexhaustible in spirits, curiosity and enthusiasm' 1

2   Baptism of Fire 12

3   'I felt indeed, as if it were all a dream' 23

4   A Diplomatic Mission 29

5   'The First Englishman I Ever Saw' 37

6   Magdalene 44

7   Revolution in South America 54

8   Knowing the 'Great Unknown' 61

9   'A Man of Extraordinary Talents' 71

10   North American Journey 83

11   'That Curious Fellow' 96

12   'A Delightful Companion' 102

13   Death of a Countess 111

14   Serving up a Good Hot Dinner 126

15   'A Crusty Old Author' 131

16   'My Dear Dickens…' 146

17   To Discover which Methods are Best 157

18   'As a Captain, Happiest!…' 173

Appendix 1 179

Bibliography 183

Index 189

Foreword

by John Hall (15th Baronet Hall of Dunglass)

I have only one qualification for responding to the invitation to provide a foreword for James McCarthy's excellent account of the life and writings of Captain Basil Hall R.N. and that is, if I may use a present tense posthumously, that Hall is my grandfather's grandfather. As a descendant, I also feel connected with him because I too try to put words together for publication, though with a very different purpose.

Basil Hall is known to a number outside the family because he was a writer and also – to quote James McCarthy – a tireless networker, visiting and corresponding with writers, engineers and scientists whose names are now better known than his, and in many cases making it his business to provide active support for the projects of others, ranging from his attempts to provide material for Dickens to use in his novels to getting a friend's recipe book published.

He was born on the last day of 1788 in circumstances vividly described in the opening pages of his *Fragments of Voyages and Travels*, into an environment ideal for someone who wished to become a writer, scientist or philosopher, since his father – Sir James Hall – played a very active part in the group we now think of as the Scottish Enlightenment, and his mother Helen, was a hugely competent manager of an estate. At the very age when he might have begun consciously to have absorbed this atmosphere, he made the decision – with the full support of his family – to take on a naval career. He was 13.

> On the day of 16th May 1802 I left home; and next day my father said to me, "Now you are fully afloat in the world, you must begin to write a journal" and, suiting the action to his word, he put a blank book into one hand, and a pen into the other, with a hint to me to proceed at once to business.

And thus was inaugurated the alternative education of Basil Hall as writer, with the 'world' as his topic, and with the developing impulse to suit words to the actions required of him in his new profession. He is not short of opinions on any topic that might arise. Many of these opinions I am very happy to admit into my genealogical claims of affiliation; they indicate a spontaneous libertarianism, born it seems from an unprejudiced assessment of his rich experiences, including ones that are explicitly political or diplomatic. Others – and James McCarthy does not spare us these – reflect the unconsidered certainties of class position, and were no doubt encouraged by the success of the paternalistic and pedagogic tone and purpose of some of his publications.

At his best he is very good, because he looked and noticed and, thanks perhaps to his father's gift, developed the skilled habit of recording his observations and finding the prose appropriate to them. He did not keep himself out of these writings, and that is part of their charm. But contradictorily, and there is so much contradictory – I think symptomatically so – in the man and his writings, there is a detailed clarity about his observations that cuts through the opinions and make them feel trustworthy as records.

I am unlikely to be the only one who is grateful to James McCarthy for this account. Apart from the insight it offers into Basil Hall himself, it is valuable for what it offers on the context of exchanges between writers and thinkers at the time and on the practicalities of publishing and funding work. Unlike his subject, James McCarthy does have the skill of keeping himself out of the way, offering commentary and judgements with the lightest of touches, but preferring to allow the sources – whether these be Hall's own published writings or his private letters or the letters to or about him (those for example of Scott, Dickens and Maria Edgeworth) – to do the talking.

I can not think of a better way of prompting a return of readers to Basil Hall's writings than this biography.

John Hall

Acknowledgements

I am very much indebted to a number of institutions for use of their manuscript resources including: the British Library; the National Archives; the Royal Society; the Royal Society of Edinburgh; the Royal Geographical Society; the Geological Society, London; the Bodleian Library, Oxford; Huntingdon Library, California; the libraries of the Universities of Edinburgh, Trinity College Cambridge, University College, London, and St. Andrews; Lilly Library, Bloomington, Indiana, University of Kansas; Somerset Archives and Records Service; the Centre for Kentish Studies; Devon Record Office; the National Army Museum, and the Public Records Office, Scotland.

In addition, the following have kindly provided or indicated sources of illustrations: David Miller; National Maritime Museum; National Library of Scotland; National Portrait Gallery; Yale Center for British Art; Edinburgh City Library; Museo Historico Nacional, Buenos Aires; Glasgow Museums and Art Galleries; the White House Historical Association; and the National Trust for Scotland. I am indebted to the staff of Bright 3D design, especially Martin Tilley, for considerable help with the illustrations.

Prof. James Grayson of the University of Sheffield and Dr. Grace Koh of the School of Oriental and African Studies, London, kindly provided information on Hall's travels in Korea and elsewhere in the Far East.

I am particularly grateful to the National Library of Scotland for their always helpful service in locating both published works and the bulk of the correspondence relating to Basil Hall, and to Elizabeth Denton for permission to access her diploma thesis on Sir James Hall. Philip Davies willingly opened his private treasure chest of correspondence on the Hall family.

To Sally Smith of Dunglass Mill, who is more knowledgeable about the Hall family of the 18th and 19th Centuries than anyone, I owe a special debt for always informatively answering my queries. Kenneth Blues Wilson has most generously allowed me to use several of his drawings. Prof. Mary Williamson of Toronto kept me abreast of Hall's travels in Canada and was a faithful correspondent, while Dr. Irene Mountjoye of Vienna enlightened me on the Styrian adventure.

I am pleased to acknowledge the continuing financial assistance of the Strathmartine Trust and a generous grant from the Society of Authors. I am delighted that Sir John Hall, the 15th Baronet of Dunglass – as a direct descendent of Captain Basil Hall – has agreed to write a Foreword.

To my wife, for her considerable forbearance, I owe special thanks.

Introduction

Captain Basil Hall was an extraordinary man whose lifetime spanned the beginnings of the French Revolution, the Battle of Waterloo and the coronation of Queen Victoria. He was directly involved in both the Peninsular War and in the liberation of South America. His friends and acquaintances provide a roll-call of some of the great scientific and literary figures of the first half of the 18th Century – from Sir Walter Scott and Charles Dickens to the astronomer Sir John Herschel, the chemist Sir Humphrey Davy and the mathematician Mary Somerville – while he also corresponded with several British prime ministers of his day. He himself became a celebrity writer with his popular books on travel and naval life. Despite all this, he is nowadays a largely forgotten figure and if only for that reason, it seems worthwhile to examine his life.

Basil Hall was born into an aristocratic family who were in many ways typical of their time and place, at the beginning of the Scottish Enlightenment. That family exhibited vigour, intellectual curiosity and a characteristic wide range of cultural interests. Yet one of the most remarkable aspects of Hall's life, given his later achievements, was that his formal academic education – ending before he was 13 years old – was perfunctory. Nor was this made good by contact with an educated milieu, since he was away from his family for years at a time from the beginning of his naval career. As the second son, he did not inherit the patrimony of his father's substantial estate, but had to make his own way in the world, albeit considerably helped by his family connections.

Although Hall himself had no title, his family background and influence seems to have given him considerable confidence in the society of his time, and he had no qualms about approaching the most eminent personages. Hall was imbued with the ethos of *noblesse oblige*, being emphatic on the point of duty and responsibility. Throughout his life he held fast to the conviction that background and social rank were important, if not essential, in commanding respect from 'inferiors', although he was by no means an autocrat and insisted on humanity and kindness – allied to effective discipline – to get the maximum cooperation from his men (his views on man-management and command responsibility would not be wildly out of place in the 21st Century). On a number of occasions in his travels, he gained the friendship of local people – even in the absence of a common language – by a combination of charm and sensitivity.

In many ways, Hall appears a complex and contradictory character. He was fiercely ambitious, but not ruthless. He describes himself as lazy, but he was energetic to a fault, verging on the hyperactive. He was praised for the clarity and conciseness of his writing, especially on practical matters (Sir Walter Scott especially commended his descriptions of the interior of a ship and life afloat), but could be numbingly prolix, particularly in his letters. Undoubtedly a man of action, he could also make impulsive decisions which he immediately regretted. Capable of arguing with his publishers over pennies on the price of a book, he could be more than generous to those who needed his help. He was essentially a humane man. Unusually sensitive to criticism, he was nevertheless opinionated in many matters.

On a personal level, Hall often demonstrated liberal and modern ideas (at least in the context of his time) – for example in the treatment of prisoners and education – yet he was in his later life notorious for his extreme political conservatism, and when riding his ideological hobby-horses he could be terminally boring. Hall could not have been an easy person to live with. His frenetic activity alone must have been an irritation to those in close proximity and he could be both naïve and intemperate in his judgements. He was impulsive and blunt in expressing his views. And yet – as the historian Sir John Allison describes – his curiosity, lively imagination and sheer range of interests and knowledge made him the liveliest and most entertaining of travelling companions. He could also be the staunchest of friends.

Hall served over 20 years in the Royal Navy at a time when that service established British supremacy throughout the world: Britannia really did 'rule the waves'. It is difficult to overestimate the importance of this command of the seas in the development of the British Empire – and not simply in terms of military dominance. The navy was instrumental in promoting new navigational methods, in hydrography and the charting of coastlines worldwide, in supporting trading links and diplomatic missions, in the protection of commercial enterprises, in the suppression of the slave trade, and in a wide range of scientific studies from astronomy to meteorology. At different times and places, Hall played a full part in these activities, being both observant and an excellent *rapporteur*, with a genuine interest in science and technical innovation well above the average. Although he was not uninterested in natural history, he was most attracted to the physical sciences such as geology and astronomy. His voyages resulted in the name of Hall being attributed to far-flung points around the globe, from Sir James Hall Island off Korea to Basil Hall Bay in Arctic Canada and on Isla de los Estados in Argentina. The world was undoubtedly his oyster.

Having been enjoined by his father to keep a diary on first leaving home, Hall wrote copiously throughout his voyages, maintaining a veritable library of journals that he drew upon for his published narratives (only one or two of these original journals appear to have survived). He seems to have recruited his brother-in-law and lifelong friend Major Henry Harvey and his younger brother James to assist him in editing his drafts for publication, and later his wife (this could well explain the readability of his published works compared to his often repetitive lengthy letters). These early years provided rich material for descriptions of the steep learning curve for any young recruit to His Majesty's fleet, rivalling those of the celebrated Tobias Smollett. Although a number of these publications were apparently intended for a young readership, there is no condescension and they obviously appealed equally to adults.

Some explanation is required for the treatment of this biography. Although an attempt has been made to maintain the logical sequence for the major episodes of his life,

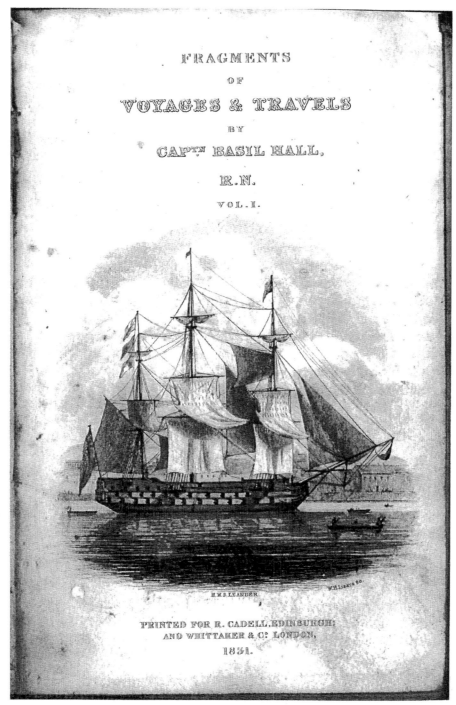

FRAGMENTS
OF
VOYAGES & TRAVELS
BY
CAPTᴺ BASIL HALL,
R.N.
VOL. I.

H.M.S. LEANDER.

PRINTED FOR R. CADELL, EDINBURGH;
AND WHITTAKER & Cᵒ LONDON,
1831.

Hall's first ship, HMS Leander *on which he spent five years at Halifax, Nova Scotia.*
Image produced by Kenneth Blues Wilson.

this has not always been strictly adhered to. For example, his association with Sir Walter Scott and others spanned a number of years, but it has been expedient to contain such connections within a single chapter. Because of the sheer number of such associations, it has proved a considerable challenge to know how best to fit those into their appropriate slot within the narrative. For one of Hall's outstanding characteristics was the time and effort he devoted to establishing connections between people. In modern parlance he was a 'networker' *par excellence*, and he assiduously cultivated not only the 'good and the great' but also those who shared his interests.

The same problem of the ordering of events in Hall's life has been exacerbated by a number of his published works which themselves do not form an orderly time sequence. He was for example, inclined to go back to earlier journals to extract previously unused material for a new publication, such as his last compendium *Patchwork* – different editions of the same original title can contain different material. Hall embellished many of his publications with his own sketches – he was clearly an accomplished artist – and popularised the use of the *camera lucida* as a drawing aid (it had been re-invented by his friend Dr. William Hyde Wollaston from an older device).

Ignoring the popular author Maria Edgeworth's advice to Hall regarding writing – 'to cook a good hot dinner, without inviting guests into the kitchen to see how it was done' – I have inevitably made much use of Hall's many published works in their various editions. However, Hall was also a prolific letter writer and his correspondence is widely scattered, from scientific institutions in London to local libraries throughout the country. Material from American libraries has been particularly useful, for example the correspondence with Dickens in the Huntington Library, California. The National Library of Scotland, Edinburgh, holds by far the largest repository, but there are important sources in the libraries of the universities of Edinburgh and St. Andrews (the latter being notable for the letters exchanged with the precocious glaciologist Professor J. D. Forbes).

Hall was an inveterate joiner of societies and clubs, not infrequently as a founder member – for example of the very exclusive Athenaeum and the prestigious Royal Geographical Society (of which he was a Fellow and member of the first Council of the Society). He was also a council member of the London Geological Society and a very young member of the Royal Society of Edinburgh (of which his father was President in the early years of the 19th Century), as well as a member of the Royal Astronomical Society. All of these affiliations established a network of influential connections.

While many of the boards and committees on which he sat are obviously linked to his scientific and technical interests, it is more difficult to see the connection with, for example, the Society for the Diffusion of Useful Knowledge and its sub-committees on 'The Life of Galileo' or on 'The New Zealanders', both of which include his name; or the committee which deliberated on the *faux*-Grecian monument on Calton Hill in Edinburgh to those who fell in the Napoleonic Wars and which was never completed, despite the eminence of its patrons.

In the course of his travels Hall became involved – deliberately or inadvertently – in a wide range of issues that characterised the first half of the 19th Century. While he intuitively decried slavery which he saw at first hand in America, he stridently opposed Parliamentary reform at home. He took a considerable interest in the working of public institutions, such as asylums for the insane and in education. He was keenly interested and directly involved is such innovations as improved illumination of lighthouses and steam power for ships.

While many naval men in Hall's time made important contributions to the natural sciences – Hall's friend, the Admiralty Hydrographer Captain Francis Beaufort was an outstanding example – rather fewer made a significant mark in the field of literature. The exceptions include Tobias Smollett and Joseph Conrad – before and after Hall's time respectively. If not unique, Hall was unusual in combining a very active naval career with a prolific authorship of popular works of travel. During this time, one wonders how he had time to write in such detail, given that he took his professional responsibilities very seriously.

In effect, his life can be broadly divided into two 20-year periods. The first – from 1802 to 1823 – as an officer engaged in a variety of naval adventures across the globe; and the second – till 1842 – as an independent traveller, consolidating his reputation as a writer but combining this with scientific investigations and a wide range of social activities (his later journeys were often in company with his wife and family, supported by a modest entourage usually including a nursemaid and a governess). What is of interest is that Hall epitomised an age when men of scientific inclination readily accepted the arts and literature as a natural part of their range of interests, while a number of the writers and poets of the time were inspired by scientific and technological developments – as Richard Holmes has illuminated so well in his *Age of Wonder*. It might well have been the *leitmotif* of Hall's own life.

Given that his faults were perhaps equal to his merits, the question might be raised as to why anyone should be interested in delineating his life. This author admits that he has always been attracted to those characters that combined a taste for practical action with a literary inclination, melding poetry and philosophy. Notwithstanding his political obsessions and tendency to be a busybody, Basil Hall was an honourable and open-hearted man. Above all, for me he has a particularly redeeming characteristic: he is up for any adventure and quite prepared – as so well demonstrated by his acceptance of the invitation to visit Countess Purgstall in her remote Styrian castle – to alter his plans and take what comes by way of experience. It does at least make for an eventful and colourful life.

'Inexhaustible in spirits, curiosity and enthusiasm'

On the night of Hogmany 1788 a violent storm was raging on the rugged Berwickshire coast just north of the English border. The old crumbling mansion house of Dunglass – a short distance from the sea – shook and creaked in the eastern gale sweeping across the mouth of the Firth of Forth from the North Sea. It was thought prudent to move Lady Hall, now in advanced labour, from the most exposed part of the house to the less vulnerable landward side. Even the first cries of the new-born Basil, her second son, were drowned out by the howling wind rattling the slates and shutters, not helped by his mother's insistence on having the windows open at all times.[1]

Location of Dunglass

Some six miles of the rugged Berwickshire Coast was owned by the Dunglass Estate, including the romantic Fast Castle. T. Atlom, engr. by S. Fisher.

1

The house lay close to the Great North Road, not far from the ancient Dunglass Castle – then a ruin from the days of Cromwell's invasion in the mid-17th Century, but still in the Hall family ownership. Indeed, the Halls had owned Dunglass for 237 years from 1687 onwards when the first baronet Sir John Hall became Provost of Edinburgh[2] (Hall is a border surname, known in both Scotland and England). Close to the road lay the remarkable old fortress of Ravenswood Castle, some 50 feet high with six-foot thick walls, sometimes known as Cockburnspath Tower – James VI slept here on his way to become James I of England and it is said to be the setting for Walter Scott's 'Ravenswood' in his *Bride of Lammermoor*.[3] The estate included some six miles of coastline, ending at the spectacularly situated Fast Castle

The Hall family Coat of Arms

on its isolated rock outcrop to the north. In 1837 George Stephenson contacted Sir John regarding the route of a proposed east coast railway. Sir John's lawyers were very sceptical about the return to shareholders and thought it would never be built. There was consternation when the route eventually fell between Dunglass and the sea – it was his son Basil who suggested the planting of masking umbrella pines.[4]

The position of Dunglass on this wild Berwickshire coast and the history and legends surrounding the area undoubtedly influenced Basil Hall's associations with his birthplace and early boyhood – which Robert Burns on a visit to the Halls in 1787 described as one of the most beautiful places he ever saw (despite his antipathy to the 'strutting' aristocracy, Burns seems to have got on well with the democratically-inclined Halls, and even more so with Lady Helen's distinctly radical brother, Lord Daer).[5] Margaret Hall – Basil Hall's wife – claimed that the area was the most beautiful of any country known to her. Towards the end of the 18th Century the residence had become seriously dilapidated. Basil's father, Sir James Hall, at great expense (the equivalent of two million pounds today) replaced it with what was regarded as one of the finest mansion houses in Britain – albeit in a variety of architectural styles. It was completed in 1813, the year in which Sir James published his *Essay on the Origin, History and Principles of Gothic Architecture*. The distinguished geologist Sir Charles Lyell described it as 'a very elegant and stylish place'.[6] The dilapidated house was demolished in 1958.

Sir James Hall, the 4th baronet of Dunglass, was an unusual and even eccentric man, but with the broad cultural and scientific interests which marked the 18th Century Scottish Enlightenment. He was described as 'a man not actually crazy, but not far from

Above: Dunglass House after rebuilding in 1813. J.P. Neale, engr. F.R. Hay

Right: Hallway and stairs, the Dunglass House in 1920s. Country Life ipc Magazines.

Basil Hall's father, Sir James Hall. Drawn from an original by Kenneth Blues Wilson.

it … so given to his scientific pursuits as to be incapable of attending to his private affairs'.[7] He had gone on the traditional Grand Tour in the years 1783–5 as far as Sicily. In the course of this he stayed with his cousin William Hamilton (the son of the 3rd Baronet's sister, whose husband – William Hamilton of Bangou – had been obliged to flee Scotland for his Jacobite sympathies as expressed in his poetry). Hamilton's *chateau* was near to the French military academy of Brienne. Here Sir James studied French and mathematics, and met Napoleon (some ten years younger) who had come to the school in 1778 and apparently – even in his last years – remembered him well (as the former Emperor of France told Basil many years later).[8] Sir James travelled abroad again in 1789, taking with him his brother-in-law Basil William Douglas Hamilton, the future Lord Daer after whom Basil was named (Daer was sufficiently sympathetic to the revolution in France to stay on to watch the assault on the Paris Bastille, after the others considered it too dangerous to remain).

Henry Thomas Cockburn's *Memorials of My Time* (Note 1) referred to Sir James as 'the most scientific of our country gentlemen … held in great admiration by all our deep philosophers … a person of great intellectual vigour and considerable originality', and describes his house at 128 George Street, Edinburgh as 'distinguished by its hospitality both to science and fashion' (Note 2). Together with Dunglass, it also housed labora-

Notes

1   Henry Thomas Cockburn (1779-1854). An eminent judge, Cockburn became Solicitor-General for Scotland in 1830 and in the following year was elected Lord Rector of Glasgow University. Among his several works, the *Memorials of My Time* (published in 1856) was a highly acclaimed and intimate picture of Edinburgh and its most prominent citizens.

2   After Sir James Hall's death in 1831 the family appeared to have relinquished this house in favour of the nearby 132 George Street – Sally Smith *pers comm*.

tories in which Sir James made significant geochemical experiments. At the early age of 23 Sir James was elected a member of the prestigious Royal Society of Edinburgh in 1783 and was to be its President between 1812 and 1820, having also been elected a Fellow of the Royal Society in London (it was at his suggestion that his friend Sir Walter Scott succeeded him). He was an intimate colleague and friend of the scientists James Hutton (Note 3) and John Playfair (Note 4), and like them was much concerned with new agricultural methods and improvements, including stock breeds. As Member of Parliament for a distant Cornish constituency, he was renowned for his assiduous research prior to any debate.

Sir James and his wife led a very active social life (he was a noted dancer), entertaining guests in Edinburgh, Dunglass, London and Bath. He utilised the recently improved stagecoach service that provided Sir James with opportunities for indulging his interests in

Basil Hall's mother, Lady Helen Hall. Drawn from an original by Kenneth Blues Wilson.

geology, architecture, and farm improvement.[9] He also travelled widely to meet European scientists.[10] It was against the threat of a Napoleonic invasion that he offered to raise a troop of Yeomanry Cavalry, which would be summoned at a signal from the sentry post established at Fast Castle on the Dunglass Estate. From family correspondence, it appears that Basil Hall was very close to his father, insisting that his portrait be placed in a prominent position in the principal room at Dunglass. He was particularly solicitous during his father's serious illness towards the end of 1818.[11]

Basil Hall also collaborated with his father in scientific matters, as his father's letter (to Basil) of 13 November 1815 indicates:

Notes

3   James Hutton (1726–1797). Hutton's main work *A Theory of the Earth* (published in 1785) completely overturned accepted notions of the age of the world and formed the basis of modern geology. He went on a number of expeditions from Dunglass along the Berwickshire Coast with Sir James Hall to obtain the evidence for his theories. Like Hall, he was a landowner with interests in agricultural improvements.

4   John Playfair (1748–1819). Playfair's *Illustrations of the Huttonian Theory* (published in 1802) supported Hutton's work and was a landmark in British geological writing. He was a Professor of Mathematics at Edinburgh University and subsequently Professor of Natural Philosophy.

…we shall send you also the entire VII volume consisting of two parts of the R. Society's transactions. Now that we have published so much in that collection, I suspect it will be necessary in the same, tho' it must be admitted to be no better than a magnificent sort of tomb. If our papers had once become of late scarce it may come to be worth while for us or some of our posterity to publish a separate collection of what belongs to our fireside … I have met with nobody who has done half so much justice to my views as you have in one or two of your letters from India, when you have taken up the question of the crystallisation of rocks and the theory of granite, etc. I am desirous of stating my new views on that subject and shall endeavour to do so before you set sail.

Sir James then sets forth his theories over several pages.[12]

Basil Hall's mother, Lady Helen Douglas, was a daughter of the fourth Earl of Selkirk and was present at St Mary's Isle, near Kircudbright, when the noted scourge of the British navy, Paul Jones, descended on the coast of Galloway with the intention of seizing her father – finding him absent, he was obliged to allow his people to carry off the family plate, every piece of which however, he chivalrously restored some years afterwards (Note 5). A representation of Lady Helen – around 1791 by the foremost Scottish portrait painter of his day Henry Raeburn – shows a very attractive and intelligent-looking woman, who habitually rose before dawn to spin, supervise the household and busy herself with estate matters in which she took an active part – including the management of the farms, tenanted houses, and shops. She was greatly respected for her energy and competence. In addition she was a copious letter-writer, usually before breakfast, and entertained frequently.[13] It was through the joint efforts of Sir James and his wife that the estates were improved from a previously run-down condition, deploying new agricultural methods so that the means were sufficient enough to invest in the building of the new mansion house in 1807.[14]

Lady Helen produced a large number of children – only some of whom survived infancy – and unusually for the times, she insisted on education for the girls as well as the boys. She and Sir James had four sons and six daughters. The eldest son (John) was destined to inherit the estate, and in time became a Fellow of the Royal Society, while the youngest (James) became an indifferent artist who nevertheless painted a portrait of the Duke of Wellington, employing a *camera lucida* which Basil was later to use for his travel sketches. He also completed a portrait of Sir Walter Scott (now on display in the Scottish National Portrait Gallery) from initial sketches drawn by Basil utilising the same device.[15] There is a record of a fourth son (William) born on 3 June 1800, who was still alive in the 1820s (but no other information has been found relating to him).[16]

During his formative years – and despite his absence from school in Edinburgh – Hall would have absorbed much from his parents and their friends and their place in the unusually intellectual and cultural background within the general milieu of the Scottish Enlightenment – of which they were exemplars. This is reflected in his own very broad range of literary and scientific interests. Apart from his established social

Notes

5   In a letter to Basil Hall from his father of 3 November 1815, the latter says: 'I cannot help at this moment being very anxious about the Selkirks, as there seems to be a ship which set out on the same day with them, put back by two successive tempests of great severity.' (J.D. Forbes Collection, St. Andrews University). The Red River settlement in Canada was established in 1811, but this could have been a return visit by Selkirk.

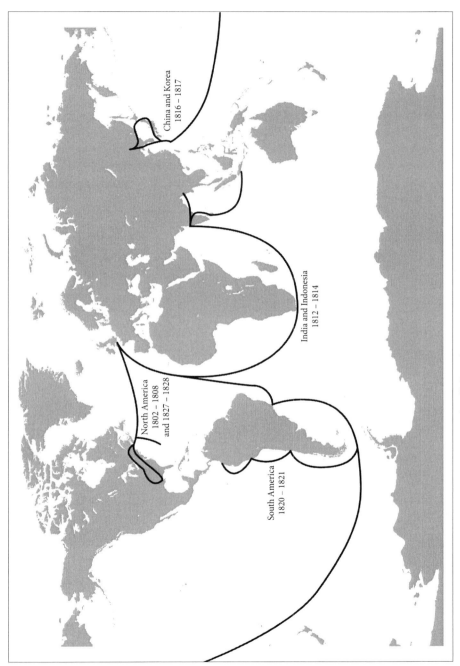

Some of Hall's long distance voyages 1802 – 1828.

China and Korea
1816 – 1817

India and Indonesia
1812 – 1814

North America
1802 – 1808
and 1827 – 1828

South America
1820 – 1821

standing, he would also have felt a sense of security and confidence from the support of his family – his parents being known for their close devotion to their children. Walter Scott characterised the family as 'inexhaustible in spirits, curiosity and enthusiasm' – an epithet which would have applied in particular to their most adventurous younger son.[17]

Hall was to claim, somewhat whimsically, that his coming into the world under the influence of such wind and waves engendered in him a passion for the sea. Certainly as a boy, whenever he could escape from his Edinburgh school he spent nearly every waking hour on the windswept northern shore, or joining the local fishermen in their small cobbles where despite his invariable seasickness, he seemed to be happiest. This was partly because the amused fishermen appeared – at least in his young eyes – to treat him as

Sir Walter Scott. Drawn from an original by Kenneth Blues Wilson

an equal, in contrast to his experience at school in Edinburgh, where he was held of no account and was deeply unhappy. Something of Hall's attitude was much later expressed in a letter to an old friend when he visited her sons being taught: the harsh attitude of their tutor made 'his blood boil' and he admitted that he himself hated school discipline and only responded to 'gentlemanly encouragement'.[18]

The High School – which had educated Walter Scott and Lord Cockburn among many other luminaries of the Scottish Enlightenment (and coincidentally, the admiral Sir Andrew Mitchell (Note 6) of the flagship on which Hall first sailed) – had a high reputation for the rigour of its teaching and discipline. The renowned Edinburgh cartographer Alexander Keith Johnston described how on his first day, his schoolmaster laid out on his desk no less than seven sets of *tawse* (or leather thongs) of different sizes, saying that he did not wish to be forced to use these instruments of punishment.[19] The classes of blue-coated boys were often huge, and senior pupils were used to instruct the juniors. The system was competitive, with constant testing to allocate everyone according to the grades achieved in the most recent examinations – their locations in the classroom reflecting this.

The imaginative and rebellious Basil was like a fish out of water, and his gloomy countenance was noted by at least one master. Questioned by him, the youngster complained that under this rigid scholastic regime, his personal feelings were given no

Notes

6   Sir Andrew Mitchell (1757–1806) was a distinguished Scottish naval officer who was given the North Sea command in 1799 under Lord Duncan. He was known as the trial judge at the court martial of the Spithead mutineers, most of whom were executed. In 1802 he was appointed Chief of the North American Station at Halifax, Nova Scotia (ODNB, Vol 24, 391–392, J.K. Laughton, rev. P.L.C. Webb).

consideration: he was quite prepared to work hard, but to his own timetable – to allow him to adequately indulge his interests outside his work hours (these interests did not include the usual sports and games of his schoolfellows). Not surprisingly, this attempt to achieve some autonomy was unsuccessful, but it does indicate a certain independence of character that was to be a lifelong trait. Hall was an indifferent scholar and all his thoughts were on the sea, the prospects of travel to exotic lands, and the holidays that would release him – at least temporarily – from his bondage. Later, Hall was to say: 'If it is certain that my future life is to be more wretched than this which is now so full of misery, what, alas! is existence worth?' He rejected what he considered the fallacy of these days being the best of life, asserting that happiness depended on oneself doing one's duty, especially if one could do so cheerfully. 'Look on the bright side' was his motto – somewhat contradicted by his downbeat statement above.[20]

At Dunglass he was entranced by the beauties of this dramatic coast, not least the romantic associations of the ruined Fast Castle on its rocky stack near Dunglass, which was claimed to be the Wolf's Crag of Scott's *Bride of Lammermoor*. Hall would later say that after world-wide travels, nowhere could excel the Forth seascape framed by the blue hills of the north. This environment provided what he most wanted: freedom and a degree of independence. He describes how he and a local carpenter's boy constructed a rough raft from logs and waste timber and sailed it across his father's horsepond, using the gardener's mat as a sail. His sense of achievement was a turning point in his young life – he described the event as the first unalloyed happiness he had ever known. The enterprise also demonstrated a characteristic sense of adventure and ingenuity which was frequently remarked on by others.[21]

Hall convinced his father that his career lay in the Navy, which he joined at the tender age of 13. This decision may have been influenced by a meeting (that his father arranged in Edinburgh) with the great hero of the Battle of Camperdown, Admiral Duncan. Duncan not only showed him the flag of the Dutch Commander de Winton (whom had been defeated at the battle in 1797 [when Basil would have been ten years old]) but also an affable kindness to the impressionable young boy. Hall seems also to have been greatly stimulated by a reference in Shakespeare's *The Tempest* to a young sailor boy 'reposing on a high and giddy mast'. This led him to read all of the great bard's works from cover to cover, which says something for an apparently unscholastic boy. Later he was to claim that Shakespeare's knowledge of seamanship was 'wonderfully correct'.[22]

Hall's enthusiasm for the sea was undeterred by the sight of the many wrecks along the Berwickshire coast – a number of them caused by their attempts to avoid the notorious Bell Rock some 30 miles from Dunglass (it was his later friend, the engineer Robert Stevenson, who greatly reduced the hazard by his building of a lighthouse on the rock). Although Hall had no memory of the incident, the story is told of how as a boy he organised a cart to take a boat some considerable distance to effect a rescue of a ship-wrecked crew, and not having sufficient funds Hall successfully persuaded the driver to undertake the venture by a promise of a guinea from his father. This is quite typical of the initiative and public-spiritedness of his later life.[23]

Other influences played a part in Hall's enthusiasms. His father was a noted geologist who had been with James Hutton when he made his momentous discoveries at Siccar

Point on the East Lothian coast, and passed on his interest to his son. Sir James Hall, as President of the Royal Society of Edinburgh, had many scientifically inclined friends and introduced Basil to the kindly Professor Playfair. He had taught mathematics to Sir James and introduced the young Hall to the science of astronomy. With a bowl of treacle, he showed Basil how to create an artificial horizon for the determination of time, stimulating the boy's interest in astronomy, and later specifically nautical astronomy, to which he made several worthwhile contributions.

When the time came to leave home on 16 May 1802 – and he realised the finality of his decision – Basil almost regretted his previous determination, worrying that the experience might be like that of school. With some prescience, his father pressed a pen in one of his hands and a notebook in the other, enjoining him to start now on his journal. This he duly did, recording the unremarkable journey to London to join his first ship. Recalling this, Hall later emphasised that readers were more likely to be interested in the writer's feelings and opinions than in a dry log-book account – an approach which in time was to make him a popular author, not least among young people. Certainly, he was not to be short of opinions on a wide variety of topics. But his description of life as a young cadet or 'squeaker' as they were known, could hardly be bettered in its intimate detail and revelation of life between decks for raw recruits to His Majesty's Navy.

Hall joined the flagship of Sir Andrew Mitchell – the 50 gun *Leander*, bound for the important naval station of Halifax, Nova Scotia – together with a dozen boys of about his own age. When his father left the ship after shaking his hand, and finding that despite his aristocratic connections no one apparently cared a button for him, the sensitive youngster was desolate. He suffered under the dual handicap of being small for his age and speaking with what he described as 'the hideous patois of Edinburgh with the delectable accompaniment of the burr of Berwick'. He was therefore marked out as an undersized 'Scotchman', ripe for ribaldry, not helped by a 'testy disposition.' The untrained 'squeakers' were regarded as something of a nuisance, but were quickly introduced to the harshness of life in the cockpit. When young Hall was displaced from the mess table by an officer requiring the place for his papers, he complained that he had lost his due portion of coveted suet pudding and was dubbed 'Mr. Justice Gobble', from a gourmandising theatrical character of the time.[24]

But there was mettle in the young navyman. In his first letters back to his father he specifically avoids mentioning the discouragements and rigours of his new life, and keeps up a cheerful front. Later, the more mature Hall was to elevate cheerfulness in the face of any circumstance as one of the most important attributes of a serviceman and that even the expression of this could induce real cheerfulness. He was also to make out a cogent case for the appointment of a schoolmaster – preferably combining this with a chaplain – to teach the young cadets, since other officers had neither the time nor often the inclination for this (Note 7). Insisting on 'solid religious instruction' he was very much concerned with the moral welfare of the teenagers and what he described as their possible 'contamination', which may be a rather coy way of indicating possible

Notes

7   On page 51 of his *Fragments* Hall refers readers to an article on the subject in the *United Services Journal* Part XI for October 1830, by Captain The Hon. Frederick Filygrald de Ros, whom he much admires, and after whom he named one of his sons.

sexual abuse.[25] He was a strong advocate of not confining instruction to strictly technical naval matters, but recommended the inclusion of the humanities and arts – which could provide a foundation for a liberal education, befitting young gentlemen. This issue of the importance of social rank and assumed associated qualities informed many of Hall's opinions and conservative attitudes to the end of his life.

References

1. Hall, 1852, *second series,*1
2. Smith, 65
3. Hannah, 69
4. Rankin, 88
5. Miller, 2008, 92
6. Lyell, Vol. I, 158
7. Grant, 1911, 310
8. Miller, 2008, 85
9. *Ibid.*, 87
10. Rankin, 86
11. Magdalene Hall to Henry Harvey 24 February 1819: Private Collection
12. J.D. Forbes Collection No. 33, JFOR/3/29 msdep 7, St. Andrews University *passim*
13. Miller, 2001, 90-91
14. Rankin, 87
15. ODNB Vol. 18, 621-622, Iain Gordon Brown
16. *pers comm*. Sally Smith
17. Grierson (ed.) (1932-79) vol. 8, note 1 Letters of Sir Walter Scott Centenary 12 vols.
18. MS 14196 Letter to Lady Jean Hunter of 24 December 1824 ff. 16–17
19. McCarthy, 24
20. *United Services Journal*, 1831, Part 2, 385–91
21. Hall, 1852, *second series*, 3
22. Miller, 2008, 96
23. Hall, 1852, *second series*, 4
24. *Ibid.*, 15 *et seq.*
25. *United Services Journal*, 1831, 524–526

Baptism of Fire

During his five years with the *Leander* based in Halifax, Hall had an adventurous time patrolling the eastern seaboard of America, with visits to New York and the West Indies (there is a certain coincidence that Hall's first posting should be to Nova Scotia, since the Hall baronetcy was as Baronet of Nova Scotia – a royal money-making ploy in the 1600s and 1700s). His ship engaged in a long chase of the Spanish *Ville de Milan*, which was a prize capture. Here amidst the rejoicing of the British crew at the prospect of profit, Hall shows his sympathetic nature, describing both the dignity and tragedy of the Spaniards, now about to lose their precious cargo of dollars and gold dust – 'the property of an old Spanish merchant, who with his wife and family, on their return to Cadiz, after 20 long years of honest industry in the colonies. The next boat brings the white-headed old gentleman and ladies on board, calm and dignified under their calamity, according to the noble spirit of their country, although totally and irretrievably ruined.'[1]

Halifax, Nova Scotia was the most important station for the British Navy in the early part of the 19th Century. Illustrated London News.

It was the practice to have captured ships returned to the nearest British naval station, under the command of a midshipman, accompanied by one of the young recruits as second in command, together with a skeleton crew. This was considered a signal honour – especially as a first command – and over his five years based on Halifax, Hall was to carry out these duties on a number of occasions. He describes vividly a near disaster when his 'prize' was only prevented from wrecking on the rocks by the timely intervention of its captured American master. Halifax itself, where the British had retreated to after the American War of Independence, had been the most important fortress in the British Empire since 1749 – bustling with naval vessels and contingents of troops. Contemporary accounts indicate an equally hectic social scene, with parties and lavish dinners for anyone of rank. The arrival of a prize ship was an excuse for general celebration, and Hall and his shipmates were fêted accordingly.

During his time based at Halifax, Hall was introduced to long-standing friends of the Hall family, General (later Sir) Martin Hunter and his wife Jean Dickson Hunter. General Sir Martin Hunter (1757–1846) had a distinguished military career across the globe, before he took up the position of *de facto* Lieutenant-Governor of New Brunswick in 1808. He married Jean Dickson in 1797. The Dicksons were a long-established family who lived at Anton's Hill, near Coldstream in the Scottish Borders, not far from the Hall's seat at Dunglass. The two families had been friendly for many years and there was regular correspondence between several members of the family, notably with Lady Hall and Mrs (later Lady) Hunter. The Hunters clearly took a paternal interest in the welfare of the young midshipman while he was in Canada, and kept in touch with Basil and his family throughout his life.

No doubt Lady Helen had asked the Hunters to keep an eye on the young sailor so far from home, and Basil developed a close friendship with them – reflected in long and quite intimate letters which he wrote to Mrs Hunter.[2] Although the Hunters had no less than seven sons and four daughters, she took a very motherly interest in the young midshipman's welfare and kept his own mother informed. It would seem that for his part he was an irregular correspondent with his parents, for on 23 August 1807 Lady Helen writes: 'now I have got into your company again, my dear boy'; and goes on ask for her regards to be given to Mrs Hunter for her friendship to him, sending a copy of Hall's journal in her own hand, which she had faithfully copied. On 3 January 1808 she writes to Mrs. Hunter, thanking her for her kindness to Basil, who apparently never fails to mention the solicitude of the family towards him, continuing:

> I wish I heard of Basil's return from that island [Bermuda] he has gone to. I am not above half pleased that he is so employed. I think it is taking him off his business and employing him in one for which he is not calculated and of which he can have no knowledge. You see he mismanaged matters in the first outset – for by blabbing his intentions all over Halifax, openly before he set out, he infallibly spread the report of himself and need not advert to any one channel of information as having betrayed his intention – I cannot help fearing that if he got amongst dishonest people with a view to detect them he may run some danger. And even viewing the matter in the best light, I apprehend he may be

Hall took part in the notorious incident of the boarding of the Chesapeake when several American sailors were killed. Courtesy of the U.S. Navy.

out of the way, at the time Sir Borlase Warren (Note 8) arrives [the new Commander-in-Chief of the North American squadron] – and when Adml. Berkeley leaves the station – he will not have the choice to come home or remain as circumstances dictate. I long much to see him as you may easily imagine.[3]

This reference to Hall acting apparently as some sort of spy remains obscure. Whatever the truth, the death of Admiral Sir Andrew Mitchell at Halifax had created a new situation. Hall and the other young officers had been fortunate in being appointed to Admiral Berkeley's (Note 9) flagship in the first instance, since they came not only under his eye but that of his senior commanders, thereby having an opportunity of showing their paces in an influential quarter. It is clear that Hall – who from day one on board the *Leander* had shown his keenness by being one of only two boys to volunteer for keeping the four-hour night watches on board – was bent on advancement, and had been marked out as a promising midshipman. From his mother's comments above it would seem that the young navyman might have been indiscreet in talking about his ambitions. There was much manoeuvring to be reappointed to the flagship under its new admiral, and Hall admitted: 'I laid myself out with all industry for this object, and thanks to my active friends at home, succeeded in obtaining a place of the list of the commander-in-chief appointed to the Halifax station.' Clearly, under the prevailing system of patronage, it did no harm to have connections in the right places. Early in 1808, writing to Mrs Hunter from Bermuda, Hall thanks her for her three lengthy letters, asking her forgiveness for his manner of writing in which he indulges himself in riding his hobby-horses – the most important of which is clearly his chances for advancement.[4]

Notes

8   Sir John Borlase Warren (1753–1822) succeeded Vice-Admiral George Berkeley as Commander-in-Chief of the North American squadron based at Halifax in January 1808.

9   Admiral George Berkeley (1753–1818). Having served under James Cook and others, Berkeley – through his political connections – was made rear admiral in 1805 and appointed to Halifax in the following year. It was under his direct orders that the incident between the *Leopard* and the *Chesapeake* took place on June 1807 on account of the *Chesapeake* taking British deserters aboard. This was one of the sparks which ignited the Anglo-American War of 1812–14.

It was Berkeley who had transferred his flag to the HMS *Leopard,* and who gained some notoriety by ordering the infamous attack on the USS *Chesapeake* by the *Leopard* on 22 June 1807, searching for deserters from British ships (or possibly attempting to impress US sailors) while blockading the French in American ports. Three American sailors were killed, and 18 others wounded, resulting in a crisis in British–US relations. The dates suggest that Hall may well have been on the *Leopard* at this time, since he returned to England on this vessel in March 1808, but he makes no mention of the incident. However, a letter from Baron Grenville (Note 10) compliments Hall warmly on the success of the blockade of the *Chesapeake*:

I congratulate [you] on the success you have had in the blockade of the *Chesapeake* and the destruction of so large proportion of the Enemy's trade. I beg you to be assured that there is no one of your friends who participated more in their credit, and I hope I may add in the advantage resulting to you from services so distinguished.

In the same letter Grenville discourses on Canadian politics and the prospects of that country, now that Upper and Lower Canada had been brought together (the advantages of which he had foreseen as early as 1790). He ends with warm greetings to Hall. Hall was then a 26-year-old lieutenant, who was not to achieve his captaincy till some three years later. It says something for his reputation that he should have been addressed in this way by a previous Foreign Secretary – and for a short period, Britain's Prime Minister.[5] Hall was later to write cogently against the practice of blockading neutral ports and suggested that it was this – together with the impressments of American navymen – that gave rise to the British-American War of 1812.

Hall's supervisor Captain Humphrey had advised him not to make any decision on his future till he saw how the admiral was disposed towards him. Hall remarks:

Some days after, I dined with Adml. B [Berkeley] who by the by keeps the command still – Adml B's family are as good as ever and a stranger would not have imagined was there such a thing as a prospect of him going home, but as lively as ever. Saw Capt H [Humphrey] who told me he had last seen Sir John [Borlase Warren] who had mentioned to him that I had been recommended to him by Lady Napier – that if I liked I might go with him.

It appears that Berkeley was being sent home under duress, and there was some friction between him and his successor. In his letter, Hall admits regret that he had made grand resolutions till the facts were known: 'I waited anxiously for the letters before I had any conversation with myself – that I might know what my friends at home wished.' He received a letter from his father and 'was weak enough to tremble at the breaking of the seal of my Fathers' and the prospect of visiting 'the land which gave me my birth – besides many many things I promised myself from returning home, contrasted with the tedious sameness of Chesapeake & Bermuda, Bermuda & Norfolk.'

In his letter to Mrs. Hunter, Hall hints at something which may have been an association with the opposite sex when he says that: 'one of my reasons for not wishing

Notes

10 William Wyndham Grenville (Baron Grenville) (1759–1834). A cousin of Willliam Pitt the Elder and Foreign Secretary (at the age of 32) from 1791 to 1801 in Pitt's administration. He himself was later Prime Minister in 1806–7.

to stay or rather wishing to go, may play across your mind – don't give it weight! It has none <u>there now</u>! [Hall had quoted an acquaintance: "What more is wanting of a young gentleman of your acquirements of insinuating manners?"] (spare my blushes) … I believe there is a young lady in the case so that you may take off the first edge of your finish … by falling in love with her … What can the man mean? Does he imagine I am foolish [?] enough to have fallen in love?' There is a strong suspicion that the lady in question might have been a Miss Callbeck, whose acquaintance Hall was to make again in Scotland – now as Mrs. Dalgairns – whose popular cookbook he later actively promoted.

His father had remarked in his letter:

> …it is a tragedy that Adml Berkeley should be recalled so near to the expiry of your time and since he is so kindly disposed towards you. –––– B may not get another command since he is not one of the party in power. Sir John Borlase Warren certainly just out in his place. I have just seen Lord Napier's Lady who is sister to Harris [?] – she has promised me to write immediately in your favour. And as Ld Napier's family have always been on the best footing I have no doubt she will do so warmly; so that I [?] concur your recommendations to the Adml will be as good as might be looked for.

But later in a letter to Mrs. Hunter, Hall reverts to his constant pre-occupation:

> Angels and ministers of Grace be! What the deuce, me! Why not so surly me – Yes, tis so indeed. An invitation to dine with Lady Warren, by her pardon, Admiral Warren, tomorrow Monday – I can hardly write, the greatship of the honour overpowers my weak nerves. I go however with a determination of refusing to stay, but if they are civil – I shall be happy to come out after … in England and getting Admiralty recommendations. I shall also go with a firm intention of carrying by force the heart of the beautiful Miss Parkins … don't you pity her – what a poor way she is in, I will, after getting her most violently in love – trash her like Amurath.[6]

This is typical – at a crossroads in his career and emotional life – of the young man's rambling immature seven-page letter, with Mrs Hunter acting in the capacity of an 'agony aunt'. Incidentally the dinner at Cedar Hill in Bermuda went off well. He was agreeably surprised by the kindness of Admiral Warren – who approved of his plans to return home – but hinted that he would be welcomed back to Canada. Hall took this as promising for his promotion – it was obvious that Lady Napier had spoken well on his behalf. The admiral asked him in some detail about his circumstances and matters at the Halifax station. The whole tone is very different from the previous despondent letter to Mrs. Hunter.[7]

By 23 March 1808, when he arrived back in England he had been at sea for six years, with only 12 days at home.[8] After being welcomed in foreign ports in their fine uniforms and cockaded hats, Hall and the 'jolly young reefers' were dismayed at the lack of attention paid to them in the home naval ports, where naval officers were 'two-a-penny'. Having lost their flagship, the crew were cast adrift to find whatever posts might be available: some left the service, others sought influential patrons, while Hall returned to Scotland, knowing that in seeking an Admiral patron he was under stiff competition from more experienced officers. Promotion beyond post-captain – which could not be rescinded – was by seniority, but up to that rank was by examination. He makes the astute point that a contender for patronage had to establish a fund of goodwill among the naval authorities, while avoiding any suggestion of servility. It was a delicate tightrope to walk, with many able aspirants.

On the 1 June 1808, accompanied by his father, Hall presented himself at Somerset House for examination as a potential lieutenant and the first step on the ladder to promotion. The many other candidates were frantically reading up their nautical textbooks and 'making buttons' (as nervous fingering of uniform buttons was described), including an apprehensive Hall. He was even more nervous when candidate after candidate was taken, so that having arrived promptly at 10.00 am, it was not until after 3.00 pm that his name was bawled down the oak corridor. He had in his hand a letter from a kindly old admiral asking that Hall be seen early not to inconvenience his father who had a travelling schedule, but Hall was not aware of its contents. Assuming that it might be a plea in his favour, he delayed giving it to the board until after the interview. Despite his anxiety, he answered what he considered to be ridiculously easy questions with confidence and passed without difficulty. However, when the board knew the contents of the letter, he was upbraided for the delay in bringing it to the members' attention. When he explained that he wished to succeed on his own merits, the board jocularly chastised him for harbouring any suggestion that they would be persuaded by anything else.[9]

Hall still did not have a post and needed influential friends at court. In the end, he could hardly have been better served. His father was a Member of Parliament, but had not aligned himself with either of the two main parties (Whigs and Tories). He decided to side with the Tories on the basis of his detailed research into the case of Richard Wellesley, the 1st Marquis of Wellesley, then under attack in Parliament for his conduct as Governor-General of India (Note 11). Sir James Hall made a brilliantly successful speech in Wellesley's defence. As a result many of Arthur Wellesley's friends and family were introduced to Basil Hall's father. One of these just happened to be Mr Wellesley Pole, the Secretary of the Admiralty.[10] Basil lost no time in begging for an introduction and at his meeting 'put his best foot forward', indicating that he was very much ready to go to sea again. Hardly surprisingly, he was shortly given an appointment to HMS *Invincible* – a 74-gun battleship launched that year. In his elation Hall made the erroneous assumption that further promotion – with comparable patronage – would come within a couple of years, but it took some six years of hard work before he achieved the coveted rank of post-captain.

Not only was the Marquis of Wellesley duly grateful to Sir James Hall for his crucial support, but it introduced the Halls to the Marquis's brother Arthur – none other than the future 2nd Duke of Wellington and the hero of Waterloo – who was to correspond subsequently with the newly-minted naval lieutenant.

Notes

11   The Marquis of Wellesley (1760–1842) as Governor-General of British India in the years 1797–1805 had fallen foul of the East India Company in his attempts to discipline their staff, and especially his efforts to control the education of junior civil servants through the establishment of the Fort William College in Calcutta. He was considered by the Company to have exceeded his authority (ODNB Vol.58, 1 – 29 Norman Gash).

But Hall had other ideas:

After the first burst of rejoicing was over, at this extraordinary good fortune, I began to disquiet myself, and not in vain, about my appointment, and to wish that, instead of being named to a line-of-battle ship, I had been ordered to join some active vessel – a frigate for instance … this change was what my whole heart was set upon … all my thoughts and wishes, asleep or awake, ran so entirely upon frigates, that I badgered the tailors' lives till my new coat was made, after which I set off, to take up my commission, at Chatham.[11]

Frigate command meant lower pay than service aboard a battleship, but offered more adventure and the possibility of both glory and prize money, apart from independence of action – by the end of the Napoleonic Wars the frigate captains were considered an elite. Hall was successful in securing a post on board the *Endymion* – one of the finest frigates in the navy and commanded by Captain the Honourable Thomas Bladen Capel (Note 12) – and he was to serve under this illustrious officer for a number of years.[12] In keeping with Hall's notions of who was most likely to provide a good officer, Capel came from a very eminent family – one anscestor was Lord Mayor of London in 1493 – and was himself the youngest son of the Earl of Essex, having been made a post Captain at the ridiculously young age of 22 after only one year's service as a lieutenant.

At Vigo on 23 December 1808 the fleet supporting the British army during the Peninsular War against the French first heard of the retreat Sir John Moore's forces. That retreat began in earnest during appalling winter weather in the last week of December, while battle ships and no less than 300 transport ships under Sir Samuel Hood sailed for Corunna on the north Spanish coast. When they arrived, they could see the French forces massing behind the town. Nevertheless, as a lieutenant aboard the frigate *Endymion,* Hall surprisingly obtained leave on the 17 January to go ashore to visit the British soldiers, just as a last battle seemed imminent.

They appeared far from ready for another bloody engagement, weary and haggard from the privations of the long retreat. Even the officers around their campfires exhibited a 'profound and melancholy silence'. Their eyes and hearts were on the ships offshore, waiting to carry them back to England. However, Hall was astonished that when a furious French bombardment started these same exhausted men sprang into action in their battle positions, no longer silent, but cheerfully jesting with one another while he listened to the hair-raising sound of bayonets being fixed. Hall and his companion – the purser Oughton – moved slightly back, just in time to see the place they had occupied blasted by cannon. In Hall's words, if they had remained there the 'story of this great battle might never have fallen into naval hands'.

The French *tiralleurs* under General Soult were pouring down in their thousands from the ridge above the town – the most imposing sight Hall had seen before or since.

Notes

12   The Honourable Thomas Bladen Capel (1776–1853) was Nelson's signal officer at the Battle of the Nile and delivered the Admiral's despatches overland after that engagement. He was present at Trafalgar. Capel was on *Endymion* from February 1806 to July 1810, in the Mediterranean Sea and off the Spanish coast (ODNB Vol. 9, 985 – 986 J.K.Laughton, *rev.* Roger Morriss).

The 7th Light Dragoons at Corunna. Illustrated London News.

Sir John Moore's tomb at Corunna. The Graphic.

He was in the centre between the opposing forces and was quite near enough to see the close combat fighting in the fields and olive groves around the village of Elvina. This key position was retaken by the 42nd Highlanders (The Black Watch) after an English regiment had been forced back. When a cannon ball fell between the two sailors, showering them with dirt and stones, they realised they were in a very different situation from what they had expected to be as mere spectators. On their way back to Corunna, Hall describes very poignantly the route littered with the dead, dying and wounded soldiers crying out for their help in reaching the ships. He also caught sight of the Commander-in-Chief, Sir John Moore, being carried off the field, mortally wounded, before he was buried on the ramparts of the town. Moore's last words commending his men gave them heart, but his death cast a melancholy shadow.

Hall's detailed description of this battle and its aftermath is an historic document in its own right, representing his most acute and sympathetic observation while he himself was in no little danger. He was clearly impressed by the orderly conduct of the men during the night embarkation while they were still under fire – a situation that has remarkable parallels to the retreat from Dunkirk over 130 years later. All the regiments were allotted specific transports, being taken offshore in small boats – the whole operation superintended by Sir Samuel Hood (Hall became close to the Admiral while under his command in India five years later). By the morning of 18 January some 15–20,000 men had been taken on board the ships bound for England. (The story of his extraordinary meeting with his sister Magdalene's future husband Sir William Howe de Lancey during this evacuation is told elsewhere).[13]

Not long after the return from Corunna, when they were treated as heroes and retold their stories many times over, Hall and his shipmates were anxious to return to the Spain for more adventures. By March 1809, he was again aboard the *Endymion,* cruising off the coast of the Peninsula. On their route home, off Cape Finnisterre in Galicia, they were beseeched by the inhabitants of the small town of Corcubion, to help them ward off the French. Like many others, the inhabitants had suffered the ravages and pillaging of Napoleon's invading army, who simply took what they needed in the way of supplies and provisions without payment, not infrequently at the point of a bayonet. All they needed, the local people claimed, was arms to rout the French, now headquartered at the historic city of Santiago de Compostela.

Although the *Endymion's* captain (an experienced officer) was initially sceptical about what his men could contribute – and more so about the trustworthiness of the Spaniards in any contest with the formidable French forces – he agreed to provide muskets and other arms. The townsfolk were ecstatic and showered the British sailors with praise, claiming them as liberators. Some of the less experienced of the officers almost began to see themselves in this light, such was the wild enthusiasm and bravado of their new Spanish friends. They were eager for some heroic action. But they were soon

The first recorded landing in 1811 by Hall on the remote rock outcrop of Rockhall from HMS Endymion. Redrawn from Hall's Fragments of Voyages and Travels.

to be disillusioned. Among the Spaniards there were violent disputes over leadership, while the peasants – often armed only with pikes and staves – had no notion of either military discipline or the essential preparations for action against a professional army. Hall is trenchant in his comments on their lack of organisation and indecisiveness: at one point, urged to take a ship's cannon to ambush the French at a position described as a defile, his reconnaissance revealed a hopelessly wide valley.

The end was predictable. The local authority had refused the French the demanded supplies, and the latter were not inclined to take no for an answer. Despite the best efforts of the British officers, the Spanish inexplicably allowed their forces to leave Corcubion and they could not prevent the destruction of the town, although many escaped by boat. Those who did not were most brutally treated, with women and children being slaughtered out of hand. The *Endymion* escaped by the skin of its teeth, and only by the failure of the French to push home their advantage. Hall, while admiring many Spanish qualities – not least their sincerity and courtesy – is quite realistic about the military capacity of an untrained peasant force other than as guerrillas in favourably rugged country. But the experience also stripped away, as far as he was concerned, any romantic notions of war as might be gleaned from sanitised reports, revealing its true horror and devastation – especially of those innocent civilians caught up in its aftermath (as Goya depicted so graphically).[14]

On its return to Britain, the *Endymion* continued to patrol in the Atlantic and on 8 September 1811 Hall characteristically became one of the first men ever to climb up the steep face of the remotest island within the United Kingdom: Rockhall, lying about 200 miles west of St. Kilda. To this day, a ledge on this tiny rocky outcrop is known as 'Hall's Ledge.' The description of the event, which took place in a thick mist, indicates how hazardous this enterprise was, with a real risk of becoming benighted on this most inhospitable islet.[15] Subsequently the rock became a subject of international contention when Britain claimed sovereignty over it in 1955.

References

1. Hall, 1852, 64
2. NLS MS 14196
3. *Ibid.*
4. *Ibid.*, Hall to Mrs Hunter, 1808 ff.1–7
5. Lord Grenville to Basil Hall, 14 February 1814, NLS Acc. 10453
6. Hall to Mrs Hunter, 1808, (n.d.) ff. 1–7 NLS 14196
7. *Ibid.*, 15 February 1808, ff. 8–11 NLS MS 14196
8. Hall, 1852, 77
9. Hall, 1852, 83–84
10. Wareham, 33
11. Hall, 1852, 207
12. *Ibid.*, 89
13. *Ibid.*, 108–115
14. *Ibid.*, 116–134
15. HMS *Endymion*, Captain's Log, PRO ADM 51/2324

'I felt indeed, as if it were all a dream'

Hall arrived on the west coast of India in mid August 1812. He had been transferred to the East India Station and journeyed on the old *Volage* as part of the escort of a convoy of East Indiamen, carrying with him the new Governor of Bombay Sir Evan Nepean. He was hugely excited at the prospect of a new continent and an exotic environment: 'No buccaneer indeed ever sought Eldorado in the sky with more fervour than I longed to visit those brilliant scenes.'[1]

At 24 years of age, he was still young enough to look forward to new adventures in what was for him a quite unknown country: 'I was thrown into a high fever of wonder and enjoyment.'[2] He was not disappointed. His first encounter with the sheer colour,

During his travels in India, Hall described the extraordinary physical feats of the fakirs. Engraving by Charles Gold from Oriental Drawings No. 35, 1806. Yale Center for British Art, Paul Mellon Collection.

smells, sounds and cultural diversity of the Bombay market was overwhelming and his rich descriptions express his delight in finding himself for the first time in this great city of the East. He claimed that 'of all the places in the whole range of countries happily called the Eastern world … there are few which can compare with Bombay.'[3]

Hall compared his initial confusion at the sheer diversity of Bombay life to the multitude of ideas stimulated by being shown the great nebulae of stars by Sir John Hershel through his giant telescope at Slough. He continued: 'the dresses, in endless variety of flowing robes and twisted turbans, flitted like a vision before me. The Hindoos of innumerable castes were there, each distinguished from the other by marks drawn with brilliant colours on his brow. There stood Persian merchants with shawls and other goods from Cashmere, mingled with numerous Arab horse-dealers careering about.' Hall felt that he was in a scene from *The Arabian Nights* – or from the Bible. He was overwhelmed by the newness and variety of his impressions, noting that the island 'was almost the only exclusively British possession within several hundred miles in any direction'.[4]

Hall had come to India at a crucial time in its history. The British East India Company – more concerned with commerce than administration – had dominated British involvement there, but after the break-up of the Moghul Empire from 1776 onwards, the British government took a more active role. By the mid-18th Century the French, Portuguese and Dutch had largely lost their claims. There was considerable expansion of British interests between 1786 and 1805 and increasing control over the Company by the government. Richard Wellesley's appointment as Governor in 1798 saw the defeat of Tipoo Sultan and the incorporation of Mysore, while by 1803 Wellesley's brother General Arthur Wellesley had overcome the powerful Marathas (it was Sir Hall who had stoutly defended Richard's record in Parliament). By 1813 – during Hall's time there – Britain had taken more of the country into its possession, so that ten years later it had established supremacy over the entire native states and was the *de facto* ruler of the whole country. He was soon transferred as fifth lieutenant to the *Illustrious* – the flagship of the renowned Sir Samuel Hood (Note 13) – at Trincomalee in Ceylon, where the admiral had reserved a place for him on the ship's company. Hall was delighted. The veteran Hood was a member of a naval dynasty, all of them contributing in their respective lifetimes to the world-wide reputation of the British navy. Hood had fought at the battle of the Nile and was very favourably regarded by Admiral Nelson for his energy and courage, losing an arm blockading the French at Rochefort in 1805. Not surprisingly, Hall was in awe of him, although they had a number of traits in common, notably insatiable curiosity and a hearty enthusiasm for any adventure.

'There was ever observable' writes Hall, 'a boyish hilarity about this great officer, which made it equally delightful to serve officially under him, and to enjoy his friendly companionship; in either case, we always felt certain of making the most of our opportunities'.[5] They had also shared the experience of the evacuation of Corunna, where Hood had played an important part and was especially noted for his personal

---

Notes

13   Sir Samuel Hood (1762–1814) entered the navy in 1776 and earned a reputation as a consummate naval commander. He had fought against the French in the West Indies in the early 1780s and particularly distinguished himself at Abu Qir Bay, supporting Nelson. He was renowned for the respect accorded to him by his officers and men (ODNB vol 27, 936–8, J.K. Laughton, *rev.* Michaeld Duffy).

solicitude for the wounded soldiers.[6] However, Hall's description of the barbaric slaughter of alligators in the course of a hunt in Ceylon – organised for his admiral's benefit and carried out by the local regiment with spears fashioned by bayonets on poles – in the presence of European women, is stomach-turning.

There is no doubt that as a young lieutenant Hall hero-worshipped his battle-scarred superior, in company with many others who served under him. As a relevant aside, the very first writing of Hall to appear in print was the obituary of his commander, which appeared in the *Bombay Courier* of January 1815, following the Admiral Hood's death in Madras from malaria. However, it was Hood who had to break the doleful news to Hall that he was not on the recently arrived navy list indicating promotions (Note 14). Hall was devastated, despite him knowing that his prospects were slender and notwithstanding the kindness and sympathy of the admiral.[7] Although the latter was to provide Hall with one of the great experiences of his life when he authorised him to cross the sub-continent to rejoin his ship, the *Theban*, on completion of repairs at Bombay:

> I felt indeed, that it was all a dream, and could scarcely persuade myself that I was really and truly on the eve of making a journey through the interior of India, and that, in a week or ten days I might really be sleeping in the palace of Tipoo and scrambling over the breach where that formidable enemy of the British name was found slain, under a vast pile of his devoted adherents (Note 15).[8]

Hall set off from Madras to penetrate Mysore (then under the administration of the East India Company) in a *palankeen* – a sort of horizontal sedan chair, of which he gives in his usual detailed fashion, an inimitable description. Hall's account of attempting to get under a mosquito net and his subsequent night-long torment by a single insect is – probably unintentionally – quite hilarious.[9] Typically, he had learnt enough Hindustani to make himself understood, commenting that the learning of important languages should be laid down by the Admiralty. Hall admired the skill and toughness of his bearers and, unlike many of his compatriots, the dedication and general honesty of all Indian servants. It is not difficult to understand the popularity of his travel descriptions of India – where many in Britain would have friends and relatives – which give such an intimate picture of conditions there, in a language which is remarkably modern.

During the week-long Dessera festival, during which he was entertained by the Maharaja, he was astonished by the sheer opulence of his Highness' throne of gold, silver and ivory festooned with huge pearls, while his turban in Hall's words, 'blazed in a battery of diamonds'. Combined with gold ornamentation and more pearls, this headgear 'gave his majesty a slight list to starboard', while 'from each ear was suspended a thick ring of virgin gold fully three inches in diameter carrying a huge ruby'. While

---

Notes

14   In his *Fragments* Hall described the system of naval promotion, differentiating between those in an admiral's gift and the much more political Admiralty List, which depended on patronage. He found out that his failure to achieve promotion at this time was because of a change of administration, resulting in his claims being overlooked in the course of the changeover. He claimed that full reparation was later made when the error was uncovered.

15   It was the Scottish general David Baird who led his Highlanders against the army of the formidable Tipoo Sahib the Sultan of Mysore at the famous victory of Seringapatam in 1799.

this display of wealth was impressive, the visitors might have been less enamoured by the subsequent baiting of wild animals, including leopards and a splendid royal tiger, deliberately provoked by thunderous noise from competing bands and fireworks placed behind the tormented beast.

In a later similar demonstration, Hall asked to put a cruelly wounded tiger out of its misery by shooting it. On that occasion he was also obliged to watch a gladiatorial contest which resulted in severe injuries, if not actual death. Animals also featured largely in Hall's visit to the Raja of Coorg. Here Hall became distinctly nervous when a couple of tigers were brought into the room on very thin leashes, which were then removed to allow the animals to wander at will unrestrained (they were followed by a couple of buffaloes and a pair of lions). It was here also that a tiger and a bear were chained together with predictable results when the tiger jumped out of a window. The *piece de resistance* however was a troupe of elephants imitating the pretty young dancing girls in front of them, while the animals tapped out the beat with the ends of their trunks on the heads of their kneeling mahouts.[10]

More civilised was what can only be described as a week-long archaeological picnic at the famed caves of Elephanta on an island in the Bay of Bombay. These housed an extraordinary series of huge carved statues cut into the rock and dating back to the 8th Century AD.[11] A mixed party of local expatriate residents was assembled to spend some time investigating and recording the caves and their contents. The group included several historians and antiquarians, among them the distinguished orientalist and surveyor, William Erskine. Although Hall himself knew little if anything of the significance of the cave's treasures, he was typically one of the most enthusiastic investigators and was to make a significant contribution to the interpretation of the cave, which was subsequently published in the *Transactions of the Bombay Literary Society* in 1819 (now acknowledged as the definitive description), with fine illustrations by the noted artist Mrs Ashburner.

According to the author of that long and scholarly article, Hall was no passenger, being the only one of the party specifically mentioned. The elephant after which the caves were named was a crude stone sculpture cut out of an isolated rock outside the caves. By the time of the expedition it had partially collapsed, but Erskine reports that 'I had, however, in the November preceding taken an accurate measurement of all its dimensions in company with Captain Basil Hall of the Royal Navy, to whose friendship I owe the annexed very accurate drawing of its appearance at that time' and agreed with Hall's suggestion that the

Hall assisted in an early exploration of the famous Caves of Elephanta (near Bombay), including this grand altarpiece. James Forbes. Yale Center for British Art.

creature on its back was actually a tiger. Erskine was later to re-assess a comment on the interpretation of one of the deities, 'having been led to a more careful examination of it by Captain Hall, to whose unwearied curiosity the present account owes much of the accuracy it may possess'.[11]

Although the party, in deference to Hindu custom eschewed all meat, they otherwise treated themselves well, with fine wines and sherries to accompany good vegetarian food. Some took little interest in the archaeological work, but one personage made his contribution by 'playing beautifully on the violincello'. They hit on the idea of illuminating the sculptures by reflecting the sun's rays in mirrors onto the figures, which delighted the Indian servants. Hall went even further in commandeering his ship's fire engine to spray water on these, removing centuries of grime to reveal the sculptures in all their glory – a typical piece of Hall ingenuity (Hall makes no comment on the quite overt eroticism displayed by several of the sculptures). Altogether, Hall considered the convivial excursion one of the most agreeable of his life, though he was moved to comment on how few of the party subsequently survived the Indian climate and disease.

This temporary idyll was in stark contrast to Hall's experience of a disastrous famine which struck much of India at the time of his arrival in the country. It was started by a country-wide drought, compounded with an infestation of locusts, and accompanied by widespread disease. The scale of the catastrophe in districts such as Gujerat was appalling, with an estimated single survivor out of every 500 people. While the wealth and stockpiles of food in thriving Bombay insulated the city against the worst effects of the famine, its population of 160–200,000 was swollen by 20,000 refugees from the surrounding countryside. The situation was exacerbated by the export of corn to the famine-struck areas where prices were at their highest. Hall rode out of the city daily to observe the effects of this famine, and describes the roads littered with the dead and dying – his only comparison was with Spain after the Peninsular War.

Hall makes the point that because the populace at home had never been exposed to such sights, they could have no conception of the awful reality of these disasters.

At the same time, he cannot forbear from commenting (beating his usual drum) that it is the stability and continuity of institutions of both state and church, which ensure that such events do not occur in Britain – or are at least mitigated by these same institutions. Hall was fascinated – some might say morbidly so – by the daily burning of famine corpses along the shore, not least the careful re-arrangement of burning body parts to ensure complete immolation. Hall did not spare his readers: 'On every side I would see indistinctly through the smoke and flames, heads and arms, and half-destroyed bodies falling down and mingling in a confused heap with the blazing faggots, each pile being surrounded and kept in order by a group of silent, ghastly, hunger-worn Hindoos.'[13] While other expatriates deliberately avoided such gruesome sights, Hall recorded them in some detail in what might be considered a degree of voyeurism.[14]

Wherever he travelled in India (he travelled twice across the sub-continent from Madras to Bombay and several times to Ceylon), Hall wrote about anything of interest, from the enchanting architectural tracery of the giant bamboo forests of Mysore[15] – one of the most magnificent sights he had ever seen, including a carefully observed description of its manner of growth and the extraordinary 60-foot high statue of the Jain saint Gamuta Raya cut from solid rock.[16] He provides a fascinating account of a Hindu fakir ceremony in which the participants were suspended 50 feet in the air by metal hooks inserted into their naked backs, apparently without discomfort.[17]

Hall was later to write at length on the history and British administration of India with considerable insight, but it is surprising that in his *Travels in India, Ceylon and Borneo*, despite journeying over 1,000 miles in Java (now part of Indonesia) he wrote only one relatively short piece on his experiences in that territory. Professor Rawlinson said of Hall's narrative on India, Ceylon and Burma that: 'Hall is the ideal travel-writer. He never wearies his readers; he makes them not only read him, but love him.'[18]

References

1. Hall, 1852, second series, 15–19
2. Rawlinson, 1931, 17
3. *Ibid.*, 20–21
4. *Ibid.*, 24–26
5. *Ibid.*, 6
6. *Ibid.*, 269
7. *Ibid.*, 38
8. *Ibid.*, 169
9. *Ibid.*, 168 *et seq*
10. *Ibid.*, 232–237
11. Erskine, 223–232
12. Rawlinson, 55
13. *Ibid.*, 120
14. *Ibid.*, 115–119
15. Rawlinson, 2005, 223–4
16. *Ibid.*, 218
17. *Ibid.*, 161
18. *Ibid.*, 15

A Diplomatic Mission

O n 9 February 1816 a small convoy of His Majesty's ships sailed from Spithead bound for the Chinese capital of Peking (present-day Beijing). It comprised the frigate *Alceste*, commanded by Captain Murray Maxwell (later Sir Murray Maxwell [1775–1831]) and the 10-gun accompanying brig *Lyra*, commanded by Basil Hall – then still a lieutenant (he was promoted to captain on his return in late 1817). The provisioning ship was an Indiaman, the *General Hewitt*. Sir James Hall wrote to his eldest son John, then in Florence:

Corean Chief and his secretary. From Account of a Voyage of Discovery to the West Coast of Corea (1818).

We have just had your brother Basil with us for a very short time, as he was called immediately upon service, having got the command of a little vessel (I do not know her name correctly) that accompanies the embassy to China. He is full of life & spirits, & by all accounts is now sure of promotion; thanks to Sir J. Montgomery [Sir James Montgomery, M.P.] thanks also I hope to his own merit which seems to be felt. Basil's ship is the Lyra, a sloop of 10 guns. He thinks it probable that they may make use of him as a messenger to send home with any extraordinary news of worth order to stop nowhere – this would really be an exploit worthy of his genius.[1]

The *Lyra* was to complete a voyage of over 41,000 miles in some 20 months. Hall had written to his friend from his Nova Scotia days, Mrs Hunter of Anton's Hill while he was in London, expressing his regret at not seeing her while he was in Scotland:

…my visit was abridged without my wishes being consulted, and I have quitted home after a visit of only 12 days, having seen any but my own immediate family. But now he has the prospect of promotion 'in these dark times' – he accepted the offer of a sloop of war (Lord Amhert's expedition) and will be absent for about two years. Was there not a young Lady send sundry … [kisses?] to me long ago in your letters? If my memory deceives me not, such things actually did take place in sly corners – and some matrimonial engagements which it were safer perhaps to make in New Scotland than Old Scotland. I suspect however that Anny Hunter [eldest daughter of Mrs Hunter] knows nothing of all this but I will bring Ian [?] and Robert to witness it![2]

At that time Britain had an uneasy relationship with China's Qing Dynasty. A previous mission in 1793 led by Lord McCartney had foundered on the assumption that China wanted commercial and diplomatic intercourse with foreigners. The Government which sent Lord Amherst to re-open negotiations in 1816 made the same mistake. The Chinese, who still considered all outside their borders as barbarians, simply assumed that the British had come to pay tribute to Chinese suzerainty. The Chinese Emperor made it clear that he expected the British ambassador extraordinary to pay him obeisance in the form of *kowtow*. Lord Amherst, badly advised, considered this demeaning to his status. The result was that he was not granted an audience in Peking, and his mission fell at the first diplomatic hurdle.

The ships reached Madeira on 18 February, when the *Alceste* went on to Rio de Janeiro, re-joining *Lyra* and the *General Hewitt* at the Cape of Good Hope in mid-April. The *Lyra* was detailed to take despatches to the Governor of Java. *En route*, Hall took the opportunity in a Malay village to describe very accurately a choreographed ceremonial 'battle' between two boys armed with canes to the accompaniment of attractive music, later followed by older men. It was typical of Hall's sympathetic and careful observation of local customs. In late July the mission anchored off the Pei Ho River (the 350 mile river which flows though Peking), to where the *Lyra* was despatched to warn the English Factory under Sir George Staunton and the Chinese authorities of the impending arrival of Lord Amherst and his retinue. Traditionally, the Chinese discouraged foreigners from visiting the capital at Peking and the British Mission suspected that the authorities would designate Canton as the permitted landing place, over 1,000 miles away.

Requiring renewal of their water supplies, the ships found a fine accessible waterfall near Hong Kong Island. Hall gives a dramatic description of fish being driven into nets:

> It was almost dark when we anchored, but the moon, which was nearly at the full, rose shortly afterwards above the hills ... the mountains appeared to form a continuous barrier. The nature of the ground also being black and unbroken, it seemed as if the ships had been transported by some magical process, to the centre of a solitary lake, lying in the bosom of a Highland glen. Soon after we had taken up our station near the waterfall, but before this curious basin was lighted by the moon, and when the most perfect silence prevailed over the whole scene, a fleet of several hundreds of Chinese fishing-boats suddenly advanced, in large groups of forty or fifty each, from behind the islands. They were rowed about with great celerity from place to place, and in each boat two or three men stood in the bow, with flaming torches in their hands, which they waved backwards and forwards, while others in the crew were employed in beating, in the most furious manner, large gongs, suspended to the masts; and to give full force and finish to this extraordinary serenade, a chorus of yells and shouts were set up from all the boatmen at the full stretch of their voices – an uproar which awakened the echoes on all the surrounding hills, and rendered the whole scene so diabolical, that the sailors, astonished and delighted at this sudden irruption, insisted upon it, that a legion of Chinese devils must surely have been let loose, to frighten away the Ambassador.[3]

In fact mandarins were received cordially with the help of much cherry brandy (although, as amusingly described by Hall, some had their pigtails surreptitiously tied to their chairs by seamen intent on fun) and an initial favourable reply was received from the Emperor. He had sent such useful presents as ten bullocks, 20 sheep, an equal number of hogs, 100 fowls, vegetables and many boxes of tea. The ships subsequently sailed through the Straits of Formosa to North China, the *Lyra* being sent ahead to take soundings between the many islands. Lord Amherst anticipated protracted negotiations and directed the *Alceste* to meet him at Canton in November, after he had travelled overland from Peking. Both the *Alceste* and the *Lyra* then proceeded northwards on a voyage of discovery – in Hall's words, 'to fill in the time'.

On 9 August the Ambassador landed at Tacoo about a mile from the mouth of Pei Ho River, where the ships took leave of the Embassy for the next five months.

Hall was interested to explore areas which had not previously been penetrated by Europeans and was delighted to find the Chinese he met along the coast of Shantung – despite the formidable language barrier – honest and hospitable, in contrast to received opinion derived from visitors' limited experience at Canton. Here they were the object of almost overwhelming curiosity, but also kindness.[4] Hall records how he was able to retrieve a lost watch – a very valuable object – which the villagers willingly returned. The ships' company was very short of vegetables but the difficulties of explaining this need almost defeated the sailors, until Hall encountered a cart loaded with green-stuff. Unwilling to accept Hall's proffered money, the carter was persuaded when Hall ingeniously cut off the silver buttons of his coat, which were readily received.

Hall was anxious to show the local people how much he appreciated their hospitality, but they would accept nothing (not even his gold epaulettes, which they much admired)

– until he offered to write something in the form of a note to any later voyager, extolling their kindness. He was escorted to the immaculate local schoolhouse and with some ceremony provided with ink and brushes to write his short letter of praise. Here, as elsewhere, Hall demonstrates a degree of both ingenuity and sensitivity in his dealings with local people.

In early September the ships commenced their voyage around Korea, surveying as they went along this quite uncharted coast. Hall landed at three points on the Korean coast, the first of which he named after his father as the Sir James Hall Islands, identified as Maryang-jin off Seochon County in the province of South Chungcheong. Other names included Helen's Island (after his mother) and Basil's Bay. The British expedition was only the second to reach Korea, following the voyage of Captain William Robert Broughton (1762–1821) in the *Providence* in 1797. They were received in a similar fashion – the local people wanted to see them off their country as quickly as possible, although no aggression was displayed. It became clear that the authorities did not welcome foreigners, for whatever reason – this may have been under the orders of China which demanded tribute from the Koreans.[5] As a result of this and the almost complete lack of communication between the visitors and the local people, very little information on their country and its customs was obtained (Hall was later to be critical of the preparations for the voyage in not providing someone with knowledge of the language, which severely hampered their investigations). Characteristically, Hall noted all the information he could and the beauty of the archipelago, which a later writer described, would have entranced him:

> In these virgin waters, Captain Hall sailed over imaginary forests and for the first time explored an archipelago which he found to be one of the most beautiful on earth. A later visitor states that from a single island peak, one may count one hundred and thirty-five islets. Stretching far away to the north, and to the south, were groups of dark blue islets, rising mistily from the surface of the water. The sea was covered with large picturesque boats, which, crowded with natives in their white fluttering robes, were putting off from the adjacent villages, and sculling across the pellucid waters to visit the stranger ship.[6]

However, there was great danger in such seas with hidden underwater coral reefs. Hall makes a point about the responsibility of command when he says that while his officers and crew were able to sleep when their watch was over, for two or three months he himself got little or no sleep, because of his concern for the ship and its crew's safety.[7]

Hall was greatly impressed by the manners and nobility of the Chief of one district:

> The politeness and ease with which he accommodated himself to the habits of people so different from himself, were truly admirable; and when it is considered that hitherto, in all probability, he was ignorant of our existence, his propriety of manners should seem to point, not only to high rank in society, but to imply also a degree of civilisation in that society. Be that as it may, the incident is curious, as showing, that however different the state of society may be in different countries, the forms of politeness are much alike in all … he certainly would be considered a man of good breeding, and keen observation, in any part of the world.[8]

Loo-choo Priest and Gentleman. From Account of a Voyage of Discovery to the West Coast of Corea (1818).

Although Hall is re-iterating his well-worn theme of the importance of 'good breeding', it also demonstrates a genuinely sympathetic understanding of the old chief's position and he is later quite distressed when the Chief breaks down in tears, apparently indicating that he is likely to be put to death by the authorities for allowing this incursion of foreigners. The ship's s surgeon, John McLeod wrote a parallel account to that of Hall and records the event succinctly:

> The old chieftain hung his head, and clasped his hands in mournful silence; at last bursting into a fit of crying, he was supported, sobbing all the way, to a little distance, where he sat upon a stone, looking back at the officers with the most melancholy aspect. His feelings appeared to be those of a man who imagined some great calamity had befallen his country in the arrival of strange people; and that he was the unhappy being in whose government this misfortune had occurred.[9]

The two vessels than sailed south to the Ryukyu Archipelago (Note 16) (now known as Okinawa but then designated as Loo Choo) and anchored off the island of Naha. Here the islanders, although still most anxious to prevent excursions beyond the immediate shore, were more welcoming than the Koreans. They were polite and good humoured, and after their initial apprehension at the arrival of these strange visitors, increasingly proved helpful, supplying the ships with hogs, vegetables and foodstuffs, refusing all payment. Two local chiefs in particular were welcomed aboard, examining everything with great curiosity but behaving with the greatest propriety, which Hall much approved of.

A friend of Hall, Herbert John Clifford – a lieutenant on half-pay – began to learn the language to good effect, becoming a favourite of the islanders as a result. Hall paints a very empathetic picture of the local people, their complete honesty and kindness, especially to invalid seamen brought ashore for recuperation. He describes their attractive dress and their apparent intelligence, at least the more important personages. One of whom, Madera, delighted and astonished the sailors by imitating their dancing exactly. For their part, the sailors modified their usual 'rough manners' according to Hall, to reciprocate those of the ever-polite inhabitants. They appeared to have no use for money and seemingly no weapons (it was later to become known as 'The Peaceable Kingdom' although the absence of all arms was found to be a myth). Hall makes the observation that in this company, dropping pretensions to *amour propre* and false hauteur paid dividends, as the islanders responded in a more relaxed way to lack of pretension, with the ordinary seamen to the fore in establishing a good rapport.

Nevertheless, as in Korea, the chiefs became almost panic-stricken when Maxwell and his officers expressed a wish to see the local town or indeed to go anywhere other than the immediate landing beach. Throughout their stay, which included a survey of the whole island coast by the *Lyra*, women were hidden from them and it appeared later that this was the reason for the embargo on visiting habitations. They were eventually successful in obtaining an audience with the local prince (whose existence was initially denied by the chiefs) and after presenting him with gifts and allowing him to examine their vessels in detail, became overtly friendly. Throughout, Hall remarks on the good manners of all whom they met, and is clearly impressed with their reception.

He describes very amusingly shipboard parties and picnics at which both saki and cherry brandy, not to mention champagne, oiled the wheels of conviviality despite the language barrier. He gives a delightfully intimate picture of the developing relations between the islanders and ships' crews. All in all it was a very happy visit, greatly helped not only by the courtesy of the islanders, but by the sensitive behaviour of the visitors – Hall pays special tribute to the good humour and patience of Captain Maxwell. Their eventual departure after a stay of 40 days was highly emotional, with tears and expressions of friendship by the chiefs and their attendants.[10]

On his return to China in early November, Hall found that the British mission had been unsuccessful. They moored at the mouth of the river which flows through Canton, only to learn that the British Factory there had been abused by the local authority and

Notes

16   A grandson of Basil Hall's – Basil Hall Chamberlain – became an acknowledged expert on the language and customs of Japan and an authority on Ryukyu. See his work 'The Luchu Islands and Their Inhabitants' *The Geographical Journal*, Vol. 5 No. 4 (April 1895).

would not allow Lord Amherst's Embassy to embark in the river. Captain Maxwell in the *Alceste* forced his way upriver, silencing the shore batteries *en route* and instructed Hall, then at Macao, to follow him in the *Lyra*, but not on any account to engage the Chinese. Hall successfully navigated upstream some 40 miles and proceeded to Canton to meet up with Maxwell, not without obstruction from local Chinese. Taking advantage of a ship sailing shortly to England, he also sent a detailed report of the whole event to the Admiralty, emphasising in particular Maxwell's restraint and justification for his action.[11]

He remained with Maxwell at Canton for several months, claiming that their resolution in dealing with the authorities had been effective, especially distinguishing between the king's boats (i.e. the Royal Navy) and other merchantmen. Eventually Amherst's Embassy was allowed to embark at Whampoa, supported by a show of force from all the British long-boats that could be mustered, the men loudly cheering their Ambassador. Lord Amherst re-embarked at Whampoa on 21 January 1817, while the *Lyra* was sent to Calcutta with despatches. (The *Alceste* was subsequently ship-wrecked in the Straits of Gaspar and Amherst had to make his way to Batavia in a long-boat).

In a letter to the governor of Bombay, Sir Evan Nepean, Hall says that he intends to provide him shortly with an account of the Embassy, reporting that Lord Amherst had sailed from China and was in good health (Hall was not to know of the shipwreck of the *Alceste*). Hall records that while Amherst felt some anxiety concerning the failure of his mission, he was certain that by not *kowtowing* to the Chinese he had maintained the reputation of the British. Hall declares that while the Ambassador was in China their own voyages had been productive. He goes on to say: 'You will be pleased to hear that Lord Melville settled my promotion previous to my leaving England', but this was not to commence before his return.[12] For a lieutenant this suggests an unusual intimacy with Nepean, although he would have got to know him quite well on his voyage to India in 1812 to take up his post as Governor of Bombay, following a number of high Government appointments in Britain, including being Secretary of the Admiralty.

In his assessment of the value of Hall's account, Professor James Grayson of the University of Sheffield is quite unequivocal on its importance, describing it as 'perhaps the last British account of East Asia before the advent of full-blown Victorian industrial and imperial expansion', when Europeans were still in 'the Age of Discovery' – as indicated by the title of Hall's narrative. He commends Hall's thoroughness and precision in his scientific and cultural observations, which are at the same time often sympathetic. In particular, Grayson emphasises the fact that Hall's account is the earliest hydrological and geological description of parts of the west coast of Korea, while simultaneously giving a first-hand account of ordinary rural and political life in a previously unknown part of the world. Despite its incompleteness, it is a primary account of an early British encounter with Korea. Much of Hall's scientific observations he credits to the early influence of his father and the milieu of the Scottish Enlightenment.[13]

Hall's account of this voyage was an immediate success and established him as a popular travel writer with a gift for conveying detailed information in an entertaining way. This may have been partly because he was describing territories and people almost completely unknown to European readers (his narrative was translated into Dutch, German, Swedish and Italian) and partly because of his readable style. It is worth mentioning that the Koreans also recorded this visit in writing.[14]

The *Quarterly Review* said of Hall's work: 'The principal value of Captain Hall's book is in his able delineation of individual character and the dramatic effect arising out of the action and dialogue with which he has skilfully invested the narrative'[15], while The *Edinburgh Review* claimed[17]: 'We do not know when we have met with two more pleasing works … they make us proud of our country, and put us in good humour with our species. They contain a great deal of curious information too; but it is their moral interest that forms by far their greatest attraction.'[16] The other work referred to is by John McLeod, who as ship's surgeon wrote his own account, very similar to that of Hall (Note 17). The eminent Alexander von Humboldt in his groundbreaking *Cosmos* said that Hall's description of Sulphur Island (or Bird Island of the Japanese) was 'admirably described'.[18]

The Edinburgh publisher, Archibald Constable, realising the appeal of the first two editions, succeeded in bringing out a popular third edition in 1826 (omitting the original technical appendices), as the centrepiece of his much-heralded first *Miscellany* with a dedication by King George and composed by no less than Sir Walter Scott. That acute observer of Edinburgh life, Elizabeth Grant of Rothiemurchus, in her acclaimed *Memoirs* declared that her sister Jane had 'carried off' one of Elizabeth's intended social captures, Basil Hall: 'He had this very year [1817] returned from Loo Choo, had published his book, brought home flat needles, and cloth made of wood, and a funny cap which he put on very good humouredly, and chop-sticks with which he ate very obligingly; in short he did the polite voyager to no end. Jane was quite taken with him, so was Jane Hunter; Margaret Hunter and I used to be amused with him, and wonder how they could wait on the lion so perseveringly.'[19] The Margaret Hunter referred to was in fact Basil Hall's future wife.

References

1. Sir James Hall to John Hall, 12 November 1815, GD206/2/319/3
2. Hall to Mrs Hunter, 5 November 1815, NLS MS 14196, ff.12–13
3. Hall, 1826, 23
4. *Ibid.*, 45
5. Koh, 124
6. Griffis, 197
7. *The Scotsman*, 16 May 1829, 3
8. Hall, 1826, 94
9. McLeod, 44
10. Hall, 1826, 119–267
11. Lt. Basil Hall, 1 December 1816 to Admiralty from Canton, ref. 152M/C1816/OF4
12. Hall to Sir Evan Nepean, 1 April 1817, Lilly Library, Bloomington, Indiana
13. Grayson, 1–18
14. Paik, *passim*
15. *Quarterly Review*, Vol 18, No. 36 (January 1818) 308–324
16. *Edinburgh Review*, Vol 29, 1818, 475–97
17. McLeod, *passim*
18. Humboldt, 277
19. Grant, 110

Notes

17 The *Edinburgh Review* article is preceded by another article that reviews *The Journal of the Proceedings of the Late Embassy to China* by Henry Ellis, Third Commissioner to the Embassy (433–453), which is a damning indictment of the whole basis of this mission and of British attitudes towards Far Eastern countries (not least China) and in particular the corruption of the East India Company.

'The First Englishman I Ever Saw'

O n 11 August 1817, on his return from the Far East expedition, Hall dropped the *Lyra's* anchor off St. Helena. For weeks previously all on board had been eagerly anticipating seeing the former-Emperor Napoleon Bonaparte, now imprisoned on the island, although only a very select few would have this opportunity. According to Hall: 'as a curious fact in the history of curiosity … by which every individual on board, high as well as low, was infinitely more occupied about this one man, than he had been with all the incidents of our singular voyage put together – I landed with two gentlemen [Capt. Harvey of the Madras Army and Lieutenant Clifford of the Navy] who were passengers in my ship, in a state of greater anxiety than I ever experienced before or since.'[1] Part of this anxiety was the knowledge that Bonaparte could be difficult. If the names laid before him and the account given of what they stood for did not interest him, he declined the honour. Count Bertrand, who attended to these matters, was civil but firm, indicating that the Emperor was not inclined to see them.[2] Countess Bertrand – to whom the officers had been presented in the Emperor's anteroom – was hopeful and encouraged them to try again. Several days passed without a response.

Although Hall's name had been mentioned to Bonaparte, he had apparently taken not the slightest notice of the communication and Hall spent a sleepless night. When

Longwood – Napoleon's crumbling, rat infested residence on St. Helena where Hall met him. Unknown artist.

Unusual portrait of Napoleon as a prisoner on St. Helena by James Sant,
RSA. Courtesy of Culture and Sport, Glasgow (Museums).

the disappointed party was riding off for the last time, Hall happened to mention that his father had met Napoleon at Brienne, which quite changed Napoleon's attitude. He was interested in everything connected with Brienne, where he had received his own military training. They arranged to meet the great man at his gloomy rat-infested residence 'Longwood' on the following morning – Hall on his own and Captains Clifford and Harvey together (Note 18).

Notes

18   In his book *The Dark Room at Longwood: A Voyage to St. Helena*, Jean-Paul Kaufmann gives an intimate picture of Napoleon's ménage at 'Longwood' and the affect on him of seeing there the Emperor's unsettling portrait *St. Helena - The Last Phase*. This striking – and relatively little-known – portrait of Napoleon executed in oil on canvas by the English artist James Sant RA, (1820–1916) was shown at the Royal Academy in 1901 and is probably drawn from other previous portraits. It was intended to illustrate the book of the same name by Lord Roseberry describing Napoleon's time on St. Helena, and was gifted to the Glasgow Art Gallery in 1907.

Hall says: 'As the opportunities which his exalted position had given Napoleon of obtaining information on almost every subject, and his vast power of rapid and correct observations, had rendered it a matter of much difficulty to place anything before him totally new, I considered myself fortunate in having to speak of beyond the mere common-places of a formal interview.' He was relieved that Bonaparte was fascinated by the Far East and cross-examined Hall on the position of Loo-choo in relation to bearings from Manila and Japan, accurately deducing its location. Hall had taken with him Havell's drawings of the scenery and costumes of Korea and Loo-choo, which Bonaparte examined carefully. He then went on to enquire very minutely about the islands, from climate to agriculture and the customs of the inhabitants 'in a manner which exceeded everything I have met with in any other instance', such was his probing. Hall felt quite exposed, but full of admiration for this active and persistent mind – Napoleon in fact 'robbed me of my story' by anticipating his conclusions. What thoroughly perplexed Bonaparte was Hall's assertion that the islanders carried no offensive weapons – whether muskets, swords or spears – and he declared his disbelief that the inhabitants did not conduct any wars. However, Hall had been misled on this, perhaps out of a desire to see good in everything concerning those hospitable people. When told that the inhabitants knew nothing of Europe, Hall added that neither did they anything about Bonaparte – Napoleon was apparently highly amused 'by this piece of impudence'.

Hall gives an intimate picture of Bonaparte's appearance, describing his physique as:

> firm and muscular, not as corpulent as he expected, but there was not the least trace of colour in his cheeks; in fact his skin was more like marble than ordinary flesh. Not the smallest trace of a wrinkle was discernible on his brow, nor an approach to a furrow on any part of his brow … His health and spirits, judging from appearances, were excellent … he waited with great patience and kindness for my answers to his questions … the brilliant and sometimes dazzling expression of his eye could not be overlooked … it is impossible to imagine an expression of more entire mildness, I may call it almost of benignity and kindliness, than that which played over his features during the whole interview.

Hall had been astonished by Bonaparte's remembrance of his father, which had clearly opened the doors for this rare interview. Bonaparte said: 'I remember him clearly – he was very fond of mathematics and liked to converse on the subject'. He informed the captain that his father was the first Englishman he ever saw and that, 'I have recollected him all my life on that account'. Bonaparte then asked: 'Have you ever heard your father speak of me?' Hall's account states: 'I replied 'Very often.' Upon which he said in a quick sharp tone, 'What does he say of me?' I said that I had often heard him express great admiration of the encouragement he had always given to science when he was Emperor of the French. He laughed and nodded repeatedly, as if gratified by what was said … His next question was: 'Did you ever hear your father express any desire to see me?' I replied that I had often heard him say there was no man alive so well worth seeing, and that he had strictly enjoined me to wait upon him if ever I should have the opportunity.' Hall had to explain his father's duties and responsibilities, referring to his Presidency of the Royal Society of Edinburgh: Bonaparte then asked him in great detail about the proceedings of the society. He went to enquire closely about Sir James's other

Notes
of an Interview with Bonaparte,
at S.t Helena, on the
13.th August 1817.—

I arrived at S.t Helena in H.M.S. Lyra, on
the 11.th of August, about 3 o'Clock.— I immediately landed,
and having waited upon Rear Admiral Plampin, the
Commander in Chief, proceeded to Plantation House, the
residence of the Governor.— As I had known Sir Hudson
and Lady Lowe, in England, and had been invited to live
at their house, I hoped thro' their influence to succeed
in seeing Bonaparte—

I was therefore disappointed on finding
that the Governor and Bonaparte, were upon such terms
as prevented Sir Hudson's asking it as a favor of him to
receive any stranger. But he undertook to do all that could
be done with propriety, and immediately wrote a note to
Captain Blakeney, the officer charged with the immediate care
of Bonaparte, saying that I had arrived from China, and
the East Indies, and was desirous of waiting upon the
General.— Sir Hudson desired that my offer should be

wall is uncertain; but it would be an amusing question to put to Bonaparte himself. —

*   *   *

My two Companions were received together after I left the Room. He put a few common place questions, and dismissed them, — he was no less polite however to them, than he had been to me. — Observing Crape on captain Harvey's arm, he begged to know for whom he was in mourning — and on learning that it was for his father, he appeared sorry — or at all events testified by his manner that degree of respect for the feelings of his guest, which a well bred person is at all times disposed to pay — Particularly to a person in distress. —

Basil Hall
Captⁿ R.N.

Above and opposite: Original record of Hall's interview with Napoleon. National Army Museum, Chelsea.

children, their ages, occupations, etc, ensuring that he got everything correctly. Hall's father recalled that while he was at Brienne, one of the students had blown up a garden wall with gunpowder, but was unsure of whether this was Bonaparte's doing.

Bonaparte was obviously impressed that Hall spoke such excellent French, as he asked how long he had been in France. When Hall replied that he had never been in that country in his life, Bonaparte then asked 'A prisoner then?' An embarrassed Hall had to admit that his teachers were French officers captured by the ships he had served in (Hall had been very critical of Bonaparte's policy of not allowing prisoner repatriation or exchange, resulting in many deaths and much unnecessary misery on both sides).

Perhaps even more embarrassing was Bonaparte's query as to why he was not married. Hall tried to turn the question by averring that he was 'not in circumstances to marry'. This equally perplexed both Bonaparte and Count Bertrand and they pressed Hall, who then had to admit that he was too poor to marry. This apparently greatly amused the Emperor, who laughed heartily and noisily, such that Clifford and Harvey waiting in an adjoining room could scarcely believe their ears. As for Hall, he joined in the joke against himself, 'though to say the truth I did not altogether see the humorous point of the joke'. Clifford and Harvey were later granted a few minutes formal audience.

Hall's vividly described interview with the great man created something of a sensation in Britain and Sir Walter Scott had no hesitation in including it in his monumental *Life of Napoleon*. Scott – referring to Captain Maitland's narrative of his reception of Bonaparte on board the *Bellepheron* at the time of Bonaparte's surrender (which Hall had sent to him) – said: '[Hall] has made many excellent corrections in point of stile. But he has been hypercritical in wishing – in so important a matter where everything depends on accuracy – this expression to be altered for delicacy's sake, that to be omitted for fear of giving offence and that other to be abridged for fear of being tedious. The plain sailor's narrative for me, written on the spot and bearing in its minuteness the evidence of its notoriety.' This narrative (published in 1826 as the *Narrative of the Surrender of Buonaparte*) had been lent to Scott by Hall. Captain Frederick Maitland (1777–1839) received Bonaparte's surrender on board HMS *Bellepheron* in July 1815.[3] If Hall had given a unique and intimate picture of Bonaparte, the interview also said something about Hall's *sang froid* in a situation which would have discomfited many.

In August 1818 Hall wrote to the Governor of St. Helena, Lieutenant-General Sir Hudson Lowe, who had the dismal task of being Bonaparte's jailor, asking that a book by his father should be forwarded to Bonaparte as a present (Bonaparte loathed the impersonal Lowe). In the following year Hall wrote again concerning Sir Hudson Lowe's young step-daughter, Charlotte, who was also the daughter of Lady Susan Lowe (née de Lancey).[4] Hall had made travel arrangements with his sister Magdalene as a companion and very unusually arranged for his own steward to accompany the ladies to the island.

My Dear Sir,

I received your letter of 4th of May only 2 days ago. I was very happy to find that you had at last received my letter about Miss Charlotte Johnston and that you were satisfied with what had been done. Lady de Lancey – who is here – is writing to Lady Lowe in reply to her letter of 17 May and Charlotte is also writing .Therefore I need say nothing about things. Except that they are both in excellent health and Charlotte, poor thing, is in great delight at the prospect of seeing you again. Her heart is very much at St Helena and I have been exceedingly pleased and approve the pains which Magdalene has taken to keep Charlotte's affections steadily and almost exclusively towards her parents. I think you will be pleased with Charlotte who has made good use of her time and her opportunities. I have no doubt we shall be able to arrange everything about her passage in a satisfactory way and that in a few months you will have her safe and snug in your island.

I need not say with what deep interest I read everything coming from St Helena. I feel for all your trouble and anxiety inseparable I fear from your situation. But it is one of high duties, and though it has nothing noble or glorious in a military sense yet it is one of the greatest distinction & importance.

I beg to offer my best respects & remembrance to Lady Lowe & Susan.[5]

Hall had been marginally involved in the Napoleonic Wars through his naval activity in the course of the Peninsular War and in the capture of French ships off North America. He also had an indirect association with the Napoleon's nemesis, the Duke of Wellington, victor of Waterloo, and through his brother-in-law, Colonel William de Lancey – Wellington's quartermaster-general at that great battle. De Lancey was mortally wounded within feet of Wellington and which he described to Hall's brother James while the latter was painting the great general's portrait.

On 28 June 1837 Queen Victoria was crowned, and many of the Hall family were in London for the Coronation, for which Hall had obtained tickets. On 1 July of the same year, one of Hall's nieces wrote to Lady Hall: 'Uncle Basil has invited us to go with him on Monday 18th to Aspley House, to see the Duke's plate laid out for the Waterloo Dinner.' There they were joined by Hall, his brother James, Lady Hunter and the Arbuthnots and they also saw the statue of Napoleon himself (Apsley House – famously known as No. 1, London – housed the Wellington Museum with its huge collection of paintings, silver, porcelain and furniture given to the Duke in honour of his victory and where the Waterloo Dinner was given annually). As the Duke was still in residence, it says something for Hall's accreditation that he was given this privileged access.

References

1. Hall, 1826, Vol.1, 303–304
2. *Mariner's Mirror*, Vol. 66, 355
3. Anderson, 1972, 110.n.
4. Basil Hall to Lieutenant-general Sir Hudson Lowe, 2 July 1818, NLS Acc. 118955
5. Basil Hall to Lieutenant-General Sir Hudson Lowe, 2 July 1818, British Library ADD 45.517 f47

Magdalene

One of Basil's sisters plays a particular part in his story. Magdalene, born in 1793, was five years younger than Basil and a favourite sister. In Scott's *The Bride of Lammermoor* (the Lammermuir Hills lie immediately to the west of Dunglass) the description of the central character of Lucy Ashton bears a very close resemblance to what is known of Magdalene's appearance and personality. She was 'exquisitely beautiful, shy and gentle in disposition.'[1] Miller claims she would have been totally at home in a Jane Austen novel.[2] Both the fictional character and the very real Magdalene shared tragic lives. She was very much involved in her mother's hectic social activities, travelling regularly with her to the fashionable spas of England and was presented at Court in London. In a letter to Charles Dickens, Basil remembered her:

Magdalene Hall – Basil Hall's sister – whose narrative of the death of her first husband at Waterloo impressed many authors of the day. Drawn from an original by Kenneth Blues Wilson.

> the days when she was a girl and I a boy – playing in the grass walks of Dunglass before I went back and then,
>
> again, when she was growing up and I returned from the coast of Spain, in the war, and found her and her sister (my greatest friend in those days) trigged up in Spanish hats by way of showing her national sympathy with the patriots.[3]

Hall was a young naval officer during the Peninsular War, directly involved in the embarkation of troops in January 1809 after the retreat to Corunna. As escort to the transports, his ship the *Endymion* was one of the last to leave, when it was approached by a small Spanish boat with two or three British officers, asking where transport Number 139 – their allotted ship – was. By this time, the remainder of the fleet was well offshore and the captain was obliged to take them on board. Hall takes up an astonishing story:

> I was so much taken with one of these officers, Colonel De Lancey (Note 19), that I urged him to accept such accommodation as my cabin and wardrobe afforded. He had come to us without one stitch of clothes beyond what he then wore, and these, to say the truth, not in the best condition at the elbows and other angular points of his frame … he was as fine a fellow as ever lived, and I had much pleasure in taking care of him during the passage. We shortly became great friends; but on reaching England we parted, and I never saw him more. Of course he soon lost sight of me; but his fame rose high, and as I often read his name in the Gazettes during the subsequent campaigns in the Peninsula, I looked forward with a gradually increasing anxiety to the renewal of an acquaintance begun so auspiciously. At last I was gratified by a bright flash of hope in this matter, which went out, alas! As speedily as it came. Not quite six years after the events here related, I came home from India in command of a sloop of war. Before entering the Channel, we fell in with a ship which gave us the first news of the battle of Waterloo, and spared us a precious copy of the Duke of Wellington's despatch. Within five minutes of landing at Portsmouth, I met a near relation of my own, which seemed a fortunate *rencontre*, for I had not received a letter from home for nearly a year, and I eagerly asked him, 'What news of all friends?'
>
> 'I suppose you know of your sister's marriage?'
>
> 'No, indeed! I do not! Which sister?'
>
> He told me.
>
> 'But to whom is she married?' I cried out, with intense impatience, and wondering greatly that he had told me this at once.
>
> 'Sir William De Lancey was the person,' he answered. But he spoke not in the joyous tone that befits such communications.
>
> 'God bless me!' I exclaimed,' I am delighted to hear that. I know him well; we picked him up in a boat at sea, after the battle of Corunna, and I brought him home in my cabin in the *Endymion*. I see by the despatch, giving an account of the late victory, that he was badly wounded. How is he now? I observe by the postscript of the Duke's letter, that strong hopes are entertained of his recovery.'
>
> 'Yes' said my friend, 'that was reported, but could hardly have been believed. Sir William was mortally wounded, and lived not quite a week after the action. The only comfort about this sad matter is, that his poor wife, being near the field at the time, joined him immediately after the battle, and had the melancholy satisfaction of attending her husband to the last.'[4]

Magdalene was unaware that her fiancé had met Basil until the day before the wedding, as he relates:

> …in 1814, probably, De Lancey came to Scotland on the Staff, became acquainted with our family & continued the acquaintance so far as to be actually on the eve of his

---

Notes

19   Colonel Sir William Howe De Lancey – who had fought with distinction at the great battles in the Peninsular War – was one of the first professional staff officers in the British Army. He and Wellington had known each other since the 1790s.

marriage to my sister without his even having heard that she had a brother at sea or having my name mentioned! ... so it was on the eve, I believe within 24 hours of the marriage, Sir William said 'I once knew an officer of your name – I wonder if he could be any relative? – I have lost sight of him though he was very kind to me.' A great shout and laugh was now the answer upon his mentioning the Christian name of his old friend.[5]

The wedding took place in Greyfriars Church, Edinburgh on 5 April 1815. [6] Within six weeks, her new husband was dead. The Duke of Wellington, in his terse military way, described the fatal wounding of his Quarter-Master General at the battle of Waterloo on 18 June 1815, to Basil's younger brother James, then sketching the Duke for a portrait some 20 years later:

> …poor fellow, I remember well he was standing next beside me when he was struck. Yes. On horseback. His horse was shot right through the back & De Lancey was thrown violently forward beside me when he was struck … I thought he was killed. I ordered him to be taken carefully to the rear. I reported him killed. I remember two days afterwards when returning through the village of Waterloo I went to see De Lancey. I found him lying on his back but in very good spirits. I told him he would have the pleasure & advantage – like the man in Castle Rackrent – of hearing what people said of him after his death, for I had reported him dead. He seemed to enjoy the joke.[7]

It was no joke. Ten days later, De Lancey expired in the arms of his wife. Amidst the post-battle chaos she had made her way from Brussels to the broken-down hovel in the village of Mont St John, where he lay and for a week she nursed him devotedly and tenderly, under conditions of great suffering and deprivation. She herself showed her courage and resolve, which comes through clearly in the intimate narrative which she wrote of his final days, lying down to sleep with him on his last night to give him comfort. She had written this at Hall's urging and for his personal information.[8] (Hall was known to have helped Magdalene considerably in overcoming the death of her husband, and this may have been one of his stratagems to achieve that). He had several copies made of this remarkable account, which greatly moved two of the greatest novelists of the time, Charles Dickens and Sir Walter Scott, to whom he showed it in confidence. As late as 13 February 1841 Hall had sent the account to Dickens which deeply affected the author. He had asked that Dickens keep its contents 'to his own fireside circle and not to speak of it'.[9] On 16 March 1841 Dickens wrote:

My Dear Hall

– for I see that it must be *juniores priores*, and that I must demolish the ice at a blow [Dickens, 24 years younger than Hall, had been in the habit previously of addressing the older man as 'My Dear Sir'] I have not had courage until last night to read Lady de Lancey's narrative and but for your letter I should not have mustered it even then. One glance at it when (through your kindness) it first arrived here, impressed me with a foreboding of its terrible truth; and I really have shrunk from it, in pure lack of heart.

After working at Barnaby [Rudge] all day, and wandering about the most wretched and distressful streets for a couple of hours in the evening – searching for some pictures I wanted to build upon – I went at it, about ten o'clock. To say that reading that most astonishing and tremendous account has constituted an epoch in my life – that I never shall forget the lightest word of it – that I cannot throw the impression aside and never saw anything so real, so touching, and so actually present before my eyes, is nothing. I am husband and wife, dead man and living woman, Emma and General Dundas, doctor and bedstead – everything and everybody (but the Prussian officer - damn him) all in one. What I have always looked upon as masterpieces of powerful and affecting description, seem as nothing in my eyes. If I live for fifty years, I shall dream of it every now and then from this hour to the day of my death with the most frightful reality. The slightest mention of a battle will bring the whole thing before me. I shall never think of the Duke any more, but as he stood in his shirt with the officer in full dress uniform (Note 20), or as he dismounted from his horse when the gallant man was struck down.

Coming from Dickens, this is a very remarkable and emotional admission concerning a true-life narrative that greatly affected anyone who read it. The renowned diarist Thomas Moore – whom Hall much admired for his work – declared that Lady de Lancey's account kept him up reading till morning and that he 'made himself quite miserable, and went to sleep, I believe crying'.[10] Dickens goes on further at some length, telling how his own wife, on reading it, was forced to retire in 'an agony of grief'. He then says that if Hall should ever consider letting a friend copy it for himself, he hoped 'you will bear me in your thoughts'. The background to this is that Hall had very much wanted his sister's harrowing story to be published, as did Sir Walter Scott. Scott had raised the very delicate question of the publication of Lady de Lancey's narrative. Scott declared that: 'I never read anything which affected my own feelings more strongly or which, I am sure, would have a deeper interest on those of the public.' But he was most concerned that its publication might cause distress to members of the family, indicating that Hall was the only person who could make a judgement on this. Scott thought that this poignant story was a peculiarly important one in illustrating 'the woes of war' and Constable was anxious to publish it as an addition to Scott's letters from Paris shortly after the battle. Constable had written enthusiastically to Hall on 9th and 13th June on the subject of including it in the *Miscellany*.[11]

In the letter of 13 October 1825 Scott says to Hall:

Constable proposed a thing to me which was of so much delicacy that I scarce know how to set about it, and thought of nursing it till you and I meet. It relates to that most interesting and affecting journal kept by my regretted and amiable friend Mrs Harvey [Hall's sister, Magdalene after her second marriage] during poor De Lancey's illness. He thought with great truth that it would add very great interest as an addition to the letter which he wrote from Paris soon after Waterloo, and certainly would consider it as one of the most valuable and important documents which could be published … But whether this could be done without injury to the feelings of survivors is a question not for me to decide, and indeed I feel unaffected pain in even submitting it to your friendly ear, who, I know, will put no harsh construction upon my motive, which can be no other than such as would do honour to the amiable and lamented authoress.

Notes

20   This refers of the Duke of Wellington being in process of dressing on the evening before the crucial battle, for the Duchess of Richmond's ball, while looking at a map with a Prussian general in full dress uniform.

Scott goes on in this vein, to express his understanding of the delicacy of the matter with regard to others, and to suggest that the identities of the principal persons be omitted.

However On December 6 1825 Hall makes a final allusion to the subject in a letter to Archibald Constable:

> I am extremely sorry to tell you, that after using every proper argument with the person chiefly concerned, I have totally failed in obtaining leave to print the Narrative which you were so anxious to obtain, and which I was equally anxious should see the light. I regret much that it is totally out of the question. There can be no more done or said on that point, and I have only to assure you that I did all that I could.

Thomas Constable said: 'This narrative, as had been anticipated, deeply interested my father' – so deeply indeed that he proposed at a later period that it should be included in an edition of *Paul's Letters to his Kinsfolk*, and had the decision rested with Captain Hall permission would certainly have been granted, for he writes: 'I am equally desirous with you that it *should* be'; but despite this and the following solicitation from Sir Walter Scott, it was withheld.'[12]

Lady de Lancey had in fact written her narrative at her brother's request. However, Hall made a few copies for particular friends, including Dickens. A condensed version was in fact published in the *Illustrated Naval and Military Gazette* in 1888. A full narrative was subsequently published in the *Century Magazine*, New York in 1906, followed in the same year by a book-length edition by John Murray (the original bound version was not found until 1998 in an Edinburgh attic). The objection to its earlier publication may well have come from a certain Captain Henry Harvey, who now enters the story (Note 21).

The reference above to Magdalene by Scott as 'Mrs Harvey' relates to yet another extraordinary conjunction between Hall's friends and his beloved sister. Hall – returning from Lord Amherst's mission to the Chinese Emperor in command of the sloop HMS *Lyra* – called first at Calcutta to deliver despatches to the Governor-General there and then at Madras. Here, Captain Henry Harvey – Assistant Commissary-General of the Madras Army of the Honourable East India Company – was anxiously awaiting a ship to take him back to England where his father had died in 1816. He would have no doubt been delighted to have found a berth as the personal guest of the commander – then Lieutenant Hall, whom he had met at Seringapatam and elsewhere and as their friendship was cemented over the voyage of four and half months, landing in Britain in mid October 1817.

It was almost a year later that Harvey (who had accumulated considerable wealth in India quite apart from the inheritance from his father) was invited to stay with Hall in Scotland. There he was introduced to Magdalene. There was an immediate mutual attraction and by the end of December 1818 they were engaged to be married. There had apparently been considerable gossip and speculation about Magdalene and her future, which Hall was anxious to forestall. In a long letter to Lady Londonderry in

Notes

21   A very full account of the history of this work is given by Miller (2000).

June 1819 he explains the circumstances of their marriage, which he said was a 'very happy business … she was not adapted to solitude, she had no objects to look to and to occupy her with an interest sufficiently intense to direct her from ennui. Her prospects and her happiness had been so rudely broken across that she was unavoidably much shaken … but she was fully resolved not to give way, but to try to be cheerful and contented.'

Hall then reveals the attitudes of the time regarding womens' frailty when he goes on, in brotherly fashion, to say: 'It was very much my wish – and that of all our family – and we suspected her own, that she should again come into the world as an active and useful member of society: but who was now to be her guide? Into whose hands could we trust her with any rational hopes that the bright vision of the married state which was so deeply set in her imagination should be realised? Edinburgh – with all its merits and graces is more remarkably deficient in this respect than any other place I have yet visited – odd as it may seem – I really do not know above two or three in the whole society whom I should, under any present circumstances, like to see connected with us in this way.' It is not clear here whether Hall is referring to the suitability of a marriage partner *per se* or whether, as seems not unlikely, he meant acceptability in terms of social rank. Hall then gives a glowing description of Captain Harvey, including his attainments in science and literature. According to Hall, Harvey had found himself adrift on his return to England without an occupation after 17 years in India, but was still under 35 years of age. Hall asked him to come to Edinburgh and accompany him in attending his classes in natural philosophy at the University. On the developing relationship between Magdalene and his friend, Hall says:

> it was curious and perhaps singular, that I should have been during four months on the most intimate footing conceivable with both the parties – many hours of every day in each of their society – and yet that not the least word of any such matter passed – nor did they know what I thought or wished. I took no part to bring them together, nor to talk to one of the other – in that, left it completely to themselves. I felt that I had enough on my head in having brought them together – to have stirred further I should have considered almost criminal – and so they had full time to become acquainted - & if it turns out ill 'it is their look out' as we say at sea – and not mine.

Hall was delighted with the match, and his family also seemed pleased. Apparently, Magdalene 'dropped her public name … glad as she said to escape from Public notice – before which she had been too long an object of useless and exaggerated interest'.[13]

The letters between the engaged couple over the months before the wedding – scheduled for the end of March 1819 – were numerous and passionate (some 40 letters from Magdalene over this period survive). After the wedding Henry retired from the army and the couple went on the Grand Tour. Magdalene gave birth in Rome to her first child, Helen, on 1 January 1820, followed by Robert, born in Edinburgh in December 1820 and Frances in Worcester in March 1822.[14] (Helen was named both after Magdalene's mother and the sister whom she had helped to nurse through her illness and death from tuberculosis.)

The letters to her beloved fiancé are interspersed with correspondence with Basil. Hall had become very good friends with Harvey – a friendship that continued throughout his life, and on more than one occasion Hall used Harvey as his agent for business and literary affairs while he was at sea. In a letter from Basil's sister Frances to her friend Catherine Johnston at Hutton Hall, Ayton on 1 April 1824, she says: 'Basil has just completed his book on South America which we send you and hope you will like. He has been hard at work for several months past, assisted by Mr. Harvey, who is a great critic in style, composition, Scotticisms, etc. which a sailor's education does not make him quite master of' (given the success of Basil's previous work, this is a very interesting comment, but Hall himself had admitted that he had written every word of his South American narrative seven times over).[15]

Together with Basil's father, Hall and Harvey were among the founders of the prestigious gentlemen's club the Athenæum, which continues to this day. Hardly surprisingly the Harvey family became friendly with the Halls and there is a very delightful letter from Captain Harvey's sister Helen, to Basil's mother, describing Queen Victoria's coronation in 1838.[16] (Note 22)

However the triangular relationship between Basil, Captain Harvey and herself had become a point of some friction with Magdalene during her betrothal. In a series of almost daily letters (on at least one day she writes twice) to her fiancé in February and March 1819 she refers frequently to his close friend Basil, who had been responsible for their meeting. On 4 February 1819 from Edinburgh, she says:

> I make a point of not encouraging him to spend hours here, as formerly – I think it is of importance that as long as I am so near that if he really needs advice or assistance he can apply for it, at the same time as the habit of daily communication is gently broken off … Last night in Geo [George] St. Basil and I sat chatting together a while & he quizzed me a little as to why I was now let alone so much instead of being an object of compassion and care – we naturally went on to talking of my situation & I worked myself up to be almost frightened to think that I shd. presume to be a companion fit for you! & Basil made me worse, for he thinks his sister very unequal tho' capable of making the happiness of his friend … for such a man as he will make allowances.

No doubt Hall was teasing his very much loved sister, but she was clearly sensitive to his remarks – at one point he claims to a friend that there never was so lucky a woman as herself. On 14 February she writes to Harvey 'Basil is quite well and goes out a great deal – but always goes home by 12 – he is in great spirits & when he asks if I have heard from x I say no – he quizzes and says you have deserted me & I shall see your marriage in the papers'. On the following day she says: 'Basil tells me he was quizzing all the time when he followed the tone of my humility that evening, for that is a woman's qualifications for a wife he thinks I am quite <u>equal</u> to his friend – & most admirably well suited – but he adds, "a fortunate minx too."'

Notes

22   In a letter to James Hall in early 1840, Hall indicates that he is arranging tickets for a London event at which he will be wearing his uniform: it is highly likely that this was the wedding of Queen Victoria and Prince Albert Saxe-Coburg on 10th February of that year.

But against all this joshing from Basil, and claims that Basil never understood her, she also applauds her brother's sterling support for her mother during his father's illness at this time, saying that his 'affection for my father & delicacy towards him exceeds all the rest'. She also lets Harvey know that Basil is in low spirits on the eve of her departure to join him, despite 'the most fervent wish in his heart being accomplished [i.e. the marriage of Magdalene to Harvey]'. By early March Basil says: 'It makes me giddy to think of you and he being indisputably united – I am not worth of such happiness – the contemplation of your happiness, & his is sufficient for me & I repose upon it with manifest pleasure.' On the same day however, Magdalene – in a second letter to Harvey – includes a note by her younger sister Fanny. It refers to all her advice respecting Basil, but 'doubts if she [Fanny] has made little use of it. She has not gained much in his affections; I cannot understand him & seldom am at ease with him, we are now separated, & with much less of attachment than separated, when looking forward to the winter which is now passed, when we last parted in Paris'.

In one of Magdalene's last letters before Harvey's arrival at Dunglass, she says of Basil:

> I do not think I have behaved unkindly to him – I trust he does not think so. He thinks I should have been his friend in the family but we never could have remained so – I am confident we both require to be guided & when he used to torture me wt [with] asking any advice I could only look anxious & wretched & could give him no help – he needs a strong mind to influence and guide him – many of his qualities appear to me such as generally belong to the female character – Helen suited him best of any for her mind had masculine strength.[17]

This correspondence is of course revealing about both Magdalene and her brother. After the tragic death of her first husband she was the object of great pity, which eventually she came to resent. She also resented Basil's insinuation – albeit at least half jocularly – that she was unworthy of his great friend. For her part, in reporting this, she may have been seeking Henry's confirmation of his love and affirmation of her value – and at the same time attempting to secure Henry for herself, by keeping Basil at a distance. In that respect she seems to have been as 'needy' (in the modern usage) as she claims he was, both of them to some extent insecure. If however she is right in her assessment of Basil having more of the feminine characteristics and constantly requiring guidance and re-assurance (as is also shown in correspondence with Dickens and others), it reveals a most interesting character, far removed from the conventional stereotype of the adventurous and authoritative naval captain. But then his writing, with its intimate detail and exposure of personality and feelings, belies any such stereotype.

Magdalene died in August1822. She was 28, barely two years after this second marriage. She died almost certainly from the tuberculosis that had claimed her sister Helen, and not long after the birth of her last child. In a letter from Dunglass to Catherine Johnston on 12 July 1822 Basil's sister Frances says, 'poor Basil, after every voyage has had some blow – on returning from India he heard of Magdalene's marriage and widowhood all at once – When he returned from China Helen had gone; when he next returns Magdalene will be no more & his best friend a widower'. In a later letter (3

October 1822) referring to hearing from Basil – then at St. Blas in California – that he expected to be in Portsmouth early in November, 'our joy at having him near us again is terribly dampened by thinking of the sad news that awaits him'.[18]

Two years later Frances comments: 'Basil is paying visits in England to a number of the great people he got acquainted with in town who invited him to their country houses. We shall expect the accounts of the interior of these houses though somewhat different, to be almost as interesting as his researches in less refined circles & more distant climates.'[19] By early 1829 Basil was to carry this beloved sister (Fanny), now terminally ill, into the largest bedroom at Dunglass where she died on 16 June, having written a remarkably composed final letter to her sister Katherine a few weeks previously.[20] She had died at the same age as her sister Magdalene.

Through his friendship with Harvey, Hall became involved (albeit on the periphery) in the infamous incident of the 'Black Bottle', which became a notorious military scandal. Henry Harvey's ward was a promising young officer, Captain John Reynolds – then in the very fashionable 11th Hussars (Prince Albert's Own) of which the commander was the excessively punctilious and peppery Lord Cardigan (who was later to lead the famous charge at Balaclava in the Crimean War). Lord Cardigan had an irrational objection to his officers drinking porter – which a number of them had become used to in India – deeming it 'unofficer like'.

It was Captain Reynolds' misfortune to order a bottle of Moselle at a formal regimental dinner in 1839, which appeared in a black bottle similar to that which normally contained porter and which the waiter had omitted to decant. As Cardigan had – almost unbelievably – actually issued an order against the serving of porter on such occasions, he was incensed and delivered a formal rebuke to Reynolds on the following morning. Not surprisingly, Reynolds protested and as matters escalated the captain was placed under arrest, while both men applied to the Commander-in-Chief for support. In this ridiculous spat, Henry Harvey supported his ward – and incredibly, letters on the subject were sent to the Prime Minister, Prince Albert (as colonel of the regiment) and the Secretary of War, among others.

Hall was recruited in support of his brother-in-law and is suspected of leaking the whole affair and associated correspondence – which would not have been atypical – to The Globe and The Times. After Cardigan's court-martialling of an officer and fighting a duel with another of the regiment on a quite unrelated matter, the affair became a major cause celebre. Strangely, it was Hall and not Harvey who was summoned by the Military Secretary to help to sort out this unsavoury affair. It resulted, albeit 25 years later, in a very emotional rapprochement between the protagonists, with Reynolds eventually achieving the rank of major-general.[21]

What is equally interesting in this whole story are the connections between the various players, illustrating the close family networks in military and government circles. Lieutenant-General Charles Reynolds (1756–1819) of the Honourable East India Company (in which Henry Harvey had served) married (at the age of 55) the 22 year-old Scottish girl Mary Hunter – the eldest daughter of John Hunter, British Consul-General in Spain throughout the Napoleonic Wars. The latter happened to be the father of Margaret Hunter – the future wife of Captain Basil Hall. On the death of Charles Reynolds in 1819 his young widow, left with four children, appointed Henry

Harvey to be the guardian of one of them – the future Captain John Reynolds. He was to marry one of Henry Harvey's daughters.[22] Thus the families of Reynolds, Hunter, and Hall were inextricably linked both through marriage and an alliance based on unforeseeable circumstance, not to mention the fact that Basil had, most unusually, brought back to England both of Magdalene's husbands-to-be and had met them before she did.

References

1. Miller, 2008, 100
2. *Ibid.*, ii
3. Basil Hall to Charles Dickens, 1 March 1841, Huntington Library, Dickens Correspondence MS 18502, ff.48 (59)
4. Hall, 1852, *first series,* 115
5. Basil Hall to Charles Dickens, 1 March 1841, Huntington Library, Dickens Correspondence, MS 18502, ff. 48 (59)
6. Rankin, 52
7. NLS MS 3220
8. *Century Magazine*, Vol LXXI, April 1906, No. 6, 821
9. Huntington Library, MSS 18502, ff. 57(43)
10. Russell, Vol. IV, 240
11. Grierson, (1932–7) Vol IX, 1825–26, 246–249
12. Constable, T., 473–4, Letter 13 October 1825
13. Basil Hall to Lady Londonderry, 11 June 1819, Kent Records U840 C574
14. Miller, 2008, 139–140
15. Russell, Vol. IV, 240
16. Helen Harvey to Lady Hall, 1 July 1838, Private Collection
17. Correspondence between Lady de Lancey and Captain Henry Harvey, February– March 1819, Private Collection transcribed by Sally Smith
18. Frances Hall to Catherine Johnston, 12 July 1822 *et seq*, Private Collection
19. *Ibid.*, 17 August 1824, Private Collection
20. Katherine Hall to Miss Katherine Johnston, 20 May 1829, Private Collection
21. Miller, 2001, 147 et seq.
22. *Ibid.*, 146

Revolution in South America

In the first quarter of the 19th Century South America was in political ferment. Independence movements against Spanish hegemony were breaking out everywhere, partly stimulated by the French Revolution, the Napoleonic invasion of Spain and the American War of Independence. All of these contributed to Latin American unrest and encouraged nationalism. While in the early stages of these uprisings, Britain officially adopted a neutral position (it had after all supported Spain in its resistance to Napoleon). Active military action was only taken by such independent spirits as Admiral Thomas Cochrane, who is still revered on the continent. But at the same time, British merchants were anxious to have access to the vast resources of South America and to open up trade relations, which the British authorities wished to encourage.

San Martin: Hall was impressed by the modesty and manners of the great Protector of Peru. Museo Histórico Nacional, Buenos Aires.

Apart from the renowned Simon Bolivar, one of the key figures was Don José de San Martin – previously an officer in the Spanish army during the Peninsular War – who led the fight for independence in Argentina, Chile and Peru and whom Hall got to know intimately. Chile had overthrown their Spanish overlords as far back as 1810. Yet with the subsequent reassertion of Spanish authority there, the Argentineans – concerned that the Spanish might invade their country from their base in the west – decided on a pre-emptive strike and invaded Chile in 1818, making the formidable crossing of the Andes.

San Martin's victory at the bloody battle of Maypo on 5 April 1818 was decisive, but the Patriots (as they were called) still did not command the seas. This completely changed when Lord Cochrane, with British and American volunteers, took charge of the naval forces and by sheer audacity won a series of stunning victories in 1820. With a minimal force, he effectively blockaded the coast of both Southern Chile and Peru, bottling up the Spanish Royalists in the capital Lima and preventing access to the port of Callao some six miles away.

While San Martin was preparing to invade Peru, Basil Hall was secretly commissioned in 1820 by London merchants to take a shipment of goods there before other competitors reached it.[1] In fact, Hall's commission was both a diplomatic and mercantile one, which he delineates very clearly in the opening chapter of the extracts from his journal, emphasising its unusual character. Appointed to command HMS *Conway* in May of that year, he was ordered by the Commodore, Sir Thomas Hardy, to proceed to Valparaiso to look after British interests on the west coast where there was no consular presence. The only authority was the British navy, which had to be distributed around the whole of the coast of the continent, from Brazil to Mexico. With the difficulty of communications in the midst of considerable political instability and public volatility, a novel responsibility devolved upon the naval commanders assigned to such a wide-ranging task, not least to resolve any disputes between British merchants and the ever-changing local authority.[2]

It says something for the government's confidence in Hall's abilities and experience that he was assigned to this challenging commission, which involved on-the-spot decisions in a wildly fluctuating political and social situation. Hall makes the point that: 'In the end, it became obvious that the only method was, to make the officers well acquainted with the general principles by which their conduct was to be regulated, and to leave them afterwards, as a matter of absolute necessity, to act to the best of their judgement and abilities, according to circumstances, but always in the spirit of their instructions.' Hall concedes that all this, together with their numerous routine port duties left them 'with little leisure for attending to the novel scenes of a local and characteristic nature, daily passing around us'. It says much for Hall's energy and interest that he was able to do just that, and to record it in compelling detail.

Hall arrived at Valparaiso on 19 December 1820, having journeyed via Rio Janeiro, the River Plate and Cape Horn. He took the time to learn as much as possible about the customs and mood of the country, meeting people of all ranks, sipping *mate* with the poorest of the inhabitants – despite his admitted imperfect Spanish. He comments favourably on the good manners, dignity, and hospitality of the Chileans, suggesting that their demeanour was at least partly due to their newfound freedom (he was later to compare this with the situation he

San Martin in old age.

found in Peru, still under Spanish domination). He went to bull-fights, gave a delightful description of flamenco dancing, and commented on the increase in foreign trade.[3]

He was even more impressed by the manners of the residents of the capital, Santiago, and much regretted that the news of the impending arrival of a French frigate at Valparaiso forced him to depart urgently, as the citizens were in fear of what this might mean. Their anxieties were unfounded. According to Hall, 'the Frenchmen, after a short and friendly visit, sailed away again, carrying off the hearts of half the ladies of the port' (it should be said, that in true sailor fashion, Hall himself was no slouch when it came to attempting to charm any pretty women he encountered in South America).[4]

The arrival of the British frigate, the *Owen Glendower* in late January enabled the *Conway*, at the end of that month, to sail for Callao – the seaport for Lima in Peru. Here he found a very different situation. While the Spanish still commanded areas of Peru, San Martin's forces were threatening the capital of Lima while Cochrane's naval blockade offshore effectively sealed off the country from trade and reinforcements to the Royalist cause from the sea. The proud Spaniards and their local supporters were in a greatly reduced state. Suspicion was rife and not unnaturally there was considerable animosity towards the British, who despite claims to neutrality were accused of supporting the revolution. In Hall's words, referring to the decline of Lima, 'jealousy and distrust with one another, and still more of strangers, filled every breast; disappointment and fear, aggravated by personal inconvenience and privation, broke up all agreeable society; rendering this once great, luxurious and happy city, one of the most wretched places on earth'.[5]

Hall – attempting to preserve the British Government's position and to pave the way for mutually advantageous trade (in this respect Peru was much wealthier in resources than Chile) – was in an unenviable and very delicate position, usually seen to be supporting one side or the other. Things took a very serious turn when two of his officers whilst visiting Callao were accused of being spies from Lord Cochrane's ship and thrown into prison. Although Hall was allowed to visit them to confirm their identities, he was not otherwise allowed to converse with them. At one point there was a real threat that the men might be hanged, and Hall was obliged to travel to Lima (which was in an uproar over the incident) to make representations on their behalf to the Spanish Viceroy.

At Callao, despite a potentially threatening crowd (a mob had recently put a whole boat's crew to death) he was allowed to pass, which Hall attributes to a quite accidental circumstance. Before the war, there had been considerable connections between Callao and Valparaiso in Chile and before departure, Hall had collected in the latter port letters and messages from friends and relatives for personal delivery, taking care to record accurately any verbal messages in his notebook. As Hall says, 'Shortly after my arrival in Peru, I took care to deliver all these letters and messages in person'.

The letters were few, but the neighbours flocked in on hearing that tidings had come from Valparaiso; and though many were disappointed, many were also made happy by hearing of their friends, from whom they had received no other direct communication for a long time. Referring to the messages in his notebook, Hall said: 'when these little memorandums were torn out and given to the parties, they became a sort of letter, and were prized as such by the receivers. For my own part, I was well satisfied with seeing people so easily made happy'.[6]

Later, attempting to return to Lima following a visit to his imprisoned officers, Hall was concerned at the angry mood of a large crowd which had gathered round him. He very deliberately rode his horse up to the houses to which he had delivered messages and on the pretext of asking for a glass of water, engaged in conversation with the inhabitants. He was upbraided for allowing 'spies' to land from his vessel, and loudly but courteously, refuted the charge. Within a short time a passage opened for him, and in his words, he 'was never afterwards molested or threatened in the slightest degree ... at a time when the hatred and suspicion were at their greatest height'. In the event, the witnesses who had laid the charge against the officers were discredited and they were set free.

The incident says much about Hall. Notwithstanding his position as a naval captain, he had taken the trouble personally to collect these letters and messages (the latter transcribed presumably in Spanish) from poor people and equally personally to deliver them, at the time with no apprehension of profit to himself. Secondly, he had the courage not only to face the mob, but also to use his diplomatic skills to take advantage of the empathy that had developed between himself and the recipients. These were attributes which he displayed throughout his life. On his return to Valparaiso in March he was able to give news of those in Callao who had sent messages, to the great joy of the recipients (Note 23).

On 24 June the *Conway* returned to Callao, and on the following day Hall had his first meeting with General San Martin, on his small schooner. He was enormously impressed by the general, one of the two in the whole of South America accorded the title of 'Liberator' (the other of course being Simon Bolivar). Hall declared him superior to anyone he had met in South America and gives a vivid pen-picture of his host.[7] According to Hall, he was thoroughly 'well bred, but unaffectedly simple, cordial and kindly' and a man who got to the point immediately. He also states: 'I have never seen a person, the enchantment of whose address was more irresistible.'

At this time Lima was apparently about to be abandoned by the Royalists and the city was in an uproar and undergoing a panic-stricken evacuation, which Hall describes evocatively, saying that Lima was now 'a vast city of the dead.'[8] On several occasions, San Martin made it clear that he had no ambition to be the conqueror of Peru, but only to enter Lima when the time was ripe and when it was quite clear that the populace wanted him, declaring that his war was 'one of new and liberal principle against prejudice, bigotry and tyranny'. His aim was solely to liberate the country from oppression. Many doubted his sincerity, but Hall would have none of this. San Martin later evinced this when he delayed entering Lima until he felt that the people had got the message, and even then tried to enter the city with only a single aide-de-camp in attendance and with not the slightest show of pomp or glory.[9]

San Martin's most telling action was, when the city was at its most anxious, to instruct his commander to obey the orders of the Governor – even to the extent of withdrawing his troops a stipulated distance from the capital to show their good intent

Notes

23 It was at Valparaiso that Hall tracked a comet that was in sight from the 1 April to 8 June and undertook experiments with Captain Kater's pendulum to determine the shape of the earth. These enabled the orbit of the comet to be determined and together with the calculations of a Dr. Brinkley of Dublin, the results were published in the *Philosophical Transactions of the Royal Society* for 1822. These pendulum observations were later repeated at San Blas in California and in the Galapagos Islands.

and discipline. On 12 July 1821 San Martin entered the capital and 16 days later the declaration of independence of Peru was proclaimed, witnessed by Hall. Within a few days of his entry to the city and with the aid of an effective curfew, order was restored and normal business was being conducted. San Martin also made it clear to Hall that once a responsible government was in place, he intended to retire, and did precisely that: Hall records that at the time of the 1826 edition of his Journal, the victorious commander was residing quietly in Brussels.

The two men appeared to get on very well together and Hall had a most privileged position as an observer, being invited to several of the most important occasions, including San Martin's formal levée on 9 August 1821, after the General had declared himself Protector. He was again impressed by San Martin's genuine warmth and modesty towards all who greeted him – including Hall himself, who was brought forward when San Martin spotted him in the great crowd of well wishers.[10]

Hall subsequently cruised along the coasts of Chile and Peru to assess the commercial interests of the various potential trading stations and to assist British merchants there. At Copiapó the port was carefully surveyed and Hall took the opportunity to ride into the interior to witness the effects of the great earthquake of April 1819, and to visit the silver mines in the mountains near the town. Hall was astonished at the change that had taken place in Peru after four months of independence, with trade burgeoning and the harbour of Callao full of commercial vessels, while the British were received warmly.

Giant tortoise on the Galapagos Islands.

He went on to Central America, visiting Mexico via Panama and the Galapagos Islands. At the inland town of Tepic, in Mexico, as usual he gives an excellent and often amusing description of the local society and their festivities, and was most hospitably entertained.[11] Perhaps more significantly he encountered merchants anxious to do business in Britain, especially as the new revolutionary government had greatly reduced the customs dues on the export of gold and silver. Here he collected more than half a million dollars in specie – a very large sum at this time – in exchange for goods to be sent from Britain. He added comparable sums before his departure from the port of San Blas, even although there was still some resistance to what they saw as the wealth of the country being exported.[12] If for nothing else this confirmed the success of his original commission, but as in Chile and Peru it also opened the trading doors with the new governments of the continent.[13] Hall had been a witness to some of the most significant events in the history of South America.

Hall's journal does not simply confine himself to day-to-day events: he expands at length on the political situation – something which others in the naval service and government generally might have thought to be putting his career at risk – with acute and intelligent observations. While supporting the revolutionaries and their ideals, and castigating those Spaniards who could not come to terms with the new order, he was also sympathetic to the latter and made admiring remarks on their inherent nobility and hospitality as individuals[14] (he did not extend this admiration to what he saw as the pernicious effects and abuse of the practice of Roman Catholicism generally on South America).[15] Hall devotes more than a chapter on the iniquities of Spanish rule and its appalling barbarities, but comes to the conclusion – on the basis of bringing Christianity and a form of civilisation to the continent – that on balance, it was beneficial.

He was in no doubt however about the long-term benefits of the new liberty of the people – not least in their immediate release from constraints on freedom of expression – and opportunities for education, especially for women who had mostly been denied this. Later, as his more conservative and Tory views hardened, together with his opposition to Parliamentary reform in Britain, he was to recant on his support for revolutionaries.

The historian W.H. Koebel put Hall's activities in South America in perspective when he said:

> Of all those British who participated in, or witnessed and chronicled, the events of the revolutionary wars in the south of the continent, perhaps the most notable from the standpoint of their association and breadth of view were Admiral Cochrane, General Miller (Note 24) and Captain Basil Hall … Hall, as a most able and intelligent officer in charge of a British warship on the South American coast, had, as a spectator, rare opportunities of which he took the fullest advantage … very few of the other gallant men possessed, in addition to the knowledge of the war, the civil and social experience in South America of those I have named.[16]

Koebel continues:

> To my mind, the most outstanding of the records of the Pacific coast during the last period of the War of Liberation and the first few years of the independence are those of Captain Basil Hall. Hall reveals himself as an admirable type of British sailor, and it is clear that his kindly geniality won for him as much popularity as his firmness gained him respect. Enjoying as he did the intimate friendship of San Martin, the great Argentine

Notes

24   Hall was later to be responsible for introducing General Miller – one of San Martin's senior commanders – to Sir Walter Scott at his countryseat at Abbotsford. Miller made an epic journey with Simon Bolivar across the Andes and was the only field officer who stayed with him from the sailing of the expeditionary force from Valparaiso to the final crucial victory at the Battle of Ayacucho in 1824 (which secured the independence of Peru and eventually the remainder of South America).

would unbosom himself to him of his hopes and fears, plans and ideals. Much has been written of late of San Martin, and it is a little difficult to understand why Hall's first-hand and intimate testimony has been so seldom referred to. The British sailor's admiration for San Martin was by no means universally shared at the time it was evoked ... Hall was not among those who doubted [his sincerity]. His fervid pen-picture of the Liberator was justified to the full by subsequent events ... Captain Hall has provided a set of pictures of the Pacific coast which are in many respects unique ... Moreover, whether he was chatting with San Martin, being entertained ashore, protecting British interests, negotiating between Royalists and South Americans, or facing a hostile Spanish mob at Callao, as was once his lot, he appears to have risen to the occasion with the most admirable equanimity.[17]

The publication of Hall's narrative was not without its problems. The publisher Constable wanted to do Hall proud with a smart and expensive work, to maintain his reputation for quality. Hall on the other hand, wanted 'to be humble and to gain favour by the absence of pretension and to win people's good will by ministering to their amusement at small cost'. Hall despaired of agreement and at one point said, 'I am well nigh resolved to drop the whole transaction'. Later, he was to quote a Captain Bowles in support of his view – provided that Hall kept out of politics and did not give offence to anyone (in or outside the naval service), but that he would seek the opinion of his brother-in-law Mr Harvey. At the same time he declares that he did not want to do anything which was against Constable's professional publishing experience. By 16 August 1824 Hall was acknowledging the great success of the book, following Constable's original proposals regarding price and format. In a number of ways, this exchange is typical of Hall's relations with a number of publishers.[18]

Frances Trollope provides an interesting sidelight on Hall's method of constructing his South American book:

> Lea, the Philadelphian publisher, told me that Capt. Hall told him the method he pursued on the composition of his work on South America was as follows: he made copious minutes of all he saw – he brought home fifteen volumes of notes. He had them all written fair by a copier. He employed his brother and brother-in-law to read them, and to mark with a number every passage according to its value, then to select two volumes full, beginning with all the number ones and going on till they had got enough. He said these voyages had been written over five times.[19]

References

1. Bethel, 301–2
2. Hall, 1826, 30–35
3. *Ibid.,* 11–12
4. *Ibid.,* 30–35
5. *Ibid.,* 79
6. *Ibid.,* 79–100
7. *Ibid.,* 179
8. *Ibid.,* 186–7
9. *Ibid.,* 182–3
10. *Ibid.,* 205–8
11. *Ibid.,* 191–94
12. *Ibid.,* 227, 288
13. *Ibid.,* 190–288
14. *Ibid.,* 284
15. *Ibid.,* 260-61
16. Koebel,166, Note 2
17. *Ibid.,* 238
18. NLS MS 7200, Constable Collection, 1823, f.22–24
19. Smalley, 426

Knowing the 'Great Unknown'

During the Christmas period of 1824–25 Hall described Sir Walter Scott in his new home at Abbotsford in intimate detail. R. Westall, ARA, engr. E. Findon.

By the autumn of 1824 the grand mansion of Abbotsford near Melrose – Sir Walter Scott's countryseat – was now finally finished. Here he lived in the style of a laird, 'visited by the old nobility whom he loved, by statesmen, squires, judges, diplomats, antiquaries, authors and celebrities from Britain, Europe, and America'.[1] It is difficult now, perhaps when his works have become somewhat unfashionable, to appreciate the international fame of this outstanding and hospitable Scottish author. The largest party ever accommodated at his splendid new home was held at Christmas of that year. Referring to Hall's journal for that time, J.G. Lockhart (Scott's future son-in-law and his first biographer), declares of Scott that he 'was never subject to sharper observation than that of his ingenious friend Captain Basil Hall', whose writing provides one of the most important and intimate pictures of the 'Great Unknown' – a popular reference to the 'mystery' surrounding the authorship of the hugely successful Waverley novels.

The study at Abbotsford where Scott's famous Waverley novels were written. Edinburgh City Libraries.

Hall kept a very detailed journal of his time over the festive season at Abbotsford in the course of two separate visits. From this Scott's biographer J.G. Lockhart extracted copiously in his *Memoirs of the Life of Sir Walter Scott.*

Abbotsford, December 29, 1824

This morning my brother James and I set out from Edinburgh in the Blucher coach at eight o'clock, and although we heard of snowstorms in the hills, we bowled along without the smallest impediment ... we arrived in good time – and found several other guests at dinner ... The public rooms are lighted with oil-gas in a style of extraordinary splendour. The passages, also, and the bedrooms, are lighted in a similar manner. The whole establishment is on the same footing – I mean the attendance and entertainment – all is in good order, and an air of punctuality and method, without any waste or ostentation, pervades everything. Every one seems at his ease; and although I have been in some big houses in my time, amongst good folks who studied these sort of points not a little, I don't remember to have anywhere met with things better managed in all respects.

Had I a hundred pens, each of which at the same time could write separately down an anecdote, I could not hope to record one half of those which our host, to use Spenser's expression, 'welled out always'. To write down one or two, or one or two dozen, would serve no purpose, as they were all appropriate to the moment, and were told with a tone, gesture, and look, suited exactly to the circumstances, but which is of course impossible in the least degree to describe.

December 30

This morning Major Stisted, my brother, and I accompanied Sir Walter Scott on a walk over his grounds, a distance of five or six miles. He led us through his plantations, which are in all stages of advancement, and entertained us all the way with an endless string of anecdotes, more or less characteristic of the scenes we were passing though. Occasionally he repeated snatches of song, sometimes a whole ballad, and at other times he planted his staff in the ground and related some tale to us, which, though not in verse, came like a stream of poetry from his lips. Thus, about the middle of our walk, we had first to cross, and then to wind down the banks of the Huntly-burn, the scene of old Thomas the Rhymer's interview with the Queen of the Fairies. Before entering this little glen, he detained us on the heath above till he had related the whole of that romantic story, so that by the time we descended the path, our imaginations were so worked upon by the wild nature of the fiction, and still more by the animation of the narrator, that we felt ourselves treading on classical ground; and though the day was cold, the path muddy and scarcely passable, owing to the late floods, and the trees all bare, yet I do not remember ever to have seen any place so interesting as the skill of this mighty magician had rendered the narrow ravine, which in any other company would have seemed insignificant.

Hall noted the contrast between Scott's well-pruned groves with hardwood trees shooting up under the shelter of firs and the choked and ragged stand, all scraggy stems and stunted growth, belonging to an indolent neighbour. He then remarked that it must be interesting to be engaged in planting. 'Interesting!' Scott cried, 'You have no idea of the exquisite delight of a planter – he is like a painter laying on his colours … I look back to the time when there was not a tree here, only bare heath'. Scott elaborates the pleasures of forestry, comparing it very favourably with farming, which involved wrangling 'with farmers about prices, and to be constantly at the mercy of the seasons'.

Anywhere which Hall mentioned on this inspirational walk, Scott had an anecdote or story concerning it. One related to the finding of the etymology of a particular *cleuch* (ravine) and 'enchanted with the discovery he once woke his wife from sleep – to her considerable displeasure – to inform her of this new literary find, which she could not care less about'. He turned to Hall: 'Now, don't you understand this? Have you not sometimes on board your ship hit upon something which delighted you, so that you could not rest till you had got hold of some one down whose throat you might cram it – some stupid dolt of a lieutenant, or some gaping midshipman, on whom in point of fact it was totally thrown away?'[2] It was hardly a flattering reflection on his – though far from intellectual – not unintelligent wife.

Hall continues:

Over all, too, there was breathed an air of benignity and good will to all men, which was no less striking than the eloquence and point of his narrations. The manner in which he spoke of his neighbours, and of distant persons of whose conduct he disapproved, was all in the same spirit. He did not cloak their faults – he spoke out manfully in contempt of what was wrong; but this was always accompanied by some kindly observation, some reservation in favour of the good they possessed.

Nowhere was this more evident than when in a walk early in the New Year, he confided to Hall his views about Lord Byron, with whom he had spent 'Many, many a pleasant hour', but whom he described as 'being a man of real goodness of heart, and the kindest and best feelings, miserably thrown away by his foolish contempt of public opinion … he has had no justice done him'.[3]

Later Hall was to remark that he did not want to give a false impression of Scott as having nothing but goodness and forbearance, as Sir Walter describes to him a conniving father in a court case against his daughter, that he would have gladly have kicked the villain through a window and into the Tweed, were it not for the fact that the river would be polluted as a result.[4]

Hall says, 'In the evening we had a great feast indeed' and then goes on to describe Scott holding forth with a rendering of the narrative poem *Christabel* and again Thomas the Rhymer's adventures with the Queen of the Fairies, interspersed with many other stories and anecdote and the company later joining in the singing of many old Border ballads, accompanied by the harp and piano. This would have been the lowland – and somewhat upmarket – equivalent of the Highland *ceilidh* but with the important difference that Scott acted indisputably as a Master of Ceremonies – something unknown north of the Highland Line.

31 December 1824 – On the last day of the year, Hall muses on how 'keeping up old holidays by bonfires and merriment' appears to be decreasing, while suggesting that this may have to do as much with older folks having less relish for these than the younger generation actually changing the habits of their elders: 'I confess, for my part, that your Christmas and New-year's parties seem generally dull', claiming that this may be because they are ritualistic or that the company may be ill-assorted. However, Hall entered into the spirit of the occasion: 'As my heart was light and unloaded with any care, I exerted myself to carry through the ponderous evening – ponderous only because it was set apart to be light and gay.' Hall admitted, 'I danced reels like a madman, snapped my fingers, and halloed with the best of them, flirted with the young ladies … and with the elder ones … talked and laughed finely'.

But Hall objected to being obliged to join in dancing, singing or playing games when he would have preferred to have been left alone. Supper ended just at midnight, 'and as the clock was striking twelve, we all stood up, after drinking a hearty bumper to the old year' and with linked hands 'joined chorus' in a song led by Sir Adam Ferguson – 'a worthy knight, possessed of infinite drollery. Then followed other toasts of a loyal description, and then a song, a good red-hot Jacobite song to the King – a ditty which, a century ago, might have cost the company their heads, or at least their hands'.[5] But Hall notes how even Sir Walter could not prevent the party becoming dull and soporific, confirming in Hall's mind the pointlessness of such enforced jollity on set occasions.

1 January 1825 – Hall describes how on the previous day being Hogmany 'there was a constant procession of *Guisards* – i.e. boys dressed up in fantastic caps, with their shirts over their jackets, and with wooden swords' to perform an old mummer play. Scott liked to encourage these old ceremonies and gave out the obligatory penny (amounting to 70 pennies) and an oatcake to each. Hall then goes into some detail about the benefits of Scott's careful silviculture, which in thinnings alone now provided a handsome profit for him. This detail is symptomatic of Hall's perceptive observation of matters which are not necessarily within his own field.[6]

2 January 1825 – 'At breakfast today we had, as usual, some 150 stories – God knows how they came in, but he is, in the matter of anecdote, what Hudibras was in figures of speech … his mouth he cannot open without something worth hearing – and all so simply, good-naturedly, and naturally!' To counteract the impression that Scott might be inclined to dominate a company with his endless stories, Hall reveals later that 'no one takes more delight in the stories of others than he does, or who seems less desirous of occupying the ears of the company … or any wish to excel the last speaker.' Scott also let the company know that he had been reluctantly forced to put a stop to the crowds of casual tourists who descended on Abbotsford – up to 16 parties a day, some of whom forced their way in, touching objects and generally making a nuisance of themselves.[7]

3 January 1825 – 'As my brother James was obliged to return to Edinburgh, and I thought that I had stayed long enough, we set out from Abbotsford after luncheon, very reluctantly, for the party had grown upon our esteem very much, and had lately been augmented by the arrival from England of Mr. Lockhart, whom I wished to get acquainted with, and of Captain Scott, the poet's eldest son … The family urged me very much to stay, and I could only get away by making a promise to return for their little dance on Friday evening.' Hall was to get very much better acquainted with Lockhart (who became famous largely as a result of his subsequent biography of Scott) as a contributor to the influential *Quarterly Review* of which Lockhart was the editor for a number of years, and as Scott's future son-in-law.[8]

7 January 1825 – the following weekend Hall returned to Abbotsford with his sister Fanny. 'In the evening there was a dance in honour of Sir Walter Scott's eldest son, who had recently come from Sandhurst College, after having passed through some military examinations with great credit. We had a great clan of Scotts. There were no less than nine Scotts of Harden and ten of other families. There were others besides from the neighbourhood – at least half a dozen Fergusons, with the jolly Sir Adam at their head – Lady Ferguson, her niece Miss Jobson, the pretty heiress of Lochore – etc. etc. etc. The evening passed very merrily, with much spirited dancing; and the supper was extremely cheerful, and quite superior to that of Hogmany.' What seems to have escaped Hall – somewhat surprisingly – is that an important reason for the party was the engagement of Scott's soldier son, Walter, to the 'pretty heiress' (as the guest of honour) which suggests that although Hall was an honoured guest and a friend, he was not part of Scott's most intimate family circle.[9] In February, Scott was to write to his sister-in-law, Mrs Thomas Scott: 'Our young folks are wedded on the 3rd … my kindest love to Anne and Eliza. As she has lost Captain Basil [on the latter's engagement to Margaret Hunter] I intend to send her a gingerbread captain with a fine gilt sword, if he should cost me sixpence; I don't mind expense. He should be a Captain of the Navy, too.'[10]

8 January 1825 – Hall and Fanny went for a walk with Scott, when the latter told him how his estate manager, Tom Purdie, had come to appreciate the beauties of landscape. The fact that Hall was able to retell Purdie's comments in broad Scots indicates that, notwithstanding his world-wide travels, he had lost none of his familiarity with his native tongue. Again Hall was impressed by how Scott could fit his stories to the location and landscape as much by tone of voice and wording. He also told Hall about his attitude towards locals crossing his land: 'Nothing on earth would induce me to put up boards threatening prosecution' or telling them to 'beware of man-traps and spring-guns … and I will venture to say that not one of my young trees has ever been cut, nor a fence trodden down.'[11]

The branches thinned from his woods he had collected in piles to be sold cheaply for firewood to his poor neighbours. 'I am perfectly certain', he told Hall, 'they are more grateful to me … than if I were to give them ten times the quantity for nothing. Every shilling collected in this and other similar manners, goes to a fund which pays the doctor for his attendance on them when they are sick; and this is my notion of charity.'[12] But Hall notes that Scott has no time for what he calls 'meddling charity', which undermines self respect and independence: 'let them enjoy in their quiet way their dish of porridge, and their potatoes and herrings, or whatever it may be.'

He also revealed, having ascertained that Hall 'did not find shooting in particular at all amusing', that he now preferred to observe birds than to shoot them, and was never 'reconciled to the cruelty of the affair' – a very modern attitude. The exchange prompted both men to reminisce about boyhood cruelties which they had unwittingly inflicted on animals and which had greatly affected them ever since – another indication of the intimacy between the two friends.

In a way which no other writer on Scott had done, Hall reveals much of the man's character by intimate family detail, for example of how Scott took his place at table wherever one was available – and not necessarily at the head or foot, as might be expected of the head of his family – in a perfectly natural way. Hall heard how he achieved his objects with regard to enhancement of land outside his boundaries (to the aesthetic benefit of his own) by keeping good relations with his neighbours and being prepared to compromise and to allow time to take its course, without forcing issues.[13]

Fanny in a letter to her sister Katherine was ecstatic about her visit:

> This has been a heavenly day. I mean the weather, and a walk under any circumstances would have been delightful but immediately after leaving town it was truly delicious … Miss Scott thought nothing of offering up her room for me for one night. Sir Walter gave me a very pleasant welcome to his house. I have always been fancying it a dream, it seems so strange and unlikely that I should really be under the roof of his house [referring to a complement of 41 – of whom 23 slept in the house – she said they continued to dance until three o'clock]. In the course of our walk, yesterday, & in the evening I often saw symptoms of the good nature & kind disposition of our host, very frequently he brings in lines of poetry, which is so much in character, and so well done that it would satisfy you.[14]

10 January 1825 – Hall describes Scott as a most convivial man, despite his official duties at court, and the business of his house and estate and many wondered how he could possibly have time to write so prolifically. However, this did not puzzle Hall when he observed the author's habits. Scott apparently never appeared before ten in the morning, and throughout the day he would absent himself for the occasional hour. His thought came spontaneously and 'he composes his works just as fast as he can write. He never corrects the press, or if he does so at all, it is very slightly – and in general his works come before the public just as they are written'.[15] Hall then goes on to make a calculation, based on the number of pages and letters in one of Scott's novels compared to his own rate of writing his journal while at Abbotsford, and incidentally reveals his own method:

> I was in company all day and all evening till a late hour – apparently the least occupied of the party; and I will venture to say, not absent from the drawing room one quarter of the time that the Unknown was. I was always down to breakfast before anyone else … always among the very last to go to bed – in short, I would have set the acutest observer at defiance to have discovered when I wrote this Journal – and yet it is written, honestly and fairly, day by day … No mortal in Abbotsford-house ever learned that I kept a Journal.

In this he was quite wrong, for Lockhart states, 'Sir Walter was surprised, and a little annoyed on observing that the Captain kept a note-book on his knee, while at table, but made no remark'. Surely Hall would have been mortified if he had known, but one suspects he had quite a thick skin in these matters.[16]

Hall then suggests that even without the incentive of the financial return which Scott would receive for one of his novels, his own journal has cost as much time as for example, Scott's *Kenilworth* (approximately the same length). His calculation of Scott's progress was verified subsequently in the time it took him to write his novel *The Bethrothed*, with which he had been struggling.[17] He raises the question of the real authorship of the Waverley Novels, which was much debated at the time. Hall is in no doubt about this, but in answer to the question therefore of why Scott made a mystery of this, says:

> This is easily answered – it saves him completely from a world of flattery and trouble, which he sincerely detests. He never reads the criticisms of his books … Praise gives him no pleasure – and censure annoys him. He is fully satisfied to accept the intense avidity with which his novels are read – the enormous and continued sale of his works, as a sufficient commendation of them (Note 25) … he enjoys all the profits – and he escapes all worry about the matter.[18]

It would appear that Hall had at an early stage penetrated the 'mystery' surrounding the authorship of the Waverley Novels, for in a letter to Scott of 25 July 1824, Lady Abercorn (Note 26) writes: 'Basil Hall, whom I like much and [who] has published a book which of course you have read on South America, dined here a few days ago and

Notes

25 Thomas Carlyle was far less generous in his estimate of Scott in this respect when he remarks acidly: 'he has none of the weariness of royalty, yet all the praise, and the satisfaction of hearing it with his own ears … to the general imagination the 'Author of Waverley' was like some living mythological personage, and ranked among the chief wonders of the world.'[27]

26 Anne Jean, the Marchioness of Abercorn, was the daughter of the second Earl of Arran and was a frequent correspondent and supporter of Scott.

he told me he knew you wrote these Novels to a certainty, as he had it from one or two people to whom you had told it'[19] Scott wrote on 1 August: 'I can easily conceive your Ladyship must have been amused with Basil Hall, and struck with the very direct and almost abrupt mode in which he always prosecuted his object of enquiry. He has written an excellent book full of practical good sense and sound views, and I admire how as a traveller he has said so much about the manners of the people, yet avoided any breach of the confidence of private society, upon which travellers think themselves entitled to trample merely because they are travellers.'[20]

Hall then occupies several pages of his journal in a paean of praise for Scott – both as an author and as a person – and more particularly his ability to be natural and simple, while simultaneously being generous in his attitudes towards others.[21] He was apparently also very philosophical about his later financial ruin, as recorded by Hall:

> "It occurs to me," I [Hall] observed, "that people are apt to make too much fuss about the loss of fortune, which is one of the smallest of the great evils of life, and ought to be among the most tolerable."
>
> "Do you call it a small misfortune to be ruined in money-matters" he [Scott] asked.
>
> "It is not so painful, at all events, as the loss of friends"
>
> "I grant that," he said.
>
> "As the loss of character?"
>
> "True again."
>
> "As the loss of health?"
>
> "Aye, there you have me," he muttered to himself, in a tone so melancholy that I wished I had not spoken.
>
> "What is the loss of fortune to the loss of peace of mind?" I continued.
>
> "In short," said he playfully, "you will make it out that there is no harm in a man's being plunged over-head-and-ears in a debt he cannot remove."
>
> "Much depends, I think, on how it was incurred, and what efforts are made to redeem it – at least, if the sufferer be a rightminded man."
>
> "I hope it does," he said, cheerfully and firmly.[22]

This exchange on such a profound issue is another indication of the closeness between the two friends. Hall was not a fair-weather friend and recorded a visit to Scott when he was in much-reduced circumstances:

> A hundred and fifty years hence, when his works have become old classical authorities, it may interest some fervent lover of his writings to know what this great genius was about on Saturday the 10th of June 1826 – five months after the total ruin of his pecuniary fortunes, and twenty-six days after the death of his wife. In the days of his good luck he used to live at No. 39 North Castle Street, in a house befitting a rich baronet; but on reaching the door, I found the plate on it covered with rust (so soon is glory obscured), the window shuttered up, dusty and comfortless; and from the side of one projected a board, with this inscription, 'To Sell'; the stairs were unwashed, and not a footmark told of the ancient hospitality which reigned within … I turned my head … and enquiring at the clubs in Prince's Street, learned that he now resided in St. David's Street, No. 6. I was rather glad to recognise my old friend the Abbotsford butler, who answered the

door … at the top of the stair we saw a small tray, with a single plate and glasses for one solitary person's dinner. Some months ago Sir Walter was surrounded by his family, and wherever he moved, his headquarters were the focus of fashion. Travellers from all nations crowded round … Lady and Miss Scott were his constant companions; the Lockharts were his neighbours both in town and in Roxburghshire; his eldest son was his frequent guest … there was not any man so attended.

Thus Hall, very economically and poignantly, describes the descent of one of 'the mighty who had fallen' but without in any way seeming to moralise and goes on to predict his resurrection:

The distinction between man and the rest of the living creation, certainly, is in nothing more remarkable than in the power which possesses over them, of turning to varied account the means with which the world is stocked … I venture to predict that our Crusoe will cultivate his own island, and build himself a bark in which, in the process of time, he will sail back to his friends and fortune in greater triumph than if he had never been driven among the breakers.

Hall, with his brother James, then relates his meeting with Scott in intimate terms, describing the author as not being unduly bowed down under his troubles, and after a time 'he began conversing in his usual style … after sitting a quarter of an hour, we came away, well pleased to see our friend quite unbroken in spirit'.[23] This is one of the best examples of Hall's writing – rarely matched by others, simply and sympathetically, of this critical time in Scott's life.

Hall himself was genuinely flattered that Lockhart had devoted a whole chapter of his *Memoirs* to Hall's Journal (which the latter described as his 'scribble-scrabbles') of his time at Abbotsford over this Christmas and New Year period. Hall is surprisingly honest about this inclusion when he says:

For one minute or so – not more – I felt sorry to have lost hold of a chapter essentially of more value, from its topic, than all of the 150 volumes of ms in my strong box put together – but before the third minute had elapsed, I saw that, considered as a mere matter of profit and puff, the said chapter was a thousand times better placed than it could have been in any work of my own. To be associated with the Great Unknown in familiar intercourse and to be thought by you worthy of being enlisted in describing him, are circumstances which I consider fully worth of all the distinction of all my other productions put together – no great things perhaps – but 'these little things are great, you know, to little men'.[24]

Lockhart undoubtedly included much of Hall's Journal because he recognised the value of the intimacy of the picture Hall painted of both Scott and of Abbotsford which is not contained anywhere else – and Hall was a very percipient observer.

Early in 1825 the publisher Archibald Constable had mooted to Scott his innovative and hugely ambitious project to publish a cheap monthly magazine which he reckoned would have sales perhaps in the millions. This was to be called *Constable's Miscellany* with the intention of bringing out Basil Hall's *Voyage to Loo-Choo* as the first number on January 1826. He asked Scott if it would be possible to obtain permission to dedicate the entire new publication to King George IV. The King consented on Scott's recommendation.[25] In his letter of 1 October to Scott commenting on Constable's wish to put his books on Loo Choo and South America at the forefront of the *Miscellany*, Hall says:

> Constable, the great Leviathan of Book swallowers, has set my pen going again – and I wish very much I could converse with you for five minutes on the subject of this said *Miscellany*, which like a steam engine, is to carry all before it. I am delighted indeed to be in such company – but sometimes a little nervous, too. I shall be most happy to do all I can to assist your part of it.[26]

References

1. Sultana, 3
2. Lockhart, 1914, Vol IV, 192–5
3. *Ibid.*, 219
4. *Ibid.*, 220–1
5. *Ibid.*, 198–199
6. *Ibid.*, 201
7. *Ibid.*, 204
8. *Ibid.*, 209
9. Lockhart, 1898, Vol 2, 560
10. Douglas, Vol 2, 242
11. Lockhart, 1914, Vol IV, 214–5
12. Johnson, Vol. II, 893
13. Lockhart, 1914, Vol. IV, 217–223
14. Fanny Hall to Katherine Hall, 8th January 1825, Private Collection
15. Lockhart, 1914, Vol. IV, 227
16. Lockhart, 1898, Vol 2, 558
17. Johnson, Vol II, 895
18. Lockhart, 1898, Vol. 2, 229
19. Grierson, Vol. 8, 337n.
20. Douglas, Vol 2, 212 (Note 1)
21. Lockhart, 1914, Vol IV, 227
22. Hall, 1833, 308–9
23. Lockhart, 1898, Vol 8, 331–335
24. Basil Hall to J.G. Lockhart, Vol. X, Dunglass, 20 September 1837, NLS MSS 932
25. Johnson, 942, quoting Grierson (1932–7), Vol IX, 320–7
26. Constable, T. Vol. III, 487–489 & Constable Letter-Book 1829–36, NLS MS. 792

'A Man of Extraordinary Talents'

Edinburgh in the first 20 years of the 19th Century was basking in the afterglow of the Scottish Enlightenment – that flowering of scientific, literary and artistic creativity that brought the city worldwide prestige to be described by the novelist Tobias Smollett as a 'hotbed of genius'. The building of the New Town, with its wide streets and fine Adams architecture reflected this renaissance and stimulated the growth of the Scottish middle class, who were not slow to appreciate the spaciousness of its living environment and new sense of order in its grid-patterned Georgian thoroughfares. Here the Hall family had handsome residences, with houses at 128 and 132 George Street (then one of the most fashionable avenues of the city), while Basil had his own house nearby at 8 St. Colme Street (the Halls broadly divided their time between summers spent at Dunglass and winters in Edinburgh).

Notwithstanding its reputation, Hall was dismissive of the allure of the city. In a letter of 11 June 1819 to the Marchioness of Londonderry (who was described by him in 1816

The Edinburgh town house owned by the Hall family was at the west end of fashionable George Street, on the far left of this contemporary illustration. Edinburgh City Libraries.

In the elegant New Town of Edinburgh, evenings were enlivened by music and cultured conversation. Sketch by John Harden, Trustees of the National Library of Scotland.

as an 'old friend') he claimed: 'Edinburgh now is I rather think, more a mart, or place of transit for Literature, rather than the source from whence the wealth actually springs.' He lists the numerous publications such as the *Edinburgh Review* and the *Encyclopaedia Britannica* with their immense sales and circulation throughout Britain, but:

> by no means written exclusively by Edinburgh people – so far from it, that I suppose four fifths of the authors never saw Edinburgh – I do not very well see why this should be – possibly the distance between the Court and the Parliament, in their intrigues and distractions – enable a few hard-working literary men to devote themselves steadily to the collection and arrangement of materials for publication. Walter Scott could never write these books in London. Society, too, on the whole is much the better of having no court: manners, indeed are certainly much behind those of England, and this particularly with the young men, who would scarcely be tolerated in England.

While claiming that his countrymen are less polished, Hall admits that they are more free, although the 'distinctions of rank are more settled and one does not see that struggle to get up, which distinguishes the crowd that press on the footsteps of the throne'. This was a favourite theme of Hall's, who disliked the notion of people being dissatisfied with their allotted place in society. However:

> We are behind in the ordinary knowledge of the day, and assuredly are not such good company as the English. We have almost all something to do and so we attend to that

– there is less leisure to bestow on society – we are thus forced into domestic habits … they lead too often to selfishness, and almost always to narrow views. I have frequently in England met with the most sociable domestic habits, accompanied by the utmost liberality and the complete readiness to engage cheerfully in the general bustle of company, this is rare in Scotland – you see people generally destroying their happiness in Company by wishing to be snug back by their fire, in their morning dress … in their snug parties I have observed not the best manners – they all speak at once – and taunt one another, and instead of gentle discussion end every topic by a dispute. These and fifty other things English society is infinitely free from than Scotland.

Hall laments that the University had lost its lustre with the departure of Professor Dugald Stewart and others, so that there were no longer any men of great eminence. He makes an exception to the hospitality of his old friend Walter Scott 'whose house is the place where one sees Edinburgh's style. He has a nice supper and treats people admirably. He is infinitely good company himself when at the head of his own table. His eldest girl, too, is completely the Poet's daughter – rather pretty – extremely well bred … with all her father's enthusiasm … but without his talents – his genius or his soaring imagination'. Hall also relishes the company of the editor of *the Edinburgh Review*, Francis Jeffrey, whose conversational powers were 'quite magical'; and that of the ailing novelist, Henry Mackenzie (Note 27), whom he admires for his still vigorous mind.[1]

It is worth remembering that from an early age Hall had been out of Scotland for long periods of time, and that when he refers to 'company' and 'society' he is certainly not referring to the populace at large. Although his remarks on the disputatiousness of the Scots are generally accepted, there is here also more than a whiff of what came to be known as the 'Scottish cringe', or a tendency to consider themselves inferior to their southern neighbours. None of this means that Hall did not retain a deep affection for his native country, as he wrote on one of his journeys in Europe, 'I can never hear a stray note of any of our national airs, without being carried suddenly back to the mountains and valleys of old Scotland, among which I have rambled so much and so often'. He refers to hearing some lines of Smollett repeated by a Scot in the teak forests of Malabar, which gave him instantaneously 'so true a taste of the superior attractions of my own distant Fatherland'.[2]

Hall certainly seems to have relished London high society and in 1829 for example, when the family – including the new baby Frances – spent the winter in Paris, his mother claimed that Hall pined for the English capital, despite the invitations he received to the *soirées* of the Duchess of Hamilton and Lady Stewart de Rothesay, (wife of the British ambassador) while frequently meeting the previous Governor-General of British India, Lord Minto and his wife. Writing to Mrs Hunter, Lady Hall says he 'very judiciously wishes to cultivate the kind friends he has hitherto had there'. Hall resided at this time in salubrious quarters at No. 4 St. James's Place, overlooking Green Park and within a stone's throw of Buckingham Palace, and subsequently on Putney Heath.[3]

Notes

27 Henry Mackenzie (1745–1831) was an eminent Scottish lawyer, who in 1779 became the Comptroller of Taxes for Scotland. His sentimental novel *The Man of Feeling* (published anonymously in 1771) became the most popular work of fiction of the decade and was translated into many languages.

Following his South American travels, Hall retired from the Navy in the spring of 1823 and appears to have spent some time in Edinburgh. In a letter to Mrs Hunter on 27 December 1824 Hall had lamented his ageing and lack of grounded-ness in society: 'I wish I had lips insulated and that I had someone in whom I could vent my ill humour at home, without growling in public'.[4]

A month later he was writing to her again, announcing his engagement to Margaret Hunter, daughter of Sir John and Lady Hunter. He says that they 'have known each other long & loved each other almost as long – we have had many years experience of one another. We shall not be rich … but all things considered we are agreed to try the Voyage of Life together – without the slightest shadow of misgiving or apprehension on either side'. In a presumably jocular postscript he had written, 'My wifie that is to be says she believes you will be angry at this said match of mine – on the grounds that she once in your presence said something to my disparagement, which you fancied was meant in earnest. I have described to her, accordingly, the very fierce and unforgiving nature of your disposition, and have assured her that there is no hope of your forgiving her such an offence'.[5]

In fact, Margaret Hall subsequently wrote very warm, long letters to Mrs Hunter – especially in the final months of Basil's life – and they were clearly on very good terms. She was one of the first to hear of the birth of the Hall's youngest daughter, Eliza, in February 1826. During their later visit to North America, recalling the Hunters' familial treatment of Basil as a young man in Nova Scotia, Margaret says 'the little midshipman is now bald and grey'.

It is not known under what circumstances Hall met Margaret Hunter, whose father, Sir John Hunter, also had a fine house in Edinburgh's West End. He had been British Consul in Madrid during the Peninsular War but died before Basil's marriage to his daughter on 7 March 1825 in St. John's Chapel Edinburgh and subsequently at the Hunter house. Here Sir John's widow (and second wife), Lady Hunter, kept a sociable table. From an early age, Margaret and her sister Jane were accustomed to sophisticated and cosmopolitan society both in Edinburgh and Europe. Ten days before his marriage, Hall had written to his publisher, Archibald Constable, that he was now less concerned to publish since he had had an 'accession of Fortune [by the death of a relation his wife's mother] – no great sum, but considerably more than I had any immediate need for'.

Following his retirement from the Navy, Hall would be on half-pay, which at ten shillings and sixpence a day even then would not have kept him in the lifestyle he aspired to, and which he often complained about subsequently. However the 'accession of Fortune' may have encouraged him to make plans for his extended visit to North America on which he and his family embarked two years later.[6] A rare clue to Margaret's temperament is given in a letter written by Katherine Hall, then in Paris:

from something of having nobody to speak to etc. you might fancy there was some difference, but on the contrary we are better friends than ever, only I have gained a little more insight into the cause. One day, in the course of some discussion, Margaret talked of herself as being very reserved, & never having had an intimate female friend in her life, with the exception of Rose – I said 'How odd, this is, I have never discovered it,' with my usual obtuseness about character – but having got the clue, I now see plain enough, it is just so – and this, I do believe is one of the reasons we go on, without the shadow of a

Hall helped to introduce the outstanding American natural history painter John James Audubon to Edinburgh society. White House Historical Association (White House Collection).

shade of difference. Two people, who are fundamentally different, could hardly proceed far, without some clashing, if there was entire openness on both sides, but if luckily one or both happen to be reserved, it all keeps right, supposing of course there are proper principles & manners & all that – now it never enters my head to describe *sensations* … to her, & far less into hers.[7]

If Katherine's perception is correct, it would seem that Margaret's personality did not invite confidences and one wonders whether her relationships with Basil were equally reserved. She had been brought up in the social milieu of the diplomatic service in Madrid which might have been somewhat formal and restraining.

Some insight into Hall's life in Edinburgh – and the society of the capital in the mid-1820s – comes from a rather exotic source. The American John James Audubon – born in 1785 of French parentage – had through his own efforts become a very accomplished painter of American birds. In the course of his wanderings in the eastern and southern woods, he meticulously observed and sketched all the birds he encountered. By 1825 the intrepid painter had amassed a considerable portfolio, which he knew had to be exhibited in Europe if he was to make a name for himself. Following his arrival in Liverpool on 26 July 1826, he was warmly welcomed by the distinguished Quaker merchant and philanthropist William Rathbone. It was Rathbone's brother who befriended Audubon after his arrival in Edinburgh on 25 October of that year.

From a background in the interior of early 19th Century America, Audubon was shy and awkward in society, acutely sensitive to his reception (and to his art) and very conscious of his lack of formal education. Not surprisingly, he had violent mood swings. He adopted the image of a backswoodsman and dressed accordingly, allowing his hair to grow unfashionably long down to his shoulders – in fact he was somewhat vain and had an eye for female company, but many commented on his simplicity and of manners and behaviour. Although he had some initial difficulty in making connections in the capital, writers, philosophers, scientists, and many natural historians who were also artists soon lionised him, and he became very happy in the city:

'I think the time spent there was six weeks of the *densest* Happiness I have met with in any Part of my Life. And the agreeable and instructive society I found there in such Plenty has left so pleasing an impression on my Memory, that did not strong connections draw me elsewhere, I believe Scotland would be the country I would chuse to spend the remainder of my days in.[8]

He was greatly impressed by the city:

I walked a good deal and admired this city very much, the great breadth of the streets, their good pavement and footways, the beautiful uniformity of the buildings, their natural grey coloring and wonderful cleanliness of the [whole] was felt more powerfully, coming direct from dirty Manchester [he was obviously speaking of the New Town and not the old Edinburgh of the Royal Mile]. But the picturesque *tout ensemble* here is wonderful. A high castle there, another there, a bridge looking at a second city below, here a rugged mountain and there beautiful public grounds, monuments, the sea, the landscape around, all wonderfully managed … I frequently turned around to view the beautiful city back of me, rising gradually [like an] amphitheatre most sublimely and backed by mountainous clouds that improved the whole really superbly.[9]

Audubon was determined to meet Sir Walter Scott, whose works were highly popular in America. On October 26 1826 he records that he found 'James Hall advocate … absent in the country' (it is not clear whether he is talking about James Hall the advocate and artist or Basil's father Sir James Hall). He also met the renowned Professor Jameson who told him that Scott had become a recluse and thus he had little hope of meeting him. 'Not see Sir Walter Scott, thought I – by Washington I shall, if I have to crawl on all fours for a mile.'[10]

Robert Jameson was Professor of Natural History at Edinburgh University and founder of the *Edinburgh Philosophical Journal*. He was also a founder of the Wernerian Natural History Society. It was at one of their meetings that Audubon attended, where among the papers was a letter from Mr William Jameson from Lima describing a voyage round Cape Horn, and a Chart of the Course laid down in the mode recommended by Captain Basil Hall.[11] Incidentally, the young Charles Darwin – who was later to refer to Hall's geological work in the course of his famous *Beagle* voyage – met Audubon at a meeting of the Wernerian Natural History Society and also saw Scott when he chaired a meeting of the Royal Society of Edinburgh.

In a letter to his wife Lucy, dated 2 December 1826 Audubon says:

> I forgot, as I am often apt to do, that Sir James Hall and his brother [Basil] called on me this afternoon. The [latter] wished to receive some information respecting the comfort that may be expected in travelling through my dear country, and said that he would bring a map and write down my observations [Audubon was in error in assuming that Basil was Sir James' brother].

On 5 December Audubon wrote:

> I returned to the Institution and had the pleasure of meeting Captain Basil Hall of the Royal Navy, his wife, and Lady Hunter [Audubon obviously did not remember he had met Basil only three days previously]. They were extremely kind to me, spoke of the Greg family and my good old friend Mrs Rathbone (Note 28) in terms that delighted me. The Captain asked if I did not intend to exhibit by gaslight, and I replied that I could not take it upon myself to speak of it. He promised to do so at once, and told me he would write me the answer of Mr Skene, the Secretary. I received their cards and, of course, call upon them soon.[12]

This is absolutely typical of Hall, the 'fixer' *par excellence.*

Hall may have become friendly with Audubon for several reasons. Hall was interested in the natural sciences and he was something of an artist himself (like his brother James), but he also wanted to pick Audubon's brains about his own forthcoming visit to North America. Perhaps as Scott indicated, it just was about getting involved 'in other people's business.' The record of Hall's meetings with Audubon in 1826 suggests that Hall was very much part of the city's literary, scientific and artistic elite in the latter part of the Enlightenment, effecting a large number of introductions for Audubon, including Sir Walter Scott at his house in the city. According to Chalmers, Hall was 'a pillar of Edinburgh society and was able to be of great assistance to Audubon.'[13] An indication of his status was his direct personal involvement with the architect Charles Robert Cockerell in the plans for the building of the intended reconstruction of the Parthenon on Calton Hill – the proposed monument to those who had fallen in the Napoleonic Wars. This commanded the attention of the 'great and the good' of Scotland, and even in its unfinished state, still dominates the skyline of eastern Edinburgh above Princes Street.

On 6 December Audubon describes his first meeting with the Halls at home:

Notes

28   Mrs Rathbone was the wife of William Rathbone, the prominent Liverpool merchant mentioned above. The Gregs were also important Liverpool merchants.

I visited Captain Hall. He lives at no 8 Chalon Street [i.e. St Colme St] where I had the pleasure of finding him *at home!* As I ascended the staircase I distinctly heard the sweet sounds of a well-fingered piano. I entered the room and saw both the Captain and his very interesting lady, the performer on the instrument. Few women ever attracted my notice more forcibly at first sight, although by nature thou knowest well I am dearly fond of amiable ones. But her fine face was [possessed] of something more than [the ordinary] and her [demeanour] had a power that I cannot describe to thee. Her youth and form all unite to [cause] a liking. Her husband received me with great, true politeness and a degree of kindness far differing from the usual on such slight acquaintance. They spoke of visiting the United States, and I [urged] them strenuously to do so. Captain Hall, a man of extraordinary talents, a great traveller and a rich man (Note 29) professing friendship towards thy husband, was very [receptive] thou mayest be sure. If I am a *phrenologist* (Note 30) at all, they are a most happy couple. I derived this conclusion from the lady telling her husband, as I bid them good morning, to accompany me downstairs, quite low and in such a tone as I am sure she never thought I heard. He told me I would be received an honorary member of the Wernerian Society (Note 31) with acclamation.[14]

On 8 December Audobon continued: 'During the afternoon I was called on twice by Captain Basil Hall, who was so polite as to present me with a copy of his work in two volumes on South America, with a remarkably polite note. His note was this:

8, St Colme St, Friday E., 3

Dear Sir, I beg you will do me the favor to accept a copy of the work which I published some time ago on South America. This is a very feeble method which I take to express the admiration I feel for your wonderful collection.

I remain your most ob.svt., BASIL HALL

(P.S.) You will not forget to come to us at eight o'clock Thursday the 14th.[15]

Audubon did not forget and immediately wrote to his wife about the occasion:

I reached No 8 St Colme Street where Captain Hall resides. But my sweet wife, I had on beautiful new pantaloons, new splendid Lafayette coat, and over all this my own face to embellish the whole. The company was precisely what the Captain had promised me. Mrs Hall, the interesting Mrs Hall, had her beautiful babe in the room, a rosy, fat, little female urchin. [There were also] a Mr Hunter and daughter, young Hall the advocate, and Mr Hall's brother-in-law and wife. Dinner was soon announced and I led a lady to

Notes

29   Audubon must have assumed Hall's wealth from his associations and lifestyle in Edinburgh.

30   The Edinburgh brothers George and Andrew Combe obsessively promoted the cult of phrenology – i.e. the characterisation of a person from the morphology of their skull. Although much in vogue at the time, it fell into disrepute later.

31   The Wernerian Society – founded by Professor Robert Jameson of Edinburgh (see below) – was the counterpart of the prestigious Linnean Society of London. On 7 December the society made a delighted Audubon an honorary member.

it downstairs … the ladies having left, the American atlas was put on the table. I read my notes, and the Captain followed the course with a pencil from New York to New Orleans, my Lucy, visiting Niagara, St. Louis, Nashville and a hundred other places. We talk of nothing else but a voyage to America, and Mrs Hall appears quite delighted with the idea. The Captain wishes to write a book; and he spoke of it, Lucy, with as little concern as I would say "Dearest girl, beloved wife, I will draw that duck".[16]

Later, Audubon was to complain that Hall – in his usual direct and interrogative way – exhausted the artist with his questions on America.

Hall called on Audubon on his return from America, while the artist was still in London in 1828, claiming that he had seen much of the United States, 'but that he is too true an Englishman to like things there'. Audubon felt 'more and more convinced that he had not remained in America long enough, and that his judgement of things there must be only superficial'. On another occasion in Edinburgh (13 March 1827), Audubon had written: 'After an uncomfortable dinner in high company, *five gentlemen* waited on us at table, and two of these put my cloak upon my shoulders, notwithstanding all I could say to the contrary. What will that sweet lady, Mrs Basil Hall think of a squatter's hut in Mississippi in contrast with this?'[17] In fact, the Halls coped remarkably well with rough travelling conditions, but decried both the shortage and quality of servants.

On 16 December Audubon – from a dinner hosted by Basil's mother-in-law, Lady Hunter – provides a revealing picture of the style of an Edinburgh social occasion, centred on the Hall *ménage*. According to the artist in one of his long descriptive letters to his wife Lucy, many of Edinburgh's titled people were there:

Now Lucy, my dinner at Lady Hunter's. I dressed [in] all my new [finery] again, and at precisely six of the evening I took coach for No. 16 Hope Street. I was shewn upstairs and presented to Mary Lady Clark, who knew both Generals Wolf and Montgomery, a most amiable English woman of eighty–two years of age. [After] Lady Arbuthnott (Note 32), [Lady] Young, Lady *this*, Sir *that*, Lord *the other*, I reached the interesting Mrs Hall, with whom I was too stupid not to shake hands. A captain of the [military] post was there, Harvey (Note 33), young Greg, and [others]. I had the pleasure of leading Mrs Hall to dinner and was seated next her mother Lady Hunter and Lady Clark. We dined. I did not feel so uncomfortable as usual. This nobility is so uncommonly kind, affable and truly well bred. Lady Hunter and Lady Clark quite nursed me. Captain Hall had the other end of the table … I could see Mrs. [Hall?] quite well from my seat. I took frequent opportunities of doing so … Little wine was drunk.[18] About 9 the ladies rose and Captain Hall *attacked me* about America again. Hundreds of questions were put me by all those noble folks, and I had no answer to all. But as all I said was very plain truths I had no difficulty except of feeling choked through my natural defect of awkward feelings in company. When we reached the ladies, [at] perhaps 11, I was quite delighted to see

Notes

32 Lady Arbuthnott was the widow of Sir William Arbuthnott – Lord Provost of Edinburgh and brother of Margaret Hunter's mother.

33 This is likely to have been Captain Harvey – Basil Hall's brother-in-law and long-standing friend whom he brought back from India in 1817. Audubon was later to refer to 'the handsome Mrs Harvey' – Basil's sister Magdalene, widow of Colonel Sir William de Lancey, now married to Captain Harvey.

Mrs Hall making tea as simply as I have seen thee do it, without any apparent pomp or fudge. Lady Hunter brought a cup of coffee, [and] a little girl one of tea, saying that she knew that 'American gentlemen like it'. The company had not augmented to a great number, and several were still coming. Miss Monro came in. Mrs Hall, from whom I begged a little music, played sweetly for me on the piano.[19]

On 24 and 25 December Audubon records:

I get up several hours before daylight to write for Captain Basil Hall, and am glad that it is over.[20]

On 26 December he continues:

Captain Hall soon spoke of America, and strange to tell, he was a midshipman aboard the *Leander* when Pierce was killed off New York (Note 34), and when [I was] on my way from France … Lady Hunter came in, and Sir William Hunter [1788–1856 – a metaphysician, lawyer and politician]. I saw a beautiful sister of Captain Hall, the handsome Mrs Harvey, and many more, but Lucy I made my escape without bidding adieu except to the Captain.[21]

Audubon went to dinner on New Year's Eve 1826 at Basil Hall's (which happened to be the captain's birthday), where he was introduced to various Edinburgh personalities, including Francis Jeffrey – the editor of the influential *Edinburgh Review*.[22]

Writing to Lucy, Audubon ends with a commendation on the Halls:

Sunday was also spent at painting as long as light lasted, but I had to go and dine at Captain Hall's again, to be particularly introduced to Francis Jeffrey, the principal writer in the 'Edinburgh Review'… I was first at Captain Hall's. [He,] his lady, Lady Hunter and the young babe were all there in the setting room. But Mr McCulloch, a great writer on political economy soon came in … During the dinner the conversation was various. I liked Captain Hall and his lady the more I saw of them, and I found Lady Hunter very kind.

Audubon had now become something of a figure in Edinburgh society. Between 14 November and 23 December 1826 his 400 works of over 2000 birds – the culmination of 25 years work – were exhibited at the prestigious Royal Institution for the Encouragement of the Fine Arts in Scotland (now the Royal Scottish Academy). The paintings at double elephant size (75 by 100cm) became the talk of the capital and the exhibition was a triumph. Edinburgh University made one of the first subscriptions to the book *Birds of America* engraved by William Home Lizars with 435 plates costing 170 guineas – which delighted the artist (the University sold its copy in 1992 in New York for $4.1 million).

Notes

34 This was the notorious incident of the shelling of a US ship outside New York in April 1807 when the British were blockading the neutral American ports against the French and in which John Pierce, an American sailor, was killed. It was followed in June by the infamous *Chesapeake* incident (see above).

This painting of black poll warblers by Audubon was stolen by Raeburn's step-grandson. Royal College of Physicians and Surgeons, Glasgow.

It was here that a very curious incident occurred, involving Hall. It was found that one of Audubon's most attractive pictures (of black poll warblers) was missing. The thief was found to be Henry Raeburn Ingles – the deaf and dumb step-grandson of the most illustrious portrait painter of his time who was well known to the Hall family and had painted their portraits (Note 35). The painting was returned on the same afternoon that it was taken, but Audubon thought that the thief should be punished. It was Hall's intervention on behalf of the young boy that prevented this and by way of thanks he presented Audubon with a number of his own publications.[23]

However, 22 January 1827 – when Hall introduced the artist to Sir Walter Scott – was a red-letter day for the impressionable artist:

I was painting diligently when Captain Hall came in, and said: 'put on your coat, and come with me to Sir Walter Scott; he wishes to see you *now…*' [Scott at this time was staying at his rented accommodation at 3 Walker Street, much reduced from his former grand town house at 39 Castle Street – his Edinburgh home for 25 years and sold only in the previous year]. In a moment I was ready, for I really believe my coat and hat came to me instead of my going to them. My heart trembled; I longed for the meeting, yet wished it over. Had not his wondrous pen penetrated my soul with the consciousness that here was a genius from God's hand? … We reached the house … Captain Hall said: "Sir Walter, I have brought Mr Audubon." Sir Walter … pressed my hand warmly and said he was glad to have the honour of meeting me. His long, loose silvery locks struck me … I could not forbear looking at him, my eyes feasted on his countenance … he had been at work writing on the 'Life of Napoleon'. Scott's daughter was brought in and there was much conversation. I talked little, but believe me, I listened and observed.[24]

Scott himself recorded the visit in his journal: '*Jan 22, 1827*. A visit from Basil Hall with Mr Audubon the ornithologist'; and commented on his great simplicity of manners

Notes

35   Ingles was the step-grandson of Raeburn.

and behaviour.[25] Scott was to meet Audubon again when invited to a private viewing of his work and was impressed. He met him yet again at an exhibition at the Royal Institution for the Encouragement of Fine Arts, when the two conversed.

Audubon was invited on 5 February 1827 to exhibit his plates at the Royal Society of Edinburgh:

> Captain Hall took my hand and led me to a seat immediately opposite to Sir Walter Scott, the president, where I had a perfect view of this great man … Sir Walter came and shook hands with me, asked how the cold weather of Edinburgh agreed with me, and so attracted the attention of so many members to me, as if I had been a distinguished stranger.[26]

Before his departure for London, Audubon was discreetly advised by Hall and the Countess of Morton to have his hair cut, as his long locks were then unfashionable. Hall also sent a black suit to Audubon in London to ensure that he was appropriately attired. In his last letter to his wife Lucy before departing Edinburgh for London, Audubon said that Captain Hall 'has been unremittingly kind to me and has give me 20 letters all valuable introductions'.

References

1. Basil Hall to Lady Londonderry, 11 June 1819, Kent Records U840 C574
2. Hall, 1841, Vol II, 167
3. Lady Hall to Mrs Hunter, 8 November 1829, ff. 129–136 NLS MS 14196
4. Basil Hall to Mrs Hunter, 27 December 1824, ff.18–19 NLS MS 14196
5. Basil Hall to Mrs Hunter, 25 January 1825, ff. 22 NLS MS 14196
6. Basil Hall to J. Constable, 10 March 1825, f.31 Constable Collection NLS MS 7200
7. Katherine Hall to Catherine Johnston, 27 February 1830, Private Collection
8. Chalmers (2003), 33, cited in Hook, A., *Scotland and America 1750–1835*, 20
9. *Ibid.*, (2003), 35–37, citing Ford, A. (1987), 305–309
10. Chalmers, 1993, 35
11. *Ibid.*, 1993, 107
12. Ford, 369–373
13. Chalmers, 2003, 60
14. Ford, 374
15. *Ibid.*, 378
16. *Ibid.*, 392
17. Audubon, 300
18. Chalmers, 1993, 58
19. Ford, 397
20. *Ibid.*, 416
21. *Ibid.*, 424
22. Chalmers, 2003, *passim*
23. *Ibid.*, 2003, citing Ford, 398
24. Audubon, Vol 1, 206–7
25. Anderson, entry for 24 January 1827, 268
26. Audubon, Vol 1, 209–110

North American Journey

When Hall sailed from Liverpool on 17 April 1827 with his wife and 15-month-old daughter Eliza, for a stay of 14 months in North America, they were to encounter a very different country from the one he had known as a young midshipman some 23 years previously. In 1806 the Lewis and Clark expedition had crossed the continent from east to west and everywhere new routes had opened up and new methods of transportation had developed, spurred by the Federal Land Law and new cheap land that encouraged westward expansion. By 1824 with the finding of a southern route through the Rocky Mountains, Oregon and California were within reach. In 1817 the first steamboats in America appeared on the Ohio River, taking goods and passengers from Louisville to New Orleans. In 1825 the completion of the Erie Canal enabled goods from New York to be transported to the Midwest, while the resources of the interior flowed eastwards to that great port.

Politically there had also been significant changes. In 1817 Mississippi became the 20th state, while two years later the Mississippi Compromise established the balance between slave states – of which Mississippi was one – and free states. In 1818 the 49th

Two slave drivers and a backswoodsman. From Forty Etchings from Sketches *made with the* camera lucida, *in North America in 1827 and 1828 by Capt. Basil Hall.*
Trustees of the National Library of Scotland.

Chiefs of the Creek Nation and a Georgian squatter. From Forty Etchings from Sketches made with the camera lucida, *in North America in 1827 and 1828 by Capt. Basil Hall. Trustees of the National Library of Scotland.*

parallel had been fixed, establishing the boundary between Canada and USA. The Doctrine of 1823 established the principle that there could be no interference from any European state in American affairs, introduced by President John Quincy Adams – whom Hall met. In 1825 the furore over his election as president by the House of Representatives resulted in the establishment of the Democratic Party and in the year after the Hall's arrival, Andrew Jackson was elected as 7th President.

From a population of approximately 4 million on Hall's first visit, that figure had risen to almost 10 million by his second. Ten years previously 30,000 immigrants had arrived on America's shores – many of them Germans and British, the latter overwhelmingly Irish. However, the demand for land meant that by 1827 the Creek Indian nation had given up all their land in Georgia, albeit by treaty, while the Indian Removal Act was wending its way through the legislative process to restrict all Indians to land west of the Mississippi. The demand for American cotton in Britain increased production enormously, aided by the invention of the cotton gin by Eli Whitney. Meanwhile, an American middle class was developing, with a growing interest in the arts and literature – Fennimore Cooper's *The Last of the Mohicans* exemplified the American values of rugged individualism, love of nature, and physical capacity. Education moved increasingly away from the European classical tradition towards modern studies and science, although conversely, the fashionable architectural style was tending toward the classical in the American Greek revival.

This was the background to Halls' visit – ostensibly to investigate American institutions such as schools, prisons and courts. His narrative of the journey touches on all of the above topics, but also comments extensively on American mores and manners. His path was considerably smoothed by over a hundred letters of introduction to some of the most eminent men in the country, and ready access to the great national institutions. In this way they met: Daniel Webster (1782–1852), who was to become Secretary of

State; John DeWitt Clinton (1769–1828), Governor of New York; Professor George Ticknor (1791–1871), the eminent historian of Spanish literature at Harvard; Jude Joseph Story (1779–1845), Associate Justice of the Supreme Court; Gilbert Stuart (1755–1828), the foremost American portrait painter of his time; and there were many others, including the President John Quincy Adams, and many State Governors.

He would not however have needed such a letter in order to meet the urbane Sir Charles Richard Vaughan (1774–1849), appointed envoy extraordinary and minister plenipotentiary to the United States at the British Embassy. As private secretary at the British Embassy in Madrid between 1810 and 1820, he was well known to Mrs Hall, who in addition to Hall himself, corresponded with him during their travels. They particularly relished his knowledgeable company at a number of balls and dinners in Washington, while he sent round his own diplomatic cards with theirs to the *Corps Diplomatique* and the Cabinet to ensure a suitable reception. There was much talk of old times in Spain, and how she had never loved anywhere more than that country.

Hall wrote long letters to Vaughan, commenting on what he found in America. He admitted that his views on the country had quite changed since his arrival and sympathised with Vaughan in having to negotiate with 'litiginous and hair-splitting' Americans. However, in forwarding a copy of his narrative on his travels, he asks Vaughan to let him know of any favourable American reaction, but not otherwise.[1]

Hall confessed that his impressions of America on his earlier acquaintance were not very favourable, but since then he considered his views had mellowed and he was determined to go there, not just with an open mind, but to be prepared to be very kindly disposed to the country and its inhabitants.[2] He admitted that he had been concerned with the wisdom of taking his young daughter on a trip such as this, which was frequently arduous, but in the event she proved to be – as many children are at that age – a very adaptable traveller, often sleeping through the noisiest situations.[3] She was accompanied by her Scots nursemaid – a Mrs Cownie from Forfar, in Angus – whom Hall described as 'a superior kind of attendant'.

Hall felt that despite the political and geographical differences between America and Britain, the relationships towards the two countries respectively should be more cordial, but that previous travellers from Britain had displayed some prejudice that the Americans naturally much resented. Hall claimed that to avoid this, he deliberately chose not to read their works in order to go with a completely fresh mind, preferring to form his opinions only from his own experience and contacts with his hosts.[4]

Hall was determined not only to write about his experiences, but to illustrate scenes in the form of sketches, using a *camera lucida*. Some of these sketches (especially of native people) form an unusual record of the time, and were published separately.[5] His view of the Buffalo waterfront at the Lake Erie Basin became famous, and among others was used extensively on Staffordshire pottery plates. It was said that 'these prints provide us with the most transparently accurate visual portrayal of the conditions of America in the first part of the nineteenth century, a portrayal unique and of considerable historical importance'.[6]

In contemplating this long and often arduous journey, even if they were both seasoned travellers the Halls were nothing if not intrepid, although he in particular tends to gloss over the very real physical discomforts. His assessments were often skewed by his politics, but his actual observations were detailed and shrewd. He takes a special interest in American government at national and state level, in slavery, in engineering accomplishments, and in the relations between America and Britain.

His published narrative is very uneven, combining as it does interesting descriptions of incidents and events with quite tedious and lengthy polemic – usually on the same theme of the government of the country and its manners. Despite Hall's claims to objectivity, he cannot hide his ingrained Tory views. As Mark Twain observes, while Hall 'exaggerates nothing', his conclusions on those aspects of American life which he dislikes are strongly, if unconsciously, biased. Although the responses of American readers were often wildly intemperate, it is easy to understand why their feathers were severely ruffled. If they had been able to read Mrs Hall's letters to her sister at the same time (not published till 1931), their opinions would have been amply confirmed.

Hall is very readable on events such as a farm fair or eating at speed in New York and he is often funny – but his polemic on American politics – always with his conservative axe to grind – is tedious and frequently repetitive. Much of his writing attempts to be 'educational' in simply describing – for example the US systems of justice – and as a result is boring, whereas his first hand description of Auburn prison is excellent. While much of his account of American life and customs is no doubt true, his interpretation is usually skewed to fit his preconceived notions of 'democracy'. 'Methinks he doth protest too much' is very apt when assessing Hall's proclamations of disinterestedness and objectivity.

Hall goes on at some length about the difficulties of answering the constant queries of Americans on his opinion of the country and its people. Praising their hospitality and kindness, he could not come to terms with their sensitivity to even the mildest criticism, despite their urging him to be frank. It is a constant theme in his narrative – his anxiety to indicate his goodwill and yet being perturbed by the American tendency (according to Hall) of being boastful about their country. It seemed to him that everything said about England could be overtopped by them, and being highly defensive about anything implying that England in particular (other European countries were less exposed) could be finer or larger, it was an issue – exacerbated by their unjustified sense of their cultural inferiority – that dogged him throughout his journey and which cast a shadow over his reputation on his return.[7]

Mrs Hall wrote long and frequent letters to her sister Jane, which perhaps fortunately were not published till over a century later and which excoriate American manners. Where Basil (with few exceptions) eschews naming those he met, Mrs Hall has no such inhibitions. While accompanying him, she generally does not share Basil's interest in official institutions, but interestingly tells her sister 'Basil has become so used to companionship that he cannot bear to go anywhere without me' – perhaps a result of his relatively late marriage. She comments at length on the style of social occasions (which only rarely meet her approval) and is affronted by those Americans who presume to make any comparison between their country and Britain. She almost always approves of Europeans met – especially Scots – but like her husband and after the convention of the time, refers to 'England' when Britain is clearly meant. Nowadays she would be described as singularly snobbish, but that is perhaps to overlook the mores that were widely shared by her class in her socially stratified home country. She is particularly appalled by the lack of servants in the northern states, and their quality in the southern ones, where they were invariably black slaves.

Nevertheless, she praises American hospitality and in New York claims that: 'There were never people so petted and made of as we are; we have the whole town at our command … we have all at once been translated to the highest rank, for were we a Duke and a Duchess we could not be more attended to.'[8] But even after a month of travelling she had 'not yet seen *one* American gentleman' – i.e. a man with acceptable manners. One could sympathise with her after reading that 'walking upstairs to valse my partner began clearing his throat. This I thought ominous. However I said to myself, "Surely he will turn his head to the other side." The gentleman, however, had no such thought but deliberately shot across me. I had not courage to examine whether or not the result landed in the flounce of my dress.' Later, on American cooking, Mrs Hall complains about the lack of 'that refinement that becomes a second nature to English persons'. Her particular delight is Eliza's adaptability and good nature in almost every situation, and she basks in her pretty daughter's effect on eminent gentlemen: the President himself sent a locket with some of his hair to the young girl.[9]

Wherever Hall went he enquired into any technical innovation. After witnessing the ineffectiveness of the much-vaunted New York fire-service – despite their undoubted energy and bravery in quelling serious fires in the city – he addressed the New York Committee of the Fire Service proposing a tripod used in Edinburgh for directing water hoses, complete with his own drawings (on his return to Britain he sent a model of this device). He examined the naval dockyards in considerable detail and describes at length the moving of a substantial brick house by means of wooden slides. In the city he was impressed by refuges for juvenile delinquents and a school for non-whites, but did not impress the head teacher of a girl's high school when he suggested changes to their pronunciation of words. He deplored the absence of wigs and gowns in court, suggesting that such customs maintained traditional dignity.[10]

The end of May 1827 finds the Hall family travelling by steamboat down the Hudson River, where he makes the telling remark that 'country houses belonging to the ancient aristocracy … now rapidly withering away … before the blighting tempest of democracy' – blaming the evident decay of both lands and manor houses partly on the equal division of property amongst all the children of a family (as the second son he himself had personal experience of the feudal system of primogeniture in Europe). However, one of his most interesting descriptions is that of a state prison in the countryside – built by the prisoners – where the basis of correction was the enforced total lack of communication between the prisoners, night or day.[11]

On 5 June the party reached Albany – the important east entrance to the Erie Canal – and the following day entered the state of Massachusetts. Dining with the DeWitt Clintons, Mrs Hall gives her first detailed description – one of many – of the lavishness of American meals, topped off by 'a magnificent pyramid of ice, supported on each side by preserved pineapple and other sweetmeats'.[12] She later states that her husband 'had thoroughly established himself as an abstemious man … and they wonder that he neither eats nor drinks'.[13] Hall himself comments on the lack of distinction between social ranks, not least between those being served and those doing the serving. In America the whole idea of 'servants' being eschewed, other than by slaves in the southern states.[14]

Hall was later very impressed by the 41 mile long Welland Canal between Lake Erie and Lake Ontario, and argues strongly for the extension of the canal system – even if this involved the annexation of French Lower Canada – since British Upper Canada had no access to the sea.[15] Hall was continuously concerned with the possibility of US incursions into the border country of Canada and advocated the building of the expensive Rideau Canal for purely defensive purposes; and for the same reason, the improvement of military and naval fortifications at Kingston on the Canadian side, while maintaining the left bank of the St. Lawrence as a wooded wilderness and avoiding improvements of rapids to discourage invaders from the south. He emphasises the need to keep the Canadians (as loyal subjects) 'on side' by showing British support and maintaining that 'the colonies should be made permanently, as substantially British, as the Isle of Wight'. It is hardly surprising that American readers found Hall's narrative inflammatory.[16]

On their way to the bustling town of Syracuse, Hall observed every stage of development from initial forest clearance and solitary log cabins in the woods to building of villages. He was depressed by the girdling of fine woodland trees to make way for agriculture, which he thought was equivalent to having 'their throats cut', leaving blackened stumps like old teeth after the brush had been set alight.[17] He found Rochester, as a canal town, humming with activity: the villagers owned some 160 canal boats drawn by 822 horses, providing a considerable income to a fast-developing town where the creation of new streets from the clearance of virgin forest – whose timbers immediately provided the material for new houses – astonished him. Each of the townships that he visited (even at their earliest stages) boasted at least one church, despite the absence of any 'established' denomination.[18]

On 29 June the Halls reached Niagara Falls, which made the profoundest impression on him. They spent ten days here, with Basil examining each aspect of the great cataract from every angle and taking detailed measurements with a specially modified barometer.[19] He even took a boat behind the Falls and despite his scientific inclinations, appeared to be under the spell of this great natural phenomenon, raising his experience to a mystic level: he was clearly overwhelmed, claiming his final visit as the most interesting three hours in his life and likening it to being sent to Heaven.[20]

Hall with Margaret (leaving Eliza with friends) then undertook an exhausting and quite adventurous journey to the eastern extremity of Lake Ontario, covering some 463 miles. Much of this was done in rough carts with only wooden springs on abominable 'corduroy' roads over a period of 11 days, returning to Niagara by steamboat. If nothing else, it says something for Hall's wife's fortitude: at one point they were at risk of serious injury when on a steep incline their cart ran backwards out of control.[21] Where a bridge had disappeared, they were saved by the ingenuity of a small boy in a canoe who got their horse and cart across the Riviere Rouge, not without considerable difficulty.

At the end of July Hall made a special point of visiting a Government-sponsored settlement of indigent Irish immigrants at Peterborough, travelling from 3am to 7pm to reach it (Note 36). There were over 2,000 settlers sent out from Ireland in 1825 at a cost of £21

Notes

36 It is very likely that Hall made this considerable detour at the request of Sir Robert John Wilmot-Horton (1784–1841) – an English landowner and Member of Parliament who promoted emigration obsessively as a solution to poverty and overpopulation (especially in Ireland) with a particular focus on Upper Canada.

each and supplied with the necessities of life plus 100 acres of land for clearance and cultivation. In Hall's words this experiment was 'to make those useless and miserable beings good subjects of His Majesty', instead of fomenting trouble at home, at a time when 'Ireland was overloaded with paupers'.[22] The immigrants apparently prospered and despite Hall's attempts to draw out of them any complaints, they were in fact duly grateful both to His Majesty and the Governor of the Province for the improvement in their circumstances.[23]

From Kingston – where typically they were given the use of the naval commodore's house – the Halls travelled to Montreal. Here they had the great good fortune to meet Captain John Franklin (Note 37) – the renowned arctic explorer – recently having arrived back from his second 14,000 mile expedition to the north, and his Scottish surgeon-naturalist, Dr. John Richardson.[24] With Franklin, Hall and his family had the exhilarating experience of an excursion on the St. Lawrence and Ottawa rivers in a 40-foot *bateau* rowed by 14 of his stalwart *voyageurs*.

Throughout his journal Hall not only describes his travels, but spends at least as much time discoursing (often at some length) on his favourite subjects. One of these is the value of the Colonies, of which at that time Canada was one. He is in no doubt that such Colonies justify their expense partly on economic grounds for two-way trade and as a source of raw materials, especially in time of war, while the so-called Provinces were important in utilising British-manufactured goods and in absorbing Britain's 'surplus' population. Canada at that time sent raw materials (especially timber) to the West Indies, employing some 15,000 seamen, and Hall particularly commends the hardy Canadians as providing a 'nursery' for good navymen.[25]

By December 1827, the Halls had re-crossed the Canadian frontier back into the United States and were enchanted by a trip on Lake George, which contradicted Hall's previous disparagement of North American scenery (although he deplored the constant noise and disturbance created by the new steam ferry boats).[26] Later, he was to be equally delighted by the prettiness of the older New England villages, especially during the Fall.[27]

Here Hall rides one of his most frequent hobbyhorses in claiming that the lack of fellow feeling between Americans and the British is not surprising given their form of government. In claiming presumably to speak for the whole population of Britain, his statement that democracy is 'as repugnant to the English as monarchy and its class distinctions are to Americans', he is ignoring the festering discontent with limited suffrage and political and economic injustice at home. He then goes on to confirm his attitudes by declaring that the lack of social hierarchies reduces the quality of services and goods to the lowest common denominator, since there is no demand for superior provision, with lowest price being the standard.[28]

Upon hearing his first Unitarian sermon (Note 38), Hall admires its delivery but cannot resist suggesting that this is a 'Democracy of Religion' which is inferior to an

Notes

37 Captain Franklin (later Sir John Franklin) (1786–1847) was renowned for his three expeditions to find the fabled North West Passage, and became a national hero after the extreme rigours of his first expedition in 1819 were made known. When he met Hall he had just returned from his second expedition, which had commenced in 1825. Both of expeditions were with the intrepid Scottish surgeon-naturalist, Dr. John Richardson.

38 The minister in question was William Ellery Channing (1780–1842) – the foremost Unitarian preacher in the USA and a prominent thinker in the liberal theology of the day. He was very influential in American religious life.

established (i.e. state-supported) church, claiming that the Church of England (which he strongly upheld) 'is diametrically opposed to the religious institutions of America.' (in America Hall had to make do by attending Episcopalian services, while sending Mrs Cownie off to wherever a Presbyterian church could be found). Because of the difficulty of changing its doctrine or discipline, the Church of England represents the 'permanency of everything we hold dear in the country'. Apart from anything else, this Anglo-centric Scottish High Tory ignores the fact that his church's writ does not run throughout the Kingdom. It is all of a piece with his increasingly conservative views, but quite inconsistent with his previous enthusiastic espousal of political freedom in South America. What Hall is evincing – despite his frequent emphasis on his openness of mind and inclination to see the best in America – is a deep-rooted Anglo-centric prejudice, whether conscious or not.[29]

Some of Hall's observations on the American political process have modern relevance. He had arrived at a the time of a Presidential election and averred that electioneering had become a sort of field sport, where the pursuit was more important than the capture and where a candidate's policies might be overlooked in the whole frenetic business of electioneering. While this focussed on the candidate, it might ignore his actual fitness for office according to Hall.[30] Where special interests predominated, the President was as much of a puppet as anything else, made worse by frequent elections at both national and state level. In Washington, at a levée held by John Quincy Adams, he had an opportunity to talk to the President, while on another occasion, Mrs Hall had the honour of being seated next to him – which in itself says something about the Halls' privileged status.[31]

Hall had a mass of letters of introduction to people of distinction – some 20 in Boston alone. As a result of these and sending out their cards, they might receive up to 20 visitors in a day. He was very impressed by the neatness and cleanliness of Boston and comments on the huge quantities of ice transported to the southern states and the West Indies – amounting to 3,000 tons annually. He visited all the great institutions of the city. They were generally pleased with the taste of Bostonians and the attention they paid to him and his family, including a number of balls and receptions laid on in their honour. He was equally impressed by the manufacturing centre of nearby Lowell, where they were guided by Dr Kirk Boott – who was instrumental in establishing the industrial complex – with its canals, bridges, spinning mills and power looms, leading him to comment on the full employment and abundant food in America generally.[32]

At Boston, the Halls engaged in a whirlwind of visiting everything from ropeworks to printing presses, schools, alms-houses, penitentiaries and navy yards – where they were invariably guided by friends.[33] At the naval stations, Hall observes that naval discipline seems to be even more severe than in Britain, with rank distinctions being maintained. As usual, Hall puts this down to the fact that such distinctions are not appreciated generally by shore-based American society, thus US naval personnel did not have a societal hierarchy on which to condition their behaviour at sea.

At Philadelphia on 28 November he had an agreeable interview with the Count de Survilliers – elder brother of the late Emperor Napoleon and formerly King Joseph of Spain, and met the Prince of Musignano, Charles Lucien – son of Lucien Bonaparte and married to Joseph's daughter. Lucien's son – a boy of between three and four years old – immediately established a rapport with Eliza and presented her with his sister's doll. This gesture enormously impressed Mrs. Cownie, delighted that her charge now had such a gift (now christened 'Miss Bonaparte') from no less than the grand nephew of the Emperor himself.

Hall shows a special interest in slavery and the conditions of black people generally. In Washington he attended the sale of a 16 year-old slave in payment of a debt to a mean-looking prospective purchaser (the young slave had no knowledge of the whereabouts of his parents or siblings who were all slaves in the south). As the bidding reached $100, Hall was asked if he would like to raise a bid. In a rage he answered: 'No! No! I thank God we do not do such things in our country.' Both the auctioneer and some of those present were apparently sympathetic to this view, but the sale ended with a successful bid of $143. Hall fled out of doors to rid himself of his despair.[34] Hall was later to acknowledge that the problem in the northern states – with relatively few slaves – was quite different from the situation in the south, where the immediate freeing of slaves could cause considerable economic problems, not least for the slaves themselves.[35] He admits to finding the whole question very difficult to deal with objectively and to discard his own prejudices.[36]

On 18 February 1828 the Halls left Norfolk for Fayetville, commenting on the seasonal migration of all those who could afford to escape the malarial swamps of the south in summer to the cooler northern states. He gives a vivid description of crossing over many miles of swamp forest, supported only by floating roads of poles, with dark forest on either side. Here they heard numerous frogs in the inky roadside ditches, with the coach sometimes sinking up to its axles. At one river crossing they were ferried across in a punt by slaves bearing flaming torches. Everywhere in the south, they were uncertain of their accommodation and supplies of food, obliging them to carry their own emergency rations.[37]

Further south near Camden, they encountered a family of white migrants on their way to Florida, accompanied by some 40–50 slaves of all ages. Hall's daughter was delighted to find children of her own age and regally dispensed a large recently-purchased sponge cake. But here Hall was to uncover the tragedy of one slave who was chained to another, miserable because he had been forced to leave behind his wife, as a different master employed her. At Columbus, Hall had confirmation of the endless restlessness of these pioneers, when the head of the travelling party was met by his brother after a long absence, who could get no rational explanation from the leader of why he had left a prosperous farm in Maryland and moreover was quite prepared to move on again if he found his situation uncongenial.[38]

Hall himself – while deploring the inhumanity and injustices involved – raises the question of what could happen – to both slaves and owners – if the slaves were liberated under the current economic regime. He clearly deplores a system where the slave masters and plantation owners are the *de facto* administrators of the law. Hall is genuinely at a loss as to the solution of the conundrum, where violence and anarchy could follow imposed changes. He is much affected by seeing some 300 slaves in a jail, young and old 'penned up like cattle' while awaiting sale.[39] Mrs Hall – declaring blacks to be ignorant and stupid, spending their money on drink – describes their houses 'the most wretched hovels I ever saw in my life'.[40] However, at a party in Charleston she 'had as tough an argument regarding slavery with some ladies as ever Basil had on any subject with gentlemen' and comments elsewhere suggested that she shared his abhorrence of the whole system.

One of the most revealing comments made by Mrs Hall was from a conversation with an impressive black slave driver called Solomon (shown in sketch by Hall) who, in the absence of the plantation owner, looked after the Halls splendidly.

> we have asked him many questions, but frequently he stops and says that he does not like to answer such and such a question, a man may get into trouble by saying too much … Mrs Cownie and Eliza walked about the place with him whilst we were writing this morning, and he spoke more freely to them than to us. He told Mrs Cownie that he cannot read nor write but that his wife who can is teaching him, but when he hears his mistress coming he hides the book because she knows she would be so angry if she detected him. Of course, the policy of the planters is to keep their slaves in a state of ignorance, that they may not come to knowledge of their situation. In the meantime Solomon keeps all of his accounts in his head.[41]

Not only does this say something of her sympathies, it also indicates an unusual degree of intimacy with her nursemaid.

Leaving Savannah on 31 March, Hall organised his journey through the southern state to New Orleans, employing a coach with driver and his son in charge of a one-horse baggage cart, which was very successful, although expensive. Their rate averaged 30–40 miles a day (often over the roughest of roads) and across virtually uninhabited swamplands without maps. In late March, the family travelled through the seemingly endless pine barrens of Georgia – some of these on fire – encountering floods, snakes and alligators, with daily distances sometimes reduced to 25 miles. After a dangerous storm, Hall describes crossing a swollen river across a treacherous pole bridge with Eliza in his arms – the little girl apparently unaware of danger, loved all the adventure. The adults usually had execrable beds but Eliza and Mrs Cownie 'had one of those admirable travelling beds, made by Mr Pratt of Bond Street, which fold up into an incredibly small compass'. There appeared to be no inns as such, the custom being to stop at any wayside house where for a small charge, the people were prepared to offer modest hospitality to travellers.[42]

The Halls then journeyed into Creek Indian Territory, from which the native people had been removed – 'a painful chapter in the history of America', according to Hall. The land thus cleared was parcelled up and subject to a lottery for white settlement, while some five square miles was allocated for the building of the capital of Columbus which was going on rapidly at the time of Hall's visit – a complete city in the making from the virgin forest. This was part of the great movement of settlers south and west fulfilling what was to be described as America's 'manifest destiny'. Hall encountered the destitute Indians to the west, unable to change from their previous hunter-gatherer mode of life on their former ancestral lands.

At bustling New Orleans, Hall (with the guidance of the chief surveyor) made a detailed study of the system of levees and water control and was astonished to find the Mississippi up to seven feet above the streets of the town. He describes the great double-tiered paddle steamers that took passengers constantly up and down the river and the 'arks', which did likewise for the produce to and from the port. He provides a lengthy analysis of the whole system of agriculture and the river environment. Presciently, he warns of the dangers of interfering with the latter through levees, especially at times of seasonal floods. [43]

By 25 April they were on their way to Louisville, aboard one of the largest steamboats on the Mississippi. Hall details the whole operation of the vessel, including the carrying of fuel wood from loading points *en route* by passengers (who could thereby reduce their fares) as well as the hazardous business of navigation.[44] By 7 May they had reached Louisville in Kentucky – greatly admiring its greenswards, gardens and fine surrounding forest – where they spent a week with hospitable friends. It was here that the Halls visited the Berthouds: Mrs Berthoud being the sister of Audubon, from whom Hall brought letters. Likewise, they were very agreeably entertained at St. Louis, with parties in their honour.

During the Hall's absence on an excursion, Mrs Cownie and her charge quite fortuitously encountered General Clark (Note 39), who not only recognised them but presented Eliza with a pretty purse.[45] The family then had a taste of the mid-west, crossing the 'Prairies of Illinois', which Hall described as being akin the sea in its magnitude and sensation of waves. They suffered in Indiana not only from an unsprung carriage on very poor roads, but also from what Hall described as a 'want of habitual politeness' or rather taciturnity, which he ascribed to the great distances separating its inhabitants.[46]

At the end of May at Cincinnati, Eliza fell ill with what Hall diagnosed as *Cholera infantum* and they were persuaded that the only cure was to get away from the rivers and into the mountains as soon as possible. The child was apparently seriously ill with fever, but recovered remarkably in the cool air of the Alleghenies – despite the most miserable travelling conditions, covering very low mileages over long days. The family had received a fright and decided to cut their trip short, omitting a scheduled return to the Maritime Provinces of Canada.[47]

However, Mrs. Hall admits something that Basil (at least in print) does not: that they had decided this well after the child had recovered, adding 'our want of patience with this country increases daily'.[48] They therefore embarked from New York on 1 July 1828 after an absence of over 14 months, having covered some 8,800 miles in North America. According to Mrs Hall, the sight that excited Basil's admiration most on arrival in England was that of footmen in livery – 'It is so long since we have seen a well-dressed servant'.[49] No doubt these were encountered when hospitably received, they spent several days with Lord and Lady Spencer.

When Hall's three-volume narrative of his journey was published, coals of fire were heaped on his head by many American readers – most of whom took his critical remarks as denigrating both their country and countrymen (and in their vehemence tending to confirm Hall's remarks on their sensitivity to criticism). What some particularly objected to was (inexplicably) his 'moral degeneracy and coarseness' in some of his descriptions of incidents.

Notes

39   Captain William Clark – together with Meriwether Lewis – had made the first overland expedition to the Pacific from St. Louis in the years 1803–1806 at the instigation of President Jefferson. They gathered much important scientific information. It was a much-celebrated journey.

Richard Biddle – a member of the House of Representatives – in a book published in both Britain and the United States, expended 150 pages in a diatribe against Hall, dissecting almost every phrase in the latter's narrative. He wrote: '[Hall] undoubtedly stands among the foremost of those who insist upon it that Great Britain and America *do* and *shall* cherish towards each other "unkindly feelings" … it would be impossible not to smile at the completeness of the self-delusion under which he shows himself to have laboured'; and that Hall's words were 'bitterly sarcastic and contemptuous'.[50] However Mark Twain in *Life on the Mississippi* was to say: 'it is difficult, at this day, to understand, and impossible to justify, the reception which the book of the grave, honest, intelligent, gentle, manly, charitable, well-meaning Capt. Basil Hall got.'[51]

In her later book *Domestic Manners of the Americans*, the English writer Fanny Trollope expressed very similar views to Hall, and not surprisingly commended his work – not least the accuracy of his comments to this sensitivity. He in his turn supported hers. Later she was to say:

> I was in Cincinnatti when these volumes came out, but it was not till July 1830 that I procured a copy of them. One bookseller to whom I applied told me that he had had a few copies before he understood the nature of the work, but that after becoming acquainted with it, nothing should, induce him to sell another. Other persons of his profession must, however, have been less scrupulous, for the book was read in city, town, village, and hamlet, steamboat and stagecoach, and, a sort of warwhoop was sent forth perfectly unprecedented in my recollection upon any occasion whatever

Hall had 'put the Union in a blaze from one end to the other', she wrote to Miss Mitford (a novelist friend). She goes on to remark: 'the observation which, I think, struck me the most forcibly, and which certainly came the most completely home to my own feelings, was the following: "In all my travels, both amongst Heathens and amongst Christians, I have never encountered any people by whom I found it nearly so difficult to make myself understood as by the Americans."'

Referring to the hostile reception of Hall's book on North America, his friend Sir Walter Scott said that he had gone to America with a glowing 'desire to paint things *couleur de rose*'. But to anticipate perfection, he pointed out, 'is everywhere to invite disappointment. And especially when people were alike in so many ways as the British and the Americans they were apt to be impatient with each other for not being in all ways the same.' Hall, he granted, often said the wrong thing at the wrong time but nothing could be worse than bad-tempered dissension between the two countries, 'ripping up' each other's defects 'in an illiberal or insulting manner'. Scott also felt sure that both might gain 'from calmly collating their points of difference'.[52] In addition, Scott later remarks: 'Cadell [his publisher] is of opinion if I meddle in politics, and I am strongly tempted to do so, I shall break the milk pail, and threatens me with the fate of Basil Hall, who, as he says, destroyed his reputation by writing impolitic politics.'[53]

However, the *Tory Quarterly Review* heartily approved of Hall's conclusions – particularly his analysis of the political situation in America – but complained that Hall had omitted 'actual instances of vulgarity, knavery, sottishness and hypocrisy, which would have been both amusing and characteristic; and that having omitted them, he has scarcely dealt fairly with his readers'. The Reviewer then records that he thinks the book will do much good in Britain by alerting people to the perils of democracy![54]

It is unfortunate that Hall's expressed opinions on American government and differences in behaviour and manners between the countries almost completely overshadowed a valuable contemporary picture – derived from extensive travel and genuine investigation – of a country at a particularly interesting stage of its development. (Note 40).

References

1. American Papers of Sir Charles Richard Vaughan, NLS MSS
2. Hall, 1830, Vol. 1, 3
3. *Ibid.*, 199
4. *Ibid.*, 4
5. Hall, 1829, *passim*
6. Conlin, 50
7. Hall, 1830, Vol. 1, 13–17
8. Pope-Hennessey, 26
9. *Ibid.*, 50, 190
10. Hall, 1830, Vol. 1, 23–38
11. *Ibid.*, 46–50
12. Pope-Hennessey, 63
13. *Ibid.*, 91
14. Hall, 1830, Vol. 1, 122
15. *Ibid.*, 214
16. *Ibid.*, 228–251
17. *Ibid.*, 129–134
18. *Ibid.*, 151–167
19. *Ibid.*, 177–211
20. *Ibid.*, 351–2
21. *Ibid.*, 349
22. *Ibid.*, 283 *et seq.*
23. *Ibid.*, 349
24. *Ibid.*, 380
25. *Ibid.*, 406–415
26. Hall, 1830, Vol. 2, 7–8
27. *Ibid.*, 94–5
28. *Ibid.*, 20–26
29. *Ibid.*, 119–122
30. *Ibid.*, 1830, Vol. 3, 59–62
31. *Ibid.*, 13–27
32. Hall, 1830, Vol. 2, 122–140
33. *Ibid.*, 144–5
34. Hall, 1830, Vol. 1, 39–41
35. *Ibid.*, 42–48
36. *Ibid.*, Vol. 3, 75
37. *Ibid.*, 113–124
38. *Ibid.*, 128–33
39. *Ibid.*,155–170)
40. Pope-Hennessey, 204
41. *Ibid.*, 221
42. Hall, 1830, Vol. 3, 266–71
43. *Ibid.*, 336–343
44. *Ibid.*, 358 *et seq.*
45. Pope-Hennessey, 278
46. Hall, 1830, Vol. 3, 377–388
47. *Ibid.*, 391
48. Pope-Hennessey, 286
49. *Ibid.*, 302
50. Biddle, 3–6
51. Twain, Appendix C.
52. Grierson, Vol. XI, 353, 355
53. Scott's Journal, January 2 1831
54. *Quarterly Review*, Vol. 41, 417–446

Notes

40   The final insult was when a Staffordshire chamber pot manufactured in England but presumably intended for the American market was decorated on the base with a portrait of Hall.

'That Curious Fellow'

On 23 October 1831 a carriage rattled across the wet cobblestones of London streets on a day of violent wind and rain. In the carriage sat a pale elderly man, dressed in trousers of the small check pattern of his Border country, with a plaid of the same material wrapped tightly round his shoulders. In his hand he grasped the shepherd's crook which had become his 'third leg' in his increasing lameness. Sir Walter Scott was now seriously ill and on his way to Portsmouth to take ship to Malta, having been persuaded that a voyage to a warmer climate might improve his declining health, after a series of strokes: it was to be his final voyage.

The bookseller Cadell had written to Hall to ask for help. Hall felt that even a Whig administration would help this grand old Tory, and on 13 September Hall went straight to the Admiralty to see Sir James Graham, the First Sea Lord.[1] Cadell's message had not reached Hall until long after office hours, and Sir James had already gone to dress for dinner, but Hall sent in word that his call was about Sir Walter and might help preserve one of the most valuable lives in the country. Sir James received him at once; before he had read half of Cadell's letter, he said that the government would undoubtedly grant the request and to 'Leave all that to me'. Hall was to write Scott without a moment's delay: 'Pray make an effort to save tonight's post. Say to Sir Walter that his passage shall be arranged in the manner agreeable to his wishes.' The First Lord then wrote to Hall saying, 'I have had the greatest pleasure in communicating to Sir Walter himself, the gracious terms in which his Majesty was pleased to convey his consent on this occasion'.[2]

Cadell wrote to Scott referring to the letter Hall had sent immediately: 'it has kept me laughing since I received it … I am positively guiltless of saying more to the Captain … than that the mode of conveyance for you was as yet unfixed – and asked if a cabin on board a man of war was at all feasible? when lo! The Captain goes smack to the First Lord & settles the whole affair in a trice.'[3] However it is entirely typical, not only of Hall's decisiveness in practical matters, but also his confidence in approaching 'the great and the good' – particularly within the service which he knew so well.

Later, in a letter to Lockhart that begins with a paean of praise for Lockhart's *Life*, Hall asks that in the revised edition his involvement in this last voyage of Sir Walter Scott should be amended, explaining that: 'it was in consequence of an urgent letter from Mr Cadell, written to me confidentially, and asking me to discover in what way a passage in a ship of war going to the Mediterranean could be obtained – and that I moved in the matter. The statement given by you on page 298 would seem to imply that I busied myself in it, of my own proper movement. Now I deserve neither such praise

Basil Hall, Naval Captain by Sir Frances Chantrey, circa 1825–30. National Portrait Gallery.

nor (as some might think) such censure. The devil lies with Cadell – I merely acted at his request. I have stated fully at page 283 of the last volume of my 'Fragments'. I think I deserve some credit, and I take it thankfully, for having gone at once to Sir James Graham, and got the affair put in train – but no more.'[4]

   In his record of this episode Hall – a Royalist if ever there was one – delivers an encomium to King William IV: his kindness, his sagacity, etc. 'Who can forget the sensation produced at the time, by the delicacy and good taste with which the interests and convenience of a private individual were therefore gracefully converted into a public concern?'[5] As Scott had not really wanted to leave his beloved Abbotsford to go on this voyage, he was undoubtedly comforted by the apparent sincerity of his reception.

Hall was of the opinion that it was necessary to drag Scott away from his labours to which he had become addicted, but which Scott saw as fulfilling a debt of honour. Scott acknowledged this when he asked Hall if he kept a diary, which Hall affirmed. Scott said: 'I fear that a great part of my present illness has been brought on by too much working. Let me warn you, captain, it is a very dangerous thing to overwork … I may have brought on some of this illness by excess of mental exertion.'[6] Scott had previously indicated that he worked up to five and a half hours daily on creative writing – two or three of them before breakfast. But Hall suspected that he did much more now, under the burden of creditors – sometimes double the hours previously.[7]

The offer of a King's ship had undoubtedly gratified Scott, and he ascribed this very much to the exertions of Hall in the part played by him in securing his passage in the *Barham*. In a letter to a relative he declared Hall had 'done a great deal for me in this matter', describing him as 'that curious fellow, who takes charge of everyone's business without neglecting his own'.[8] Furthermore, when in London, Scott complained mildly: 'My womenkind [Jane Scott and Sophia Lockhart (Note 41)] are gone out with Walter and Captain Hall … I wish that they would be moderate in their demands on people's complaisance … a sailor in particular is a bad refuser and before he can turn three times round he is bound with a triple knot to all kinds of [engagements]'[9]

Also in London, Hall promptly waited on Scott and offered to go to Portsmouth with him and help in the embarkation – noting that often those not used to naval vessels did not always appreciate what had to be done, including the procuring of bed linen etc. Scott did not want to put Hall to further trouble.[10] Someone had suggested that at the end of the voyage Scott might give the Commander of the *Barham* a pipe of Madeira or a hogshead of sherry: 'Now, is this right?' Scott anxiously asked. 'No', replied Hall; it was unusual and would offend him. Scott supposed: 'But may I not give him a copy of the *Waverley* novels, for instance, with an autograph inscription?' This Hall approved.[11]

From that point on, recognising his usefulness, Scott agreed to Hall's proposal, especially when he offered to escort the ladies in the party back to London. Scott was later to describe Hall as 'running about among the blue jackets quite in his own element'.[12] However one suggestion by Hall – that the King's indulgence in providing a berth for Scott aboard one of His Majesty's ships would justify a few lines from Scott – went awry. Scott interpreted this as a few lines of poetry and replied accordingly. Hall was mortified to receive a letter from Scott on 26 October 1831 from the Fountain Inn, Portsmouth: 'My Dear Sir, Nothing but an absolute impossibility would occasion my declining a request of yours at this moment especially as you oblige me by saying [that] you have shewed unremitting kind[ness]'. Scott goes on to explain that he was only a good writer of occasional verses and asserts that 'if ever I see an opportunity of returning thanks for this great favour … it must be in humble prose'. Scott was clearly confused, for he admitted that a few days previously, he had broken down in an attempt to write something for Dorothy Wordsworth's album. Scott then goes on: 'Suppose for instance I should inscribe to you a Romance in my best manner, making proper mention of the King in the

Notes

41   Jane Scott was the author's dutiful daughter and Sophia was John Lockhart's wife.

dedication & supplying you with an early copy for the King's library table. This would be more easily done … etc. I am with a deep sense of your kindness, affectionately yours.'[13] Hall declares: 'You will perceive that Sir Walter in some degree, mistook my purpose, for nothing certainly could be further from my thoughts than the idea of suggesting to him to write a copy of Verses at such a time and on such an occasion.'[14]

Hall hurried ahead to Portsmouth by the Rocket coach to engage rooms for Scott's party. The *Barham's* sailing was delayed by contrary winds, and after failing to secure rooms at The George (the principal inn), Hall settled on rooms for them at the Fountain Inn, which Scott described as 'a mansion made of wood in imitation of a ship'.[15] Apparently the landlord of the Fountain Inn was so overcome at the unexpected honour of having Scott under his roof, that he prevailed on a whole family to turn out of their rooms in order to accommodate the Scott party.[16] Hall then carefully inspected the cabins, approving them all – but arranged for the gratings in a ladder to the quarter deck to be blocked over to prevent Scott's stick from catching.[17]

Captain Pigot of the *Barham* was most solicitous concerning Sir Walter's comfort and the amusement of his party, even offering them a naval barge to do a bit of sight-seeing.[18] The Lieutenant Governor of Portsmouth, Sir Colin Campbell, and other local authorities 'called upon him almost as if he had been a royal personage'. The port-admiral, Sir Thomas Foley, waited on him to say that his yacht the *Sylph* and the flagship's barge were at his orders, while the commissioner, Sir Michael Seymour, offered the facilities of the dockyard. The ladies wanted to see an anchor forged and this was duly laid on. The Lords of the Admiralty on a tour of inspection also waited upon Sir Walter's pleasure.[19]

When a deputation from the Portsmouth Philosophical Society arrived to pay their respects, Scott was at dinner, but interrupted this to receive them graciously, speaking to each one of the large party personally.[20] According to Hall The Fountain overflowed all day long with visitors to the famous man, and Scott declined no one, but remained in his usual urbanity and good humour over the several days waiting for a favourable wind.

Scott's spirits lifted with his novel surroundings, in which he took an interest – including the location of the sinking of the *Royal George*, the subsequent destruction of which Hall had recorded in considerable technical detail for the Hydrographer to the Navy, Sir Francis Beaufort. Hall thought Scott was never more cheerful and animated than on the day of his departure.[21]

Hall often talked to Scott about the Waverley Novels[22]. Hall mentions having bought the manuscript of *The Antiquary*, which Scott liked best – telling Hall that he wrote it *currente calamo* (without trouble). Hall sent for the manuscript that he owned by express and received it in time next morning. Hall asked Scott to write on the manuscript his reason for preferring this work above all his others. Scott then wrote a two page letter to Hall personally, which Hall asked to be signed and dated, realising that this was probably the last letter he would write in England and which Hall included as a facsimile of the original at the end of his text.[23] That letter explains that it was one of the few of his novels based on the life of a real person – a boyhood friend – and how an old friend of Scott's father, having read *The Antiquary*, deduced that Scott was the author of the Waverley Novels. Jonathan Oldbuck of Monkbarns was based on the late George Constable of Wallace Craigie of Dundee, despite, as Scott says, his own attempt at cover up.

According to Scott, George Constable 'dined when in Edinburgh twice or thrice with

The attempt to lift the sunken Royal George failed. Drawing by Andrew Taylor.

my father every week & used to speak of my sayings and doings as [those of] a clever boy. I was extremely surprised at this detection. For I thought I had taken the utmost care to destroy every trace of personal resemblance … At least we three walked every day in the world and the Antiquary was my familiar companion. He taught me to read and understand Shakespear. He explained the field at Preston pans at which he had witnessed the horrors from a safe distance.' Scott goes on to philosophise about the circumstances at the end of his life in a letter which is lengthy, but intensely personal. The letter ends:

The sort of preference which I gave, and still give, this work, is from its connexion with the early scenes of my life. – And here am I seeking health at the expense of travel, just as was the case with me in my tenth year. Well! I am not the first who has ended life as he began, and is bound to remember with gratitude those who have been willing to assist him in his voyage, whether in youth or age, amongst whom I must include old George Constable (Note 42) and Yourself.

WALTER SCOTT
Portsmouth, 27 October, 1831.

Of all his correspondence with Hall, this is the item which most clearly indicates the fraternity between them. Scott died 11 months later. It is easy to see why Hall treasured this rare tribute (by a curious coincidence, at the time of drafting this episode a news item appeared concerning the WWII sinking of HMS *Barham* – a successor to the 19th Century vessel that a Scottish woman medium had 'seen' despite a news blackout over the incident. As a result of her 'disclosure' to the relatives of one of the 861 sailors who died, she subsequently became the last person in Britain to be jailed as a witch in a sensational trial in 1944. With his interest in witchcraft, Scott would have been intrigued).

Notes

42   George Constable of Wallace Craigie, Dundee.

The last letter that Sir Walter Scott wrote from England was addressed to Hall. Trustees of the National Library of Scotland

References

1. Hall, 1833, Vol. 3, 285
2. *Ibid.*, 286 *et seq* & Walter Scott to Robert Cadell, 9 May 1831, ff.383/384, NLS MS 1752
3. Robert Cadell to Walter Scott n.d. NLS MS 3242
4. Basil Hall to J.G. Lockhart, 18 April 1836, f. 65, NLS MSS 932
5. Hall, 1833, Vol. 3, 287–87
6. *Ibid.*, 306–7
7. *Ibid.*, 311
8. Anderson, 672
9. Anderson, 670
10. Hall, 1833 Vol. 3, 290
11. *Ibid.*, 293–4
12. Anderson, 672
13. Grierson, 1932–37, Vol. XII, 35–6
14. Basil Hall to J.G. Lockhart, NLS MS 932
15. Anderson, 672
16. Sultana, 31
17. Hall, 1833, Vol. 3, 296–300
18. *Ibid.*, 294
19. *Ibid.*, 298
20. *Ibid.*, 302
21. *Ibid.*, 311
22. Johnson, Vol. II, 1198–2000
23. Hall, 1833, Vol. 3, 321

'A Delightful Companion'

In early summer of 1818, in the company of Sir Archibald Alison (Note 43), Hall made one of several later journeys to Europe, following the route of the fashionable 'Grand Tour'. Alison had been friendly with Sir James Hall and 'spent several happy weeks each year' at Dunglass and at Gosford House, home of the Earl of Wemyss. He was very admiring of Sir James's three daughters, Helen, Magdalene, and Fanny ('too soon cut off by consumption while still in the bloom of youth').

Alsion records: 'I made up a travelling party with Pringle, my companion in Ireland, and Captain Basil Hall, then in the zenith of his popularity on his return from Loo-Choo'. In London on 12 July 1818, Alison was joined by an old college friend and they set out 'joyously' for Rome and Naples, through Switzerland, visiting Napoleonic battlefields and touring round Mont Blanc and then continuing via St Bernard and the Simplon Pass to the Italian Lakes, Milan, Parma, Verona and Padua. They stayed in Venice for ten days where Alison writes: 'this interesting city, rendered doubly so at that time by the introductions which Captain Hall had brought to Lord Byron … living in almost total seclusion from his countrymen, for whom he seemed to have a rooted aversion' (Byron had fled London from the obloquy of English society).

Alison continues: 'As Captain Hall was a distinguished literary character, however, and had brought letters from Mr. Murray, their common publisher, [Byron] received us with great cordiality.' Apparently Byron took them to his favourite ride at the Lido and through the city in his gondola, and made his hotel their home. Alsion writes: 'I believe Captain Hall and I were the only English who saw him, at least for any considerable period of time, at this time' and then gives a succinct and perceptive analysis of Byron's personality.

The party then went on to Petrarch and the prison of Tasso at Ferrara, to Bologna, Florence, Tuscany, before arriving in Rome on 19 September 1818. After visiting Naples, the Amalfi coast and observing Vesuvius in eruption, they returned to Rome, where they visited the studios of the famed Canova (Note 44) and Thorvaldsen. Despite the

---

Notes

43 Sir Archibald Alison was an inveterate traveller who studied law in Edinburgh and contributed no less than 50 pieces to *Blackwood's Magazine* over 20 years. An historian of the French Revolution and a committed Tory – he warned against democracy – his work had huge sales in Britain and America. He was violently against trade unions although he challenged the excesses of capitalism, but was a defender of slavery – all-in-all a contradictory man (*Sir Archibald Alison (1792–1867)*, Michael Fry, ODNB Vol. 1, 739–742).

44 Antonio Canova (1757–1822) was the most famous exponent of Neo-classical sculpture, widely acclaimed for his revival of ancient Greek and Roman styles. He worked on commissions from Napoleon and produced sculptures in England. He would have been over 60 when he met Hall.

reputation of the Italian sculptor, Alison described his work as mere 'imitations of the antique' but was pleased enough to have supper with Canova, while Sir Humphrey and Lady Davy (Note 45) and Captain Basil Hall made up the party. It was one of those *noctes cœnæque Deum* (Note 46) which occur rarely in the course of life … Canova and Davy each sought to draw out the other, and each seemed forgetfulness only of his own greatness' (Hall was also to become friendly with the Davys, strengthened by their mutual interest in science and technology). The party returned to England via Florence, Bolsano, Pisa and Lucca, sailing to Genoa and visiting Lyons and Paris.[1]

Hall had dearly wished to meet Lord Byron: they were later to share the experience of supporting independence movements in South America and Greece respectively. By a series of coincidences they appeared to miss one another in Venice, although they were able to correspond, as Moore records in his monumental *Life* of the poet:

> On the last day of August, 1818 I was taken ill with an ague at Venice, and having heard enough of the low state of the medical art in that country, I was not a little anxious as to the advice I should take. I was not acquainted with any person in Venice to whom I could refer, and had only one letter of introduction, which was to Lord Byron; but as there were many stories floating about of his Lordship's unwillingness to be pestered with tourists, I had felt unwilling, before this moment, to introduce myself in that shape. Now, however, that I was seriously unwell, I felt sure that this offensive character would merge in that of a countryman in distress, and I sent the letter by one of my travelling companions to Lord Byron's lodgings, with a note, excusing the liberty I was taking, explaining that I was in want of medical assistance, and saying I should not send to anyone till I heard the name of the person, who in his Lordship's opinion, was the best practitioner in Venice.
>
> Unfortunately for me, Lord Byron was still in bed, though it was near noon, and still more unfortunately, the bearer of my message scrupled to awake him, without first coming back to consult me. By this time I was in all the agonies of a cold ague fit, and, therefore, not at all in a condition to be consulted upon anything – so I replied pettishly, 'Oh, by no means disturb Lord Byron on my account – ring for the landlord, and send for anyone he recommends.' This injunction being forthwith and literally attended to, in the course of an hour, I was under the discipline of mine host's friend, whose skill and success is no part of my purpose to descant upon; it is sufficient to mention that I was irrevocably in his hands long before the following most kind note was brought to me, in great haste, by Lord Byron's servant.

> Venice, August 31, 1818
>
> Dear Sir, Dr. Adglietti is the best physician, not only in Venice, but in Italy; his residence is on the Grand Canal, and easily found; I forget the number, but am

---

Notes

45 Sir Humphrey Davy (1778–1829) was a chemist, inventor, amateur poet, and philosophic naturalist. He first described the process of photosynthesis and discovered laughing gas. Davy often moved in the literary circles of Wordsworth and Southey, while Coleridge became an enthusiastic friend. Given a post at the Royal Institution in 1800 in London, he was elected Fellow in 1803 – his patron being the influential Sir Joseph Banks. In 1807 he was elected a secretary to the Royal Society and in 1820 became its President (ODNB Vol. 15, 506–512, David Knight).

46 The classical name for choice gatherings of congenial spirits, also known as *petits-soupers* or bachelors' dinners in modern English.

probably the only person in Venice who don't know it. There is no comparison between him and any of the other medical people here. I regret very much to hear of your indisposition, and shall do myself the honour of waiting upon you the moment I am up. I write this in bed, and have only just received the latter and note. I beg you to believe that nothing but the extreme lateness of my hours could have prevented me from replying immediately, or coming in person. I have not been called a minute – I have the honour to be, very truly

Your most obedient servant

Byron.

His Lordship soon followed his note, and I heard his voice in the next room; but although he waited more than an hour, I could not see him, being under the inexorable hands of the doctor. In the course of the same evening, he again called, but I was asleep. When I awoke I found his Lordship's valet sitting by my bedside. 'He had his master's orders', he said, 'to remain with me while I was unwell, and was instructed to say, that whatever his Lordship had, or could procure, was at my service; and that he would come to me and sit with me, or do whatever I liked, if I would only let him know in what way he could be useful.'

Accordingly, on the next day, I sent for some book, which was brought, with a list of his library. I forget what it was which prevented me from seeing Lord Byron on this day, though he called more than once; and on the next, I was too ill with fever to talk to anyone. The moment I could get out, I took a gondola and went to pay my respects, and to thank his Lordship for his attentions. It was then nearly three o'clock, but he was not yet up; and when I went again on the following day at five, I had the mortification to learn that he had gone, at the same hour, to call upon me, so that we had crossed each other on the canal; and, to my deep and lasting regret, I was obliged to leave Venice without seeing him (Note 47).[2]

Although Hall was ill for much of this trip, he made his first visit to Vesuvius with the renowned guide, Salvatore Rosa – 'one of the ablest, the most intelligent, and the most agreeable guides in Europe'.[3] They set off on donkeys in unfavourable weather, and proceeded on foot to the cone of the volcano, which quite unexpectedly erupted violently at that point:

'we felt the ground tremble, and heard the volcano tremble in most terrific style. In the next moment the great crater was heard to vomit forth a mass of fiery materials.' In the fog they could see nothing and Salvatore was seriously perturbed. When stones fell – 'much too close' – the guide said they must change course quickly. There was then an even louder explosion and Salvatore commanded Hall to stand still and look up into the air, but not to move except for a single step to left or right if a stone was to be seen falling on their heads.

The stones fell around in quantity – some bigger than a man's head, and red hot, almost hitting the guide's shoulder. But the donkey man ran when 'a larger mass of lava

Notes

47   Hall's note implies that he did not meet Byron, but Alison is quite unequivocal about this and the dates are consistent. The only explanation is that Hall regretted not saying goodbye to Byron.

than the rest was discovered by my companion whirling down from the sky, full upon his head'. Having been roped to the donkey man, Hall had to follow suit and Salvatore was convinced that they would both be killed. In the mist the stones came thundering down all around – it was possibly the closest that Hall had ever come to serious injury or even death. Nevertheless, they then went to the crater to witness the huge furnace, which was vomiting forth smoke, flames, and red hot stones, at intervals of six or eight minutes – but all shrouded in mist.[4]

Some 15 years later Hall was to observe the volcano in full eruption, which he had anticipated by observing the current weather conditions and saw 'one of the grandest sights I ever beheld', typically using the smoke of the eruption to accurately hypothesise on the course of land and sea breezes. He lost no time in meeting up again with Salvatore, who was already geared up for an expedition as if expecting a call. This time it was a family affair and even Hall's little girl Eliza was carried up the mountain in an armchair on the shoulders of one of the mountaineers. The ladies in the party were partly 'towed' by mules and donkeys.

According to Hall, 'We beheld to our infinite joy, the lava flowing from an orifice to a considerable distance', but a closer inspection was vetoed by the experienced Salvatore. Hall estimated that the jets of stones projected up to 2,300 feet. Next day, Hall returned to make a complete circuit of the outer cone with Salvatore, making very detailed observations of the rate of flow of the lava stream at uncomfortably close range, which he measured at one foot every two seconds. At one point, huge masses of red hot ancient lava broke off from a precipice, forcing a young helper to save his life by jumping into a crevice. Hall – who seems to carefully calculate his expenses – gives the cost of the whole expedition (Note 48) at £1 and 3 shillings.[5]

Alison was very complimentary about Hall, and as the most detailed description of his character, is worth quoting in full:

> During this long journey … from Lyons to London, I was much impressed by the talent and conversation of Captain Basil Hall … we were in the carriage every morning at four, and went on till nine at night. This lasted seven days, independent of a few days' rest in Paris; and during the whole of that time, our conversation never flagged, not did I experience a moment's weariness. He had inherited from his father and mother, in both of whose families talent had long been remarkable, strong natural abilities; and though he had not enjoyed the advantage of a university education, in consequence of having been sent to sea at thirteen, yet he had supplied this defect in a surprising manner by observation and conversation. His thirst for knowledge led him to enquire minutely into the circumstances, manners, and institutions of every country which he visited; his acuteness gave him an extraordinary power of discovering everywhere the persons from whom such information could best be obtained. The chances of his profession had already led him into almost every quarter of the globe – he had visited America, Canada,

---

Notes

48 Incidentally, while at Palermo Hall was horrified by a vast number of mummified monks in a convent, declaring: 'Save me from the half dried monks of Palermo!' – stuck up in rows and dressed in the identical cowls and hoods they wore when alive (Hall, 1841, Vol. II, 172). The author had a similar experience in 2008 when the corpses had been considerably augmented and had become part of the standard tourist itinerary.

the West Indies, India, and China, besides almost all the naval stations of Europe, and he had recently returned from Loo-Choo of which he had published a very interesting account. The celebrity acquired by this work had rendered him a decided lion the season before in London society; and thus his acquaintance with people of distinction in this country, equalled that which he had already acquired and turned to such good account in other quarters of the globe. These great advantages, joined to a graphic power of description, extraordinary quickness of observation, and great talents for conversation, rendered him a delightful companion. His temper was naturally passionate, which the habits of despotic command at sea had tended to increase; but he was generous, had no rancour in his disposition, and when the fit was over, his smile was like the sun emerging from the clouds.

   Such was the eagerness for information with which Basil Hall was animated, that he sought it at all hands, and often without due consideration of the sources from which it was derived. So intense was the ardour of his mind that it often led him to hurry to conclusions without sufficient regard to the premises on which they were founded. He was thus perpetually deceived as to the real character even of what fell under his own observation, and hence his descriptions of different countries are often tinged with the colours of romance.[6]

(The reference to a 'passionate temper' may well be a euphemism for the fact that Hall was inclined to 'blow his top', even if momentarily.)

Alison then retells a couple of anecdotes provided by Hall against himself in this regard, relating to Loo-Choo and the South American revolution against the Spaniards, when Hall later admitted that 'he was all wrong in his account of South America' (where he had supported the local uprisings), and he regretted the share he had in augmenting the general delusion on the subject.[7] This view of course would not now be shared either by the inhabitants of the countries involved or by post-imperial liberals. This assessment of Hall is the most rounded of the pictures we have of him, but of a piece with others. Coming from a distinguished historian – albeit a family friend – it is likely to be reliable.

The second extended trip to Europe commenced in 1833, with Hall taking a very pleasant apartment in Rome for some five months for the winter (at the very reasonable price of £4 a week, as he reported to Cadell) having followed a zig-zag course to Geneva via the Simplon Pass and thereafter to Nice, Genoa, Leghorn and Florence. *En route* to Geneva, Hall had taken time to study the physiography of mountains, including the development of the great river Rhone, the glaciers which fed it, the complex geological forces at work, and the initiation of avalanches.

He is clearly well read on his subject, quoting such authorities as the geologists Charles Lyell and Louis Agassiz and even Captain Robert FitzRoy's journal of the recent voyage of the *Beagle*.[8] Hall – writing on the huge forces of mountain building and erosion over aeons of time – said that 'this contemplation may cause pain and bewilderment, but such pursuits as geology and astronomy, properly carried out, do essentially contribute to fortify our faith in Revelation – how powerless we are, and how powerful is our Maker'.[9]

The family spent the summer of that year at an idyllic location on the shores of Lake Geneva, in a house where Sir Humphry Davy had once fished from one of the rooms directly into the lake. Here, under the shadow of Mont Blanc, Hall's first son was born.

He describes very emotionally his fevered sleepless dreams over the days and nights of waiting for this event. Perhaps presciently, he saw visions of the death of his son, Freddy.[10] Ever afterwards, he associated the birth of his son with the towering presence of Mont Blanc. In the early summer of 1833 he wrote one of many lengthy letters to Cadell – as he did throughout his two-and-a-half year 'ramble' around the Continent, much of this to do with his publications and money matters, but also:

> I have thought for a considerable time that my travel writing powers and means in other respects are gone. Since the break-down of Uncle B's letters [to a nephew] I have hardly ever got up my literary head and question much if I shall be able to make anything worthy of your new office of which you are so proud. I go on writing Journal, however, regularly…

He complains that his (European) track has been too much ploughed up by others while 'I have no classical knowledge – very little historical – and as for the scientific knowledge, I profess it is too loose and general – not profound'. Referring to his lack of background on the countries visited he admits: 'I have come to feel indifferent about all but English politics and that I love to study in an abstract style, unsuited to the multitude.' But he also claims that since retirement from the Navy, writing fills the vacuum best: 'I feel that unless I have some hard work to keep my joints in play, I shall get ill and become unhappy.'

Hall acknowledges that previous years have given him the best of opportunities for writing based on experience, but these are no longer available and 'his pen is powerless'. He makes no bones about the pleasure from being paid for his work, 'I am now travelling at a rate somewhat above the ways and means more costly than heretofore'. Unsurprisingly, he asks Cadell to look over the journals he is sending via his brother James, with a view to possible publication. James apparently thought that these did not have the 'dash and risk' necessary to attract the public, while Hall says that he has at times 'thought of trying my hand at a work of fancy [fiction]', but feared it was beyond his imaginative powers.[11]

At Rome, in November of that year, he wrote another lengthy letter to Cadell:

> [I am] afraid I am getting very old, stiff and stupid and am not very confident I shall again produce work which you will have courage to publish. I think there is the stuff in me if I could but muster strength and boldness to give it expression – come what may I shall make the trial in the hope that you will stand by me and give me a fair chance … The public have been very indulgent to me and I think would receive kindly anything which I might present to them after an interval of two or three years' silence – but it must be something new in conception.

Hall admits to needing some encouragement from his publisher while 'a word on the discouraging side sinks me as low'.[12]

In a rambling and intimate letter to Cadell of 9 July 1834, Hall is preoccupied with his financial position, and while not in debt, is concerned that he is using up his earnings, which he had hoped to leave to his family. He has made up his mind not to write up any more travels.[13] In October of that year he begs Cadell to find out details of a dividend which is due to him from investments in a water company – a request repeated in several subsequent letters as '*entre nous*, my expenses in travelling come close to the edges of my income and so cut a slice off my nest-egg'.

The issue of cost appears to have influenced his decision – towards the end of his European tour – to spend the last six months over the winter and spring of 1835–6 in Paris, letting Cadell know that he could obtain much better teaching – including dancing, music, and language – for his girls, at considerably less cost than in England. He admitted that he was now thoroughly weary of travel, but had nowhere to lay his head in his impoverished state. For this reason he was most anxious to get going on another book and asks Cadell's advice, saying that this must be small in size and as cheap as possible to attract the public. Interestingly, he indicates that this will be written extempore by himself without the benefit of the usual editorial input by his brother James and wife Margaret – who normally received each chapter as they were written for comment. He was clearly undergoing a *crise de confiance* regarding his own abilities, but needed 'to twist out of the pockets of the public a sufficient sum of cash to pay the expenses of this long journey which has reduced my purse sadly'. But this is a temporary expedient, prior to a proposed scientific biography as a *magnum opus* that he hopes will set his family up.[14]

Hall obviously uses his publisher as a general business advisor, for later on his return to London, he seeks his opinion on selling a house that he has apparently let to Sir Whitelaw Ainslie – most probably the property at St. Colme's Street in Edinburgh's New Town. He complains that the various taxes combined with repairs and redecoration and other costs are not matched by the rent. However, he had wished to use it for his wife's impending confinement in the autumn of 1836, but the sitting tenant had expressed a wish to keep it for a further year.[15] Hall also had notions of using the funds from any sale to purchase a property in London.

Hall also wrote to J.G. Lockhart at this time, expressing his gratitude to him as editor of the *Quarterly Review*, for the complimentary notices of Hall's previous works and Lockhart's comparisons with Smollett, which Hall modestly disclaims. He had made a pilgrimage to Smollett's grave at Leghorn and had discovered it disfigured by graffiti. Typically, he organised the cemetery keeper to get a bucket, brush, and pumice stone to remove the names of English tourists. He is clearly not enamoured of these visitors, nor the English reading rooms supplied with all the English newspapers of the day – confirming his view that most of these 'travellers and expatriates' were ignorant of the country they were in (by this time, the so-called 'Grand Tour' was no longer the exclusive prerogative of a cultured English aristocracy and lower-class visitors were often referred to derisively as 'cockneys'). But Hall also complains of the 'bugs, fleas, mosquitoes, ciceronis, blue stockings, fine artists and all the other worrifications of travelling'.[16]

From Lucca, Hall writes to his brother James on 14 August expressing his relief to get away from the heat and mosquitoes of Southern Italy (his daughter Eliza had been badly bitten at Naples and Leghorn). He is delighted with his comfortable accommodation in 'our house in the Casa Nobile-bagni della Villa close to the Duke's Palace', where he had regained health and spirits with nearby friends, taking walks and rides. He compared

*Hall made a detailed study of the geology and lava phenomena
of Mount Etna, viewed here from Catania.*

the cleanliness and industriousness of the inhabitants of Northern Italy very favourably with those of the south. At this time he is sending his journals of his travels (which were to form the basis of his final work *Patchwork*) to James for reviewing.[17]

In the following year Hall returned to Sicily – now with his family – where he not only ascended Vesuvius (as described above), but also Mount Etna. Characteristically he did nothing by halves, making a comprehensive tour of the base of the volcano over several days, before tackling the summit, which he was to describe as 'a noble journey': 'We accordingly landed our trusty steward Guiseppe, and packed our basket with tea, sugar, rice, bread, pickles, sauces, cold fowls and a huge beefsteak pie.' But at the main coastal town of Catania, he was irritated by the noise and melée of a local festival (complete with fireworks) that went on for several days and nights. It took the party including his family and entourage, some five and half hours to reach Aderno on the south side of the mountain.[18]

Fortunately they had brought their own iron bedstead, mosquito nets and sheet sleeping bags to the very run-down hotel there. Hall spent several hours in the vicinity attempting unsuccessfully to find the geological sites mentioned by Charles Lyell, and berated such geologists for not identifying the locations sufficiently. After three hours travel next morning they arrived in Bronte, which had just escaped a lava flow two years previously.Hall was in his element here, describing the various effects of such an occurrence. He is more admiring of this phenomenon than of the inhabitants whom he considers ignorant and dirty – as in much of Southern Europe – while the lack of facilities and provisions required any party to be well prepared beforehand (the beefsteak pie was demolished by ants).

After five days of touring the base of Etna, Hall and his party set off on the very fatiguing ascent, initially using the uncomfortable *letiga* – a crude wooded sedan chair with a mule fore and aft, which at one point overturned, tipping out the ladies, fortunately without serious injury. The guide was too old and feeble, according to Hall, to be much use, and they were hampered by lack of reliable information. Their hazardous final climb involved leaving their primitive shelter at midnight to see the sunrise from the peak, using an uncertain path and crossing a snowfield.

Coupled with mountain sickness in the party, it was a formidable expedition, but they were rewarded by spectacular views over the surrounding Mediterranean (Hall had taken his children to the Cyclopean Islands from Catania before the ascent). But it was not simply a recreational excursion: Hall made detailed notes on the effects of eruptions and vulcanicity generally, impressing Professor J.D. Forbes of St. Andrews with his comparisons of glacier movements and volcanic streams. Typically he somehow succeeded in making personal contact not only with the famous astronomer Cacciatore (then making a catalogue of the stars from the observatory at Palermo), but also the acknowledged expert on Etna – Mario Gemallaro – whom he encountered at Bosco. He was later able to – in correspondence with the distinguished astronomer Sir John Herschel and Captain W.H. Smyth, RN – confirm their previous height measurements of the mountain by barometer readings, offending the local inhabitants by reducing the original estimates.[19]

Hall had chartered a Sicilian boat for six weeks to travel round the island. To cap their landward adventures, on their return to Palermo in the Straits of Messina, they were chased by a mysterious corvette flying the French flag, the cannon shots from which landed uncomfortably close. The captain, Don Giovanni, desperately turned to Hall for advice and between them they succeeded in outpacing their pursuer, whose true nationality or ultimate purpose was never discovered.[20]

All of these European travels in the early 1830s are described by Hall in his last book *Patchwork*, generally considered below the quality of his previous works and showing evidence of a somewhat rambling pulling together of spare left-over material. Nevertheless, his narrative is symptomatic of the man, illustrating his indefatigability and adaptability, his wide range of interests and scientific curiosity, allied to a capacity for coping with challenging circumstances. On the same European tour he had yet to experience in his meeting with Countess Purgstall in remote Styria, one of the strangest episodes of his many travels...

References

1. Alison, Vol. I, 110–161
2. Moore, Vol. IV, 129–132
3. Hall, (1841), Vol. II, 135
4. *Ibid.*, 140 *et seq.*
5. *Ibid.*, 78–98
6. Alison, 139
7. *Ibid.*,171–173
8. Hall, (1841), Vol. II, 90–115
9. *Ibid.*,Vol. I, 18–19
10. *Ibid.*, Vol. II, 138–174
11. Basil Hall to Robert Cadell, ff.59-60 NLS Acc. 9849 MS 21009
12. *Ibid.*, ff 69
13. *Ibid.*, ff. 75–6
14. *Ibid.*, ff. 87–9
15. *Ibid.*, ff. 139–145
16. Basil Hall to J.G. Lockhart, Vol X, f. 50 NLS MS 932
17. Edinburgh University Special Collections 1MS, Lyell.1.
18. Hall, 1841, Vol. III, 2–3
19. *Ibid.*, 33–57
20. *Ibid.*, 72

Death of a Countess

On 28 of March 1834 the doors of the Purgstall family vault at Riegensburg Parish Church were firmly closed against any possible prying eyes. Here in a deeply wooded valley of Styria, in a remote corner of southern eastern Austria close to the Hungarian frontier, the shroud of evening mist mirrored the mood of the two men working steadily within the vault. Keeping a careful watch on their efforts were two others. One was a bent elderly man in rough peasant clothes, his tear-stained face wrinkled and worn, addressed as Joseph by the other distinctive figure – a smaller man, but with a commanding presence and a military bearing. From time to time, in broken German, he gave instructions quietly to the gravediggers – now uncovering the first of the coffins – ordering them to take care as they set this to one side, the hard-packed earth falling from its cracked lid. The man issuing the instructions was Captain Basil Hall.

An observer would have been puzzled by what happened next. The village labourers dug further down, exposing another coffin, which equally carefully they hoisted from the grave and set to one side beside the first. The top of yet another coffin was revealed and with considerable difficulty and some help from Joseph, they silently raised this to the surface. Like the others, this was placed gently on one side. When they had excavated

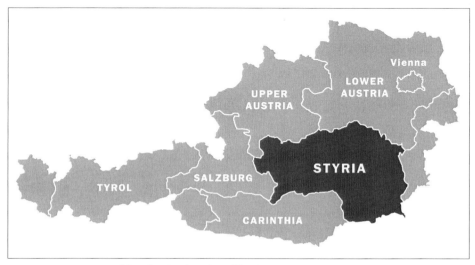

Map showing location of Styria.

another half metre they looked towards the soldierly man in his frock coat. Nodding his approval to the workmen, he indicated that the first of the coffins to be removed should be placed at the bottom of the pit. Scraping away the dust from another of the coffins, he read the inscription: 'Count Gottfried Wenceslaus Purgstall b.1774 – d.1811' and ordered it to be placed on top of the first. The next wooden coffin, which seemed distinctly lighter, had inscribed: '–––––– beloved son, aged 19 years' but the rest of the inscription was worn off.

A newly-made iron coffin lay on the ground awaiting burial. It had no identification, but Hall knew that it contained the mortal remains of a Scottish lady – Countess Purgstall – since he and the old Austrian family retainer Joseph, had helped to lay the body in place – the pale withered head supported (as instructed) by a bundle of letters. It was now past midnight and he had not only done his honourable duty, but done so in a typically practical way that had solved what had seemed an intractable problem. With head bowed, Joseph tearfully crossed himself.

Jane Anne Cranstoun came from a noble Scottish family which could trace its aristocratic lineage back several centuries. She was the middle of three daughters of the fifth Lord Cranstoun. George, one of her two brothers and as an eminent judge of the Court of Session, took the judicial tile of Lord Corehouse after his seat by the spectacular Falls of Clyde in Lanarkshire. Born in 1760 at Warriston House in Edinburgh, Jane had her youth during the most active period in what is known as the Scottish Enlightenment. A particularly congenial *coterie* developed around George Cranstoun, with his home in the capital in Frederick Street off the main thoroughfare of Princes Street.

Here, almost on a nightly basis, George would meet his brother Henry and also Thomas Thomson (the modest advocate from the west of Scotland), Dugald Stewart (who would marry Jane's sister Helen d'Arcy and become the renowned Professor of Moral Philosophy at Edinburgh University), Will Erskine (later Lord Kinneder) – a lifelong friend of Walter Scott, and the great novelist himself, among others. Lord Dudley wrote at one point to Mrs Stewart claiming that those around them said that 'the Cranstouns are the cleverest but the oddest people in the world.'[1] Among the many other distinguished persons she met at this time of great intellectual activity in the capital was Sir James Hall.

Jane acted as housekeeper to her brother George, but was clearly an active participant in their modest entertainments and lively debates. She was described by one commentator as 'witty, but compassionate'. In common with her sisters, she was apparently 'romantic, eloquent, and full of wit and sensibility'.[2] She took a lively interest in matters of the day, and from her later correspondence it is obvious that she was greatly stimulated not only by her wide reading, but by her association with these bright young men at the outset of their often distinguished careers. She was probably the first to recognise the literary genius of Walter Scott (being some 10 years older than him) and it was she who not only praised his early work, but also continued to encourage him avidly over many years.

In June 1797 Jane – much to the surprise of her friends – married Count Gottfried 'Godfrey' Friedrich Purgstall (some 14 years younger than her). He was the owner of extensive estates and a number of castles in Styria (now more often known as Steirmark). By this marriage Jane became Countess Purgstall and a member of one of the best-

Riegersburg Castle – the ancestral home of the Purgstalls – where the Countess Purgstall was taken on her arrival in Styria. Drawing by Andrew Taylor.

known aristocratic families in what was later to become part of the sprawling Austro-Hungarian Empire.

The countess was brought to Schloss Riegersburg – a fantastic edifice in the mountains of southeast Styria, with its seven-gated entrance and two drawbridges and one of the most magnificent castles in Europe. Built over 850 years ago, it rises almost 500 metres above the surrounding lush vineyards and wild chestnut forests. Here Count Purgstall had been born in 1774. Almost from the beginning of her time in this backward and feudal part of Europe – with its peasant lifestyle and lack of intellectual stimulation – she was overcome by a deep homesickness, reflected in her correspondence. At the time of the Countess's arrival, Austria was still – unlike much of the rest of Europe – a feudal state dominated by a relatively benign nobility.

Her only son was born in the year after her arrival and was described as 'a frail, beautiful boy, singularly gifted in heart and brain'. The Countess employed a nurse from Aberdeenshire specifically to induct the child into what she called 'the language of her heart'.

Sir Walter Scott received a number of letters from Jane in the summer of 1799. By this time the countess was nearly blind from eye trouble, but still wrote in her characteristic flowing hand on large quarto paper: 'Such is the electric charm of your penmanship that I declare to God that I am such an idiot I cannot look at your letter yet without crying.'[3]

The only known image of Countess Purgstall is this medallion by the famous Italian sculptor, Canova. From Sir Walter Scott and his Friends *by F. McCunn.*

The invasion of Austria by the French under Napoleon changed everything. After the disastrous defeat of the Austrians – commanded by the 18 year-old Archduke John at Hohenlinden north of Munich in 1800 – Austria was forced to sign an armistice and agree to the Peace of Luneville. Count Purgstall (according to the Countess) was committed to the service of his country and the Emperor accepted his offer of help, becoming a member of the commission charged with the reorganisation of the defence of the capital, Vienna.

He was later to urge his people to resist the invaders and paid for the formation of a company based in Riegersburg. The Count himself took the lead in this attempt to re-conquer those territories lost to the French and her allies. He was present at the victory of the Austrian forces at Sacile near the head of the Adriatic, with heavy losses on both sides. But the Archduke John failed to follow this up and allowed his forces to be ambushed in the rear by those under Eugene de Beauhanais – Napoleon's Viceroy in Italy. Together with several other noblemen, the Count was captured at Padua and imprisoned at Mantua. He died in 1811 shortly after his release (Note 49).

Near the end of April 1834, Hall had left Rome for Naples accompanied by his wife Margaret and family of two daughters (Eliza and Fanny Emily – one aged about nine, the other about five) and his baby son, Basil Sidmouth de Ros (just over a year old).[4] With them was a German governess, Fraulein Herthum, and the Scots nursemaid, Mrs Cownie (who had been with them for several years), together with a mountain of domestic baggage. At Albano they stopped to change horses, while other carriages passed or stopped to rest. One of these attracted Hall's attention and he was delighted to find in it 'our amiable and accomplished Polish friend with an unpronounceable name' – the Countess Rzewuska (Note 50) who was proceeding in the opposite direction. She had a letter from Countess Purgstall, which Madame Rzewuska had intended to deliver to Hall in Rome, where she supposed the family would still be. She had been asked to confirm that Hall was the son of Sir James Hall – one of her earliest and most intimate friends in Edinburgh. If so, on behalf of Countess Purgstall, she had been requested to

Notes

49   The Count almost certainly died of tuberculosis – the disease that also killed his son, Wenzel Rafael.

50   The Countess was Madame Evelinede Hanska (*née* Rzewuska), who subsequently married the writer Honoré de Balzac. At the time of her meeting with Hall – despite her being married – Balzac was still continuing his ardent 17-year pursuit of her, and proposing to meet her in Rome.

invite him to pay her a visit at her *schloss* in Styria, as an alternative to the much more popular tourist route homeward through the Tyrol.

The Halls had apparently made it a rule when travelling never to make too fixed arrangements and to be guided by circumstances, so that they were quite happy to accede to Countess Purgstall's wishes. Furthermore, Hall seemed pleased with the prospect of getting off the beaten track that was now being worn by English tourists in particular. He wrote to the countess and she – being under the mistaken belief that the first had been misdirected – wrote two answers. Her replies confirmed what the Halls had learnt about the old lady – now in her 74th year – including her cleverness and eccentricity. In her first reply she said:

> It will be doing me a very great favour indeed if Mrs Hall and you will bestow a visit upon me. Your little darlings surely need repose. I beseech you to let them find a home in Hainfeld; the house is large; there are thirty-nine rooms on this floor all completely furnished, though in the mode of the last century ... Hungary is only three hours distant.

But the real reason for her begging (there is no other word) them to visit her is revealed in her poignant plea:

> I dare not speak of the home of my youth. Thirty-five years of absence have sponged me from the remembrance of those dearest to me; but if you graciously visit me, you will draw back the veil and give me a glimpse of things still, alas! too dear to me ... the Governor of Milan, Count Hardegg, will please you much, and also our countryman, General Count Nugent (Note 51), at Trieste.

Her second letter apologised profusely for sending the first in error to a poste restante address in Naples. It too was in much the same pleading tone, but included the addition: 'Your excellent Scotch nurserymaid will revive me with letting me hear once more the language of my heart.' She also gave practical instructions on travel – indicating that by *eilwagon* the journey between Trieste and Graz would take about 55 hours – and something of her own domain. She suggested cunningly that as Hall had been interested in the constitution of the United States (she had relayed a very favourable opinion of his book on America), a study of the local government in her bailiwick might appeal to him. The châtelaine held the position of minor royalty under a benevolent feudal system, but the nobility had been much reduced in circumstances by the recent wars with the French.

Hall took the bait, and indicated that the family would arrive about the middle of September. He added another reason: 'It is true I am not writing a book; but I often sigh for some bit of ground to tread upon which has not been ploughed up by the merciless pens of preceding travellers ... but your account of Styria does stir up my inkhorn, and if I don't make a quarto out of it, the fault is mine.'

Notes

51   Field Marshal Laval Nugent was an eccentric Irishman who had served with distinction in the Austrian Army against Napoleon and was always in financial difficulties resulting from his obsession with purchasing dilapidated European castles to restore at whatever expense.

The Countess was ecstatic about his acceptance of her invitation, indicating that her horses would be waiting to conduct his party from Graz to Hainfeld. Knowing Hall's interests in natural history, she let him know of the curiosities en route, including the underground rivers in this country with its karst topography, the vast caves near Trieste with their unique fish life, and the geological museum at Graz founded by the Archduke John, whose huge iron works at Vordernberg might also command his technological interest. However, she adds a warning: 'Your sweet infants will be sadly disappointed when, instead of a splendid dwelling, they see a building like a manufactory, the grounds in culture to the door, and the cows lodged within a gunshot of their bed-chamber. At first they will be afraid of me, for I am now nothing like they ever saw … Alas! the ravages of time are equally visible on its possessor, and upon poor desolate Hainfeld!' This description of the castle is in striking contrast to that of the romantic splendours of Schloss Riegersburg where she had first arrived in the country as a young bride. Hall confirmed her imagery:

> At length four little sharp turrets, indicating the four corners of the long-looked-for Schloss, or castle, came in sight, and presently afterwards, the whole building which, to do its looks no injustice, and in the words of its proprietor, resembled nothing so much as a manufactory. Instead of standing boldly on top of a high rock, the family mansion of the Purgstalls was placed in the flattest part of a flat valley, far from the abundant trees and rich scenery of the adjacent high grounds, as if in utter contempt of the many picturesque situations which might have been selected on the same property … we found our aged friend in a huge antiquated bed, with faded damask curtains, in a room feebly lighted, and furnished in the style of a hundred years ago. Her wasted form was supported by half a dozen pillows of different shapes and sizes, and everything about her wore the appearance of weakness and pain. Everything, I should say, except

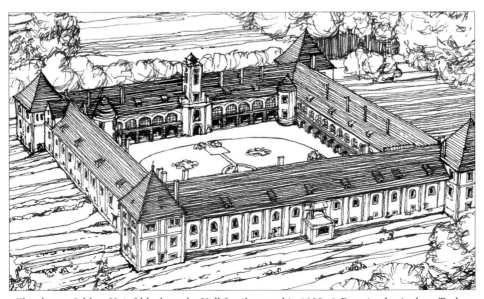

The gloomy Schloss Hainfeld where the Hall family stayed in 1835–6. Drawing by Andrew Taylor.

her voice, expression of countenance, and manners, in none of which could be traced any symptom of decay or weakness [Hall became convinced that Scott, in his novel Rob Roy, has modelled the heroine Di Vernon – a lady of great beauty and talents – on Jane Cranstoun in her youth, both from her appearance and lively personality (Note 52)]. Still less might any feebleness be detected in what she said, for nothing in the world could be more animated or more cordial than her welcome. She shook hands with each of us, as if she had known us all our lives, and expressed over and over again her joy at having succeeded in bringing us to her castle.

The family was shown to their large rooms, where the major-domo Joseph, had lit the old German-style porcelain stoves, not only in these but also in many other rooms so that they could make a wide choice. Everywhere was furnished in antique fashion, including an eight-foot wide bed with crimson silk curtains bordered with silver lace two or three inches broad, surmounted by a massive carved cornice fringed with silver tracery. The walls were hung with crimson satin and in the main room, old fashioned sofas 'with curling backs and arms like dolphins tails' were placed. All the furniture was heavy and elaborate, while the ceilings of all the rooms supported grotesque ornamental plasterwork in high relief. Hall and his entourage had walked into a decayed family museum, virtually untouched for nearly a century.

Now a solitary exile in a foreign land, the Countess appeared to have no connection with her adopted country and no purpose other than to cherish the memory of what had been lost – her country, her husband and her adored son. She was entrapped in her grief and had nothing to do but to reinforce it by allowing no changes to be made at Hainfeld. In Hall's very perceptive words,

> Every article of furniture stood exactly in its old place – not a walk amongst the grounds was altered – not a tree cut down – not a book shifted in the library. So that the castle of Hainfeld and all its old inmates, all its own usages, went on, or rather went not on, but remained as if arrested by the frost of its mistress's grief, in the very position they occupied of the period of that last and crowning disaster, her son's death, which obliterated the house of Purgstall.

The fact that the countess insisted on lying in the very bed (where she had lain for the last three years) in which her son had drawn his last breath 17 years previously, adds a touch of the macabre to her surreal existence in this ghostly and remote turreted Styrian castle.

To the initial confusion of her listeners – and despite her capacity for clear expression – she always spoke in a mixture of languages including French and German, but dominated by the older Scots tongue. Far from being a penance, the daily periods the family spent with her were enlivened by her cheerful animation and her wide-ranging conversation never flagged, such that Hall declared they were the most agreeable times of the day. She had mixed with some of the greatest minds and talents of her time, and with a superb memory was able to provide endless anecdotes from Bonaparte and the

Notes

52   W.S. Crockett (1912) casts doubt on the evidence Hall produced for this.

Emperor Alexander, or the stories of Sir Walter Scott's first attempts in literature. Lady Davy claimed that with one exception, 'she was the woman of the most powerful mind she ever knew and was adored by all in Styria from the Archduke John to the humblest peasant'. She could relate tales about Schiller or Goëthe – both of whom she had met – and describe the playing of Mozart and Hadyn: all of these part of her personal experience in cultured society at home and abroad.

She took a particular delight in the company of Hall's one year-old boy and his nursemaid, who spent hours in her room daily. All-in-all and despite her situation, she herself became a favourite of the whole family, who developed a great fondness for their châtelaine. But her melancholy was deep-seated: not only had she suffered the personal tragedy of her family, but she had personally witnessed the ravages of the most brutal warfare in her own district. Although she was visited by a number of acquaintances, she appeared not to have any truly intimate friends to whom she could unburden herself, so that she was overcome by loneliness and a sense of isolation. It is not difficult to imagine how this woman of wide-ranging intellectual and cosmopolitan experience must have felt in a rural Austrian backwater, with its deeply conservative mores.

All this reinforced her almost pathological homesickness and need for connection with her native country and people, who now provided her with her happiest memories. Hall came rapidly to understand why he and his family were now regarded as saviours in a desert of solitude and the reason behind the Countess' pleading invitations. But there was, as he found out, a much deeper reason for her anxiety to have her country folk around her at this time:

> She had the greatest horror at the idea of dying alone, without a friend to close her eyes, and under the exclusive care of servants … [she had] the most vehement desire to establish in her castle an English family, who should devote their time chiefly to her, and whose tastes, habits, languages, prejudices and so forth, might, in the main, might be found to fall in with her own.

Although she could not under normal circumstances have found such a family to permanently settle themselves under her roof, Hall subsequently realised that from the first acceptance of her invitation, the Countess saw his family in this role, and that in his words 'after she had got hold of us, and found us suitable, she never meant we should escape from the castle'. To ensure this that cunning woman employed every device, even to the extent of disguising her severest pains with the greatest fortitude, so that the family would not be disinclined to approach her. In effect, over time she wove a silken web of obligation and sympathy on their part to detain them until her last moment on earth.

The Countess ensured that they had every convenience that the castle could supply – including the services of a full retinue of servants and access to a very fine library – while she herself was confined entirely to the least comfortable chamber directly above the noisy arched entrance to the castle, simply because that was where her son had died. One device which she used to make the Hall's stay agreeable was to arrange suitable excursions for the family. The first of these was to the ancient home of the Purgstalls – Riegersburg Castle – where the Countess had first been brought by her husband after their wanderings in Europe.

Nor was this the only excursion which the countess had arranged. Off the Halls were sent to Gleichenberg (about ten miles south of Hainfeld) where they found a beautifully situated castle built atop a steep rock, inaccessible on three sides, with striking views from its windows. It too, however, had fallen into a desperate state of neglect, except for its upper floor which contained a suite of well-furnished apartments inhabited by the Countess of Trautmansdorf. She was an accomplished society lady of elegant manners, once the star of the most fashionable assemblies of Vienna and still a beautiful woman.

A very different visit was that to meet the His Imperial Highness, Archduke John – brother of Austria's Emperor – which Hall very much looked forward to, with his interest in technology. The family paid two visits. The first was to meet the Archduke at his vineyards in Lower Styria in the autumn of 1834. The second was at the end of winter in 1835 to the Archduke's industrial works in Upper Styria. Hall gives a lengthy and detailed description of these excursions and comes away full of admiration for this modest and benevolent man, who apparently worked tirelessly on behalf of those over whom he had jurisdiction.

In making arrangement for these excursions through her formidable network of influential contacts and in other ways, the countess strove to find out what the family liked best and to make suitable household arrangements for them (she was also cleverly spinning out the time before the winter snows would have made the Hall's departure impossible). The children were set to lessons as before, and the Halls established a comfortable routine, spending much time with their hostess. What became clear early on was that any discussion of their future plans – including departure – threw the old lady into such a state of agitation that they soon dropped the matter, while they quietly resolved to leave when it seemed most appropriate. They did not however reckon with the Countess' steely determination to detain them or her skilfulness in ensuring this.

The whole question came to something of a head at the beginning of November when the Halls announced that they intended to depart on the 10th of that month. The old lady had hysterics and entreated them to at least stay the winter with her, emphasising the hazards of the winter journey for the children and that she would make them as comfortable as money could provide, and so on. The Halls were prevailed upon to set 1 December as their departure date and to avoid further confrontation, put this in writing. The countess's response was characteristic:

> My Dear Sir
>
> Every day Mrs Hall and you bestow on me, I receive gratefully as a blessing. Had Heaven and you vouchsafed to grant my prayers, you would have nestled in poor Hainfeld as well as you could, till the breath of spring invited you to launch into the world.
>
> Faithfully yours, etc.

In fact, Hall's family were by now quite snugly ensconced in the castle (where Hall spent several hours each day attempting to master the German language) and were not averse to remaining throughout the winter. He himself commented that the Countess appeared to have almost magical powers, not only in knowing exactly everything that was going on within her domain (despite her bed-ridden state), but also in understanding what was thought and felt by all her guests, including several who came to stay during the Hall's residence (one of these was a young British officer, W. Raleigh Kerr (Note 53), serving in the Austrian Army and the son of Lord Robert Kerr, whom Hall subsequently recommended to the Duke of Wellington).

The Countess had made it clear at an early stage in their stay that her most important wish was to be buried with her deceased husband and son. She had built a chapel in the church of the picturesque village at the foot of the brooding Riegersberg Castle. Here she had erected a fine granite statue of her husband and son, and over the altar – quite unlike the simple elegance of the rest of the chapel – a very showy image of Saint Wenceslaus. Further, she had presented to the church a magnificent and costly piece of religious art depicting Saint Florian (made in Vienna), which far outshone anything that had decorated the church previously. To this had been added a sum of money to be distributed to the parish poor after her internment.

She had anticipated difficulties with the local Catholic priesthood in securing this, either on the grounds that she was a Protestant or that the castle might pass from her family. All of these handsome gestures therefore were to ensure compliance with her wishes. Hall delicately raised the question of the need for a leaden coffin to be available quickly if she was to be buried in the church vault. What happened next astonished Hall.

Ringing the bell, and with a curious smile, the Countess summoned her factotum, Joseph. 'Get the keys', she exclaimed, 'and show Captain Hall my coffin.' Turning to the family, she added, 'when you see it, I think you will admit that it is not likely to be refused admittance to the church on the score of want of strength, or, for that matter, for want of beauty.' What Hall was shown was not a lead coffin, but one constructed of iron, resembling nothing more than (in Hall's words) 'one of those ornamental pieces of sculpture which surmount some of the old monuments in Westminster Abbey', complete with three huge fantastically-shaped padlocks. Inside at either end and neatly sewn up in white linen lay two large bundles of papers. In the Countess's handwriting, they were inscribed: 'Our Letters – J.A. Purgstall'.

The countess had in fact indicated that her wish was, in her own words, 'to drop off while you are here to attend me, instead of being left to die alone … I may safely promise not to keep you long! … Had you not come to me so providentially, I should have been dead by this time; and I should have died wretched and alone, with no hand to close my eyes or smooth my pillow.'

The question might be raised as to how the family spent their days at Hainfeld with the worsening winter weather approaching. Breakfast was attenuated by the family insisting that they spoke German only throughout the meal, the children far outstripping their parents in fluency at an early stage. But even before breakfast, Hall had made a written report to the Countess on the health and well-being of his family – a device he arranged, to her complete satisfaction, to calm her feverish night time concerns that there was illness or discomfort among Hall's entourage.

Such was her concern that prior to the written report, she insisted on Joseph visiting the family at daybreak to ascertain their welfare. This had obliged Hall to wake the children in their nursery while they were still half-asleep to check on their condition.

Notes

53   Kerr stayed a month at Hainfeld and may have been the source of two articles on the Austrian Army that Hall wrote for the United Services Journal.

The Countess was especially concerned about the welfare of Hall's 15 month-old son, of whom she was especially fond. She and the rest of the household insisted on calling him the young Graf or Count, who required Hall to sing him to sleep for his morning nap.

Hall's early morning report to the Countess was supplemented by a daily visit around 10 am every morning, during which Hall gave a detailed description of everything that had happened in their apartments overnight. In return, the Countess attended to their every wish, including on one occasion sending a servant on horseback at 3 o'clock in the morning to Graz – some 30 to 40 miles away – to procure a special kind of chocolate made according to a recipe of the Princess of Salms, for one of Hall's daughters.

Likewise, notwithstanding the availability locally of good quality tea, she ordered nothing less than a chest of the best and most recently imported tea from as far away as Trieste. She gave secret instructions to the village shopkeepers to ensure that any of the family purchases were rendered to her account, including any postage costs. In this and many other ways, the Countess attempted with considerable subterfuge not to put her guests in her debt, so much as not to give them any excuse – such as expense – for leaving her household. The Halls were effectively trapped in a web of sugared complicity.

Propped up by a multitude of pillows, the Countess used one half of her wide bed as a sort of study, where she held court. Hall was dismayed by the accumulation here of piles of letters, journals from all over Europe, and books, all furnished by friends and numerous correspondents. She took a lively interest in anything new, but on one occasion Hall counted in a single file three dozen unopened publications in English, French and German, besides innumerable pamphlets, endless files of newspapers, and unopened letters from several weeks back. This was all mixed up with farm and household accounts, bills, and even here and there a bag of silver money!

Promptly at noon, Hall would go to the Countess's room, staying there for one to one and a half hours. He remarked that she was always cheerful and lively, whatever her travails during the night, and would converse animatedly on her experience – whether an anecdote concerning Sir Walter Scott or other European men of letters whom she knew: the literati of Austria, France and England and even the details of the Napoleonic campaigns which had devastated Austria (later, Hall was to greatly regret that he did not take notes from these conversations, such was their unique historical interest). At half-past one he would be relieved by Mrs Hall or one of the many guests who came to the Schloss. Following afternoon exercise or local excursions, the company would dress for dinner and assemble in the Countess's room – at one such assembly, the company numbered 18 – where she appeared to enjoy simply listening to the conversation.

When dinner was announced the Countess would send for the Hall's nursery-maid and his youngest son, providing her with what was clearly the happiest hour in her day. The toddler reciprocated her adoration (which may not have been unconnected to the memory of her own son) and would sit happily for hours on her bed. He would even sometimes lay his cheek tenderly on her own deeply lined one: Hall himself ensured good behaviour at this hallowed time by insisting on the youngster's late morning nap under his own supervision.

Special occasions were marked by the Countess, in her anxiety to ensure that the Halls were not inclined to raise again the vexed question of their departure. Such was the occasion of Hall's birthday on Hogmanay. Everyone (including the servants) was ushered in after dinner to the library by the master of ceremonies, Joseph. Here in the middle of a semi-circle of chairs, Hall was installed in an elaborate gilt covered chair with his children on either side of him and the youngest on his knee. Two lines of peasants facing each other were drawn up, to form an avenue for the solemn procession of title holders who now appeared. First came the hereditary gamekeepers bearing ancient fowling pieces on their right shoulders. These were followed by the foresters carrying their axes, and all of them bore a flaming torch that cast a flickering light on the dark panels and many volumes of the library.

Suddenly, the air was filled by a flourish of trumpets from remote parts of the castle, followed by the tread of 50 heavy boots (in Hall's words), 'trampling like so many horses' hooves over the bare wooden floors'. The procession was headed by the bailiff or land steward (in Scotland he would be the estate factor) carrying as an emblem of his office, a roll of papers. After him trooped in all the members of the household and home farm, each bearing some appropriate symbol of their employment. The bailiff (or *verwalter*) made a speech to Hall, which in elaborate terms extolled his fame, the honour which he had done them and the hope that he would always remember them. Hall replied, accepting their good wishes and the great attention which had been accorded to the family by the Countess and all her staff.

Each of the latter then paraded round the library in pairs in front of the Halls, to place on the table in front of them something to indicate the department they belonged to. This ranged from a shining hatchet from the woodsmen to a tub of linen from the washerwoman, not forgetting a sprig of laurel in a vase by the gardeners, while the coachmen cracked their whips and the maids twirled their brooms. Even the blacksmiths wielded their sledge hammers and the masons bore in their trowels. Finally, the bailiff's wife presented to Hall's young boy a vast bunch of shining grapes.

The evening was rounded off a dance and supper, which according to Hall, 'made the old castle shake to its foundations with long forgotten gaiety'. A great honour had been done to the Halls, since apparently no such celebration had taken place for over 20 years, ever since her son had died in the Countess' arms – although the castle had seen many such events before that as the centre of much of the social life of the district. But Hall and his family were very much aware of the shadow cast over the proceedings by the absence of the bed-ridden châtelaine. Later however, the family put on a small 'playlet' for the whole household, largely at the Countess's instigation, with the two girls demonstrating an admirable command of the German language which was applauded by all, while the proceedings were relayed to a clearly delighted Countess, who entered into the spirit of it in an almost girlish way.

By mid February the Halls were seriously considering leaving Hainfeld for home, with the worst of the winter weather over. However, by this time not only had they become very fond of the Countess, but also in the presence of their fun-loving and affectionate family she herself almost seemed to be shaking off her deep melancholy. In particular Hall's baby son had endeared himself to her by quite contentedly sitting at the end of her bed for hours, or even touching her withered face with his hands, happy to be with her. When Joseph became aware that the family were making preparations for departure surreptitiously – so as not to alarm the Countess – he solemnly declared that their leaving would spell the end for her. Hall himself, seeing the situation, could not bring himself to broach the subject with the Countess. However, towards the end of the month she went through a crisis, wracked by coughing fits, high fever and even more sleeplessness than usual. By early March, convinced of her imminent death, she rallied sufficiently to write a note to Hall.

That note was in the form of a request to Hall. It explained that during an absence of a family, advantage was taken of this to allow others to occupy the family vault. The Countess had become aware of this at her son's funeral in 1817, seeing no place for her own coffin. What she was asking Hall to do was to remove an unwanted corpse to another location, so that she could be buried with her beloved husband and son. No expense was to be spared to ensure this. Hall reassured her that he would do all that was necessary, at the same time suggested that there was no reason for thinking about this at the time. Apparently, 'she only smiled, shook her head, and said, 'You'll see – you'll see'. At this point, Hall admitted that they hoped charitably that her prophecy might come true, given her hopeless situation and her constant physical suffering. The best thing that could happen would be for the Halls to be present to carry out her ardent wishes. For her part, she had made it abundantly clear that given her worsening condition, she wished them to stay at Hainfeld till she died.

However by mid-March the Countess seemed much improved and her request prompted Hall to enquire jokingly when she intended her demise to be, as it would affect other matters, such as the family's departure. The Countess took this in good part, but assured Hall 'I shall not keep you long'. She explained that this time of year had in the past been fatal to her happiness and that the 22nd of the month of March was the date of her husband's death, some 24 years previously. She could confidently predict that she would expire on the same day. With this certainty she extracted a promise from Hall that he would stay until the end of the month, although she was adamant that her death would come at the equinox and that long before the month's end he would have laid her peacefully in her grave. But by the 20th of the month she was in sufficient good health that Hall wrote to her friends to say that her recent relapse was over and that the danger was passed. On the 23rd of the month and less than 24 hours outside her own prediction, she died (Note 54).

On the previous day Hall had carried in all his children to take a last look at the dying lady. She herself not only recognised them, but gave them affectionate farewells, thanking them for their kind company. To 'her little boy' she was especially moved and he for his part – not understanding the situation – looked her full in the face and said, as he was wont to do every evening when carried away, 'Ta! Ta!'. The faithful old retainer Joseph – who had promised on the death of her son never to leave the Countess – was inconsolable and wept ceaselessly: Hall gave him pride of place at the head of the dying woman's bed. All the household staff came to pay their respects for a time. Even the local Catholic parish priest – admired by the Countess – came to sit respectfully and tactfully

Notes

54   After her death Hainfeld was inherited by the renowned orientalist Dr Joseph von Hammer-Purgstall (coincidentally a Fellow of the Royal Society of Edinburgh), who was commissioned by the Countess to write *Denkmahl* – the memorial book on the lives of her husband and son. He took his name after the Countess's death. The *Schloss,* after being converted into a luxury hotel, is now derelict.

at a little distance. Somewhat to Hall's consternation the good Catholic Joseph placed a lit candle in the dying woman's hand, giving a changing light to her face and a surreal atmosphere to the whole scene.

That night Hall pondered on her death and the strange circumstances that had brought them together. Their quite accidental meeting was the first time they had heard of the Countess, and would no more have thought of visiting her, in Hall's words, 'than we [would have] had of visiting the Cham of Tartary' – far less spending six months in her castle in Styria. Over this time not only did the ailing woman become very fond of them, but also they in turn reciprocated that affection quite naturally. Her company was as agreeable to them as it was to her.

The result was that they became acutely aware of the affect of their departure before her death, such that from motives of real compassion, Hall and his wife believed that the best thing for all concerned would be her passing before they left. They did not of course mention such a thought – of which they were half ashamed – but they did not reckon with the Countess's acute intuition.

More than once she had said: 'Only wait a little; wait till the equinox comes, and you'll see me go out like a candle burned down to the socket.' In the event, Hall was overcome by genuine grief at her death, remembering how she had praised his eldest daughter's looks, how she had laughed at her funny remarks, how she entreated Margaret to read another chapter of a Waverley novel, and most of all, how she adored the presence of Hall's friendly little boy.

The Countess lay in state in the castle chapel for four days, on a high platform with scutcheons of the family placed in reverse position (indicating that she was the last of the Purgstalls – a previously numerous dynasty). Thousands of people from the surrounding villages flocked to the chapel to pay their respects, many of them remembering her great generosity in their times of trouble over 40 years, including the ravages of war which seriously afflicted many districts – some totally depopulated as a result of forced conscription.

At the end of the lying in state, Hall and Joseph lowered the body of the Countess into the mighty coffin, carefully placing the letters of her husband and son beneath her head as a pillow and a box of her heirlooms at her feet. Joseph was still distraught, and Hall had finally to padlock the coffin and remove the keys from the old retainer's hand. There appeared to Hall an atmosphere of desolation not only over the castle, but the whole neighbourhood with her passing.

This feeling was exacerbated by the response from the authorities in Graz when they were approached to fix a date for the funeral and to make arrangements for the family vault at Riegersburg to be opened up. Through the parish priest it was made clear that the vault was completely full and that the bodies there could not possibly be removed, despite the frequently expressed wish of the Countess to be laid to rest with her husband and son. With the help of a long-standing friend of the Countess a resolution was found: to remove sufficient soil from below the existing coffins to allow another to be placed on top, while the 'foreign' coffin was placed at the bottom, all carried out in some secrecy.

The funeral was held on a bright spring morning. The heavy iron coffin was loaded on to one of the Countess' own unpretentious wagons, drawn by four sturdy farm horses.

It was followed by 200 bareheaded men and half that number of women on foot marching four abreast, chanting Ave Marias and paternosters alternately, from time to time in chorus. It was a most picturesque scene as the whole procession wended its way through the deep forests and green valleys leading to Riegersburg. At every village, its arrival was anticipated by the ringing of bells, making an almost continuous sound along the hilly route.

At the head limped the lame prison keeper of the Hainfeld prison, complete with a huge lantern with a lighted candle in it in one hand, and the keys of the prison in the other – perhaps symbolic of the Countess' release from her pains into the 'light everlasting'. Passing through the villages, all the inhabitants flocked to the roadside to pay their respects, for she was apparently liked and respected for many miles around. The procession was made up not only of the estate tenants, but also many hundreds of others who joined it spontaneously, including swarms of children. In Hall's words: 'the whole forest through which we passed seemed alive; and as these extra attendants upon the procession observed no order of march, but made short cuts over the knolls and across the glens, they gave to the whole somewhat the appearance of a wild hunting party.'

All of the side of the rock below the magnificent Riegersburg Castle was covered with people awaiting the cortege, while the bells of the church pealed out, and the priests chanted their prayers and hymns (Hall was most impressed by the courtesy and discretion of the Catholic clergy towards the avowedly Protestant Countess in their arrangements). The chapel itself was filled to overflowing, including the pulpit, while the village choristers sang a Miserere so simply and beautifully that Hall could not refrain from comparing it favourably to the 'falsettos' he had heard in Rome a year previously, in the august company of Pope and cardinals.

Hall was just in time to avert a possible tragedy. The heavy coffin had to be tipped up at one end to be inserted into its allotted position, and at one critical point was supported by only one rope. Those below were in real danger of suffering severe injury or even death when it became clear that those lowering the coffin could not support its huge weight. Hall – using his naval skill with ropes – seized one firmly and by wrapping it round a ringlet at the other end, succeeded in having both ends supported by two men. In his words: 'Thus it happened, literally as well as figuratively, I complied with the good Countess's entreaty, that I "would not desert her at the last, but remain by her to close her eyes, and lay her poor shattered head in the grave!"'.

Hall's book on this episode was one of the most difficult he had ever written, and it was to have unexpected repercussions (Note 55).

References

1. Mccunn, 37
2. *Ibid.*, 37
3. Countess Purgstall to Walter Scott, 26 July 1799 in Partington, 7–8
4. Hall, 1836, *passim*

Notes

55   Except where indicated, all the quotes above are derived from Hall's *Skimmings: Or a Winter at Schloss Hainfeld in Lower Styria* (1836). Gibson (2007) argues that Hall's narrative was used to provide the background for Sheridan Le Fanu's *Carmilla* – a Gothic tale of lesbian vampirism.

Serving up a Good Hot Dinner

The popular novelist and short story writer Maria Edgeworth (Note 56) corresponded at length with Hall in the years 1827 to 1836 and he clearly used her as a sounding board for his draft work. Hall had sent her a copy of his book on his Far East travels in 1818, but she did not make his acquaintance personally until they met during her visit to Sir Walter Scott in Edinburgh. Here she met the notables of the city, including Sir Henry Raeburn, Baron Hume, Francis Jeffrey, Lord Meadowbank, Lord Robert Kerr, Sir Adam Ferguson, Lord and Lady Hope of Hopetoun, and other eminences.

By this time the Anglo-Irish writer had not only established a solid reputation for her wide-ranging works, but is said to have influenced novelists such as William Makepeace Thackeray, Jane Austen, Ivan Turgenev, and importantly, Sir Walter Scott – whose Waverley novels were claimed to have been inspired by her, while her publisher was Scott's son-in-law, J.G. Lockhart. Apart from literary luminaries such as Lord Byron, she counted among her friends such eminent scientists as Sir Humphry Davy (Note 57), William Herschel and the Admiralty Hydrographer Sir Francis Beaufort, all of them known also to Hall. There was an unusual convergence of literary and scientific personalities at this time, as so well illuminated by Richard Holmes in *Age of Wonder*.

Edgeworth's impression of Hall at that time was not complimentary. On their last night in Edinburgh – 23 June 1823 – the Edgeworths again dined in Castle Street. She writes:

> But the festive evening was quite spoiled by the presence after dinner of John Hall, the future Baron of Dunglass ... that odious Caledonian bore, and his pushing heiress wife, who had extorted an invitation from Sir Walter, though even his infinite good nature would not invite them to dinner. Hall's sailor brother, Captain Basil Hall, *was* at dinner, and he was bad enough.

Edgeworth thought him clever, but too eager to show off; she continued:

Notes

56 Maria Edgeworth (1768–1849) was an important Anglo-Irish author, who wrote on a wide variety of topics from women's education to Irish rural life, and was a popular writer of children's fiction. She combined this with taking a very active part in the management of her father's estate at Edgeworthstown in County Longford.

57 Humphry Davy (whom Hall also knew) was suspected of having an affair with Maria's beautiful half-sister Anna – then married to Dr. Thomas Beddoes who was Humphrey Davy's scientific partner. Davy thought that under different circumstances Anna might have become as distinguished as Maria.

[Basil Hall was] on the edge of his chair always with anxiety while anyone else is speaking to get in his own facts and observations. Then came the other two, and we wished them a thousand times in Jamaica that last evening … heaven forbid they [should] come to Abbotsford while we are there – for which they made great pushes & Sir Walter *hoped some time of other that Mrs. Hall*, etc., but Lady Scott looked blacker than November – she cannot bear any of them.[1]

Her comments on Basil Hall at that time are in keeping with his high-octane behaviour described by others – and even himself – on social occasions. In addition on 14 August 1831 she mildly upbraids Hall for his request that she only provide encouraging remarks, as he is so easily discouraged, while she insists she will remain objective for his own good.

But by 1829 Edgeworth not only mentions that her sister Fanny is connected – albeit distantly by marriage – to Hall's family, but invites him to visit them in London, hoping that 'this may lead to a good acquaintance and future happiness'. By April 20 1829, Edgeworth appears to have concluded her remarks on Hall's North American narrative with some 12 pages of detailed comments – but it is worth pointing out that by this time, Maria Edgeworth was a confident 63 year-old, 20 years senior to Hall. A year later, she is offering sincere condolences on the death of his father, insisting that only he should write an account of the latter's life and achievements.

Subsequently she had been greatly flattered in 1827 to receive Hall's private journal on London society, including observant comments on the scientific, political, and fashionable figures of the day whom Hall had met. She much approved of his pen-portrait of his friend and colleague Captain Francis Beaufort – Hydrographer to the Navy and whose sister was Edgeworth's mother; and likewise his description of Lydia White – a 'kind friend' of Maria's who was also the leading London hostess of the time. Edgeworth especially commended the good sense of Sidney Smith, the eminent preacher and editor of the *Edinburgh Review* and was glad that Hall had apparently accepted his criticism with good grace, saying that he would as a result be a good friend and advisor in future years.

She did not however think that Hall had done justice in his comments on the clever Swiss

The popular Anglo-Irish novelist Maria Edgeworth corresponded frequently with Hall.

diplomat Albert Gallatin, whom Maria had admired during her extended stay in Paris.[2] This intimate journal – which indicated the high society circles in the capital which Hall moved – does not seem to have been published, but references were made to Hall's character sketches in for example *London Society*.[3] Regardless, Edgeworth invited Hall to send more of his journals to her.

Before Hall departed for the United States, he asked Edgeworth for introductions to people known to her there, and she also referred him to books by British travellers which she thought might be helpful (in fact Hall eschewed reading any such works on the basis that these might colour his independent judgement of the country and its people). He sent chapters of his Journal to her as they were written, at her request. He must have been on terms of some intimacy with Edgeworth, as he also forwarded copies of his wife's letters to her family, describing their travels. Edgeworth responded: 'You have made us all quite love as well as admire you, my dear sir; Mrs Hall must give us leave to say *love*, young and old, and well she may, for believe me, she has her share of the love and admiration both.' She also affirmed that nobody outside her family knew that Hall had lent her his Journal. While she was full of praise for the interest of his narrative, she was also emphatic on any future publication, insisting that Hall retain the form and immediacy of his early draft – the amusement would otherwise be 'absolutely destroyed'.

Furthermore, recognising the difficulty of incorporating the more general and serious observations on American life with the lighter journalistic tone of their adventures, she advocated identifying any parts of the narrative which could be omitted, including anything which might offend individuals or the long-winded description of his experience of the Niagara Falls, which seemed to be out of keeping with Hall's usual style. The detail of this practical criticism – covering some five pages in a single letter – is impressive, based on her scribbled notes while the narrative was being read out to her by one of her sisters. There are a number of letters on the same theme between August 1838 and November of that year.

On 30 August Edgeworth refers to a visit of Francis Beaufort and was greatly tempted to show him Hall's work on North America. She had now read his fifth volume and asked for his permission to show this to Beaufort, especially for his objective criticism. By late September – Hall's permission having been received – Beaufort on another visit spent many hours perusing Hall's journal, apparently agreeing with Edgeworth's earlier remarks, not least on the need to let his views settle before rushing into publication. Beaufort was particularly seized with the difficulty of the subject – especially of not giving offence – while being truthful. She herself goes on at some length on the need for objectivity and balance, emphasising a light touch on the question of American manners.

Later, she asks him to decide clearly whether the work is to be primarily one of interesting travel, or to have a broader 'educational' purpose describing the commercial, political and social make-up of America. Her letter of 12 October 1828 extends to eight pages on much the same theme but including this comment: 'You have many excellent conversations … you might use the very words that were spoken, without names, and placed never to betray persons … the French Revolution gave us enough of the majesty of the people. But you must take care that your hatred of democracy, does not touch, or seem to affect your love of liberty.'

Edgeworth then refers to an apparent inconsistency in Hall's views on this topic as expressed in a previous work: 'Your fame as a writer and as a man rests solidly and securely, upon your last work on South America, which breathes the noble spirit of rational love of liberty … You must take care, in the first place, *to be* consistent, and in the next place to *appear* so … do not give room for any to accuse you of being the advocate of arbitrary power.' She points out the need, in any published work, to lead people to their own conclusions by presenting the facts, without pushing his own opinions, particularly on politics.

Edgeworth might be described as an enlightened conservative – and in her own writing portrayed the Irish tenantry in a more favourable light than heretofore (implicitly contrasting this with an often effete aristocracy) – and in her advice to Hall, displays a mature wisdom (she herself had been a strong early advocate of women's right to education). While she does not disapprove of Hall's strictures against universal suffrage, she is adamant that he must always point up 'the advantages of just representative government'.

In her letter to her sister Honora, Edgeworth expresses her delight at praise on her writing received from Sir Walter Scott and on 12 March 1829, she writes to Hall:

> If what you had sent to me had not pleased, gratified and delighted me to the top of my bent; saturated me head and heart, with the most grateful sense of the kindness of my most admired friend, and with the unspeakable gratification of his esteem and affection … It would I am sure, give you very great pleasure your last packet gave to all my family, as well as to myself. One and all exclaimed 'How excessively kind it was of Captain Hall to send this to you, Maria, and to think of doing so in the midst of his own work, and that he found time for it too, is wonderful.' Believe me my dear sir, I feel it all; and if I could, as you say, flatter myself that Sir Walter Scott was in any degree influenced to write and publish his novels from seeing my sketches of Irish character, I should indeed triumph in the thought of having been the proximate cause of such happiness to millions.

Her euphoria presumably stemmed from some communication via Hall of Sir Walter's estimate of her work, which would have more than gratified any author, given his international reputation at this time.

In 1834 Hall was again on his European travels and writes to her from Italy, praising her novel *Helen* and speaking of all her characters as representing real human beings – in contrast to one critic who said the opposite. Her self-belief was obviously restored by these remarks – especially as he also proposed some corrections for the second edition – describing him as her 'dear best of critics'. Having secured his favour – and to avoid any suspicion that they might constitute a mutual admiration society – she then bluntly told him that she does not like *Continental Growls* as the title of his proposed book on European travels, nor its preface and indeed actively discouraged him from writing it at all. She was obviously being deliberately provocative for (what she considers) his own good. 'You are too honestly apt to depend on the sympathy of the public in your private concerns', says Edgeworth, referring to the expression of his authorial doubts in the draft preface. This criticism is both honest and perceptive – Maria is happy to retain his confidences, but does not wish to see these in print. As in his other works, she is constantly abjuring Hall to be brief and to concentrate on quality.

By contrast, Edgeworth was entranced by his later work on the extended stay with his family at Schloss Hainfeld in Styria, attending to Walter Scott's old friend Countess Purgstall in her last months. She wrote (in reference to a letter of praise from a distinguished, but unnamed literary critic): 'I hope your mouth is wide open, and that you are desperately thirsty, for I have a fine large! Sparkling! Glorious! Assuaging draught for you of unqualified praise! Swallow it down, it will do you no harm.' Her only criticism was the inference that might be drawn by unfriendly readers from his confession that, for the very best of humanitarian reasons, he sometimes wished the Countess dead. But by the end Edgeworth and those of her family who read the narrative were convinced of Hall's genuine solicitude for his hostess. She told him: 'You now serve up a good hot dinner, and do not force the guests into the kitchen to see it cooked', referring to his previous *apologias*.

In her letter of 30 March 1837 Edgeworth is similarly impressed in Hall's translation of Baron Pelet's book on his conversations with Napoleon Bonaparte (Edgeworth was a fluent French speaker). Hall's translation was universally praised, not only for its accuracy, but also for the light it shed on the character of the Emperor in contrast, as Edgeworth remarks, to 'the trashy, manufactured, not to say fabricated, or forged, anecdotes or conversations of Napoleon's, which have passed upon the credulous, and disgusted the discerning class of readers'. Having spent some time in France among both the aristocracy and intelligentsia, Edgeworth was in an informed position, while Hall himself had the unique experience of interviewing Bonaparte in person on St. Helena on his return from the Far East in 1817.

Maria and Hall – writing in very different genres – had forged an intimate literary association on which both came to depend for encouragement and support, with the luminous figure of Sir Walter Scott providing a fulcrum around which they connected with the world of letters.[4]

References

1. Johnson, Vol. 2, 814–5
2. Hare, A.J.C., 285
3. *London Society*, 1878
4. Edgeworth, F.A.B., (unpublished), Vol. 3, 7–185

'A Crusty Old Author'

All of Hall's main publishers and editors had professional associations with one another, and he was to cross swords with most of them at some stage. He was inclined to involve himself in every part of the publishing process from proof-reading to production and printing, not excluding advertisement and promotion. At times he wrote on a daily basis in considerable detail with advice to his current publisher. He complained at some length of lack of attention, delays and poor illustrations, and wherever possible attempted to insert his own political views into his correspondence – even his proposals for advance publicity in his later works.

John Murray the second (1778–1843), following in his father's footsteps was but one of that great dynasty of eminent publishers based in London. He had been closely associated with the Edinburgh publisher Archibald Constable, but separated from him in 1813 because of disagreements with Constable's risky business methods (in 1807 their combined debts amounted to the then enormous sum of £10,000). Murray published some of the most famous travellers and authors of his time, including Lord Byron, Thomas Moore, Mungo Park, John Franklin, Jane Austen and Sir Walter Scott. In 1809 he launched the *Quarterly Review* in opposition to the *Edinburgh Review*, both journals receiving Hall's work. For much of the19th Century the firm of John Murray was the centre of the English-speaking publishing world, certainly in the field of works of travel.[1]

It was Murray who published the first of Hall's books on his travels to China and Korea, *Account of a Voyage of Discovery to the West Coast of Corea and the Great Loo-choo Island*. It was also on the return from that journey that Hall called in at St. Helena to interview Napoleon Bonaparte. Writing from Portsmouth on 16 November 1817 Hall writes to say that his father's old friend, the geologist John Playfair 'had lost his notes on Bonaparte – a serious annoyance', and that he would like some ready cash 'to pay off a plaguey debt': young lieutenants in the Royal Navy were not overpaid.[2] In fact, after the publication of this first book, he was still in need of money and claims that he has made only £58 after paying off expenses. Assuming that his book 'has had its day', he asks that Murray sell the remaining copies for whatever the publisher can get.[3]

To his delight Murray proposed a second edition, since the first had completely sold out, and Hall suggested a cheaper version (which Hall emphasised was completely different from the first) for wider circulation. By June of 1819 – when about 1,500 copies had been sold or ordered – he reports that he is sending a copy of his book to Lord Byron[4] (five years later he met Lord Byron in Venice and offered Murray an anecdote concerning this, showing Byron in 'a very amiable light').[5] However, early in the following year Hall let Murray know that he was leaving on a voyage of several years (his journey to South America) and requested that Murray settle his accounts urgently – including any profits on the second edition – in order to pay for his travel preparations (Hall had complained to Constable that 'Murray had treated him in a manner which I cannot submit to'). He was also greatly disappointed that the recently published Navy List had made no mention of his books.[6]

It is clear from this correspondence that Hall is very much bound up (somewhat anxiously) in the progress of his books, and when complaining to Murray about delays is also almost fawning to his publisher. Murray assures Hall that he (Murray) will not receive a shilling for at least 12 months on the sale of the smaller edition, but that he will give Hall 100 guineas for the copyright if he insists on closing the account – 'on the basis that I am only desirous of pursuing the principle which has regulated me throughout of making you satisfied'.[7] But Hall was adamant that he would not relinquish the copyright – since Murray was not inclined to agree Hall's terms – and he had appointed Mr Harvey, his brother-in-law, to manage his business affairs in his absence.[8] On his return from his South American travels, Hall indicated that he was thinking of writing a book on his experiences and of giving Murray first refusal, while expressing his disappointment that the *Quarterly Review* (then published by Murray) had discontinued its nautical and astronomical section, in which Hall had a particular interest.[9]

At the end of 1826 Hall became embroiled with Murray in a proposed publication that was curiously aberrant. It concerned a cookery book written by a friend from his early Nova Scotia days – now a Mrs Dalgairn living in Dundee. Hall had written a fulsome preface (and unbeknown to the main author, he had inserted a recipe of his own for 'Captain Hall's Sandwiches for Travellers'!). He recommended it strongly to Murray for publication, with an exhortation for early consideration given that he was about to leave the country. Although he commends it to Murray purely as a matter of business and asks him to put aside any personal considerations, it is clear from his lengthy justification for the book that he is exerting not a little pressure on his publisher as 'it has been on his [Hall's] mind for a couple of years'. Not having heard from Murray by early December, Hall is obviously becoming more anxious and unfortunately it all ends in tears, as Murray – after long delays – turns the proposal down.[10]

In 1826 Murray sent his son to Edinburgh for his education, and Hall took a genuine interest in the welfare of the young man, assuring Murray that he would do all to help him: 'Your son breakfasted with me yesterday morning and in the course of conversation I learned what your wishes were with respect to his studies here.' Hall then went on to recommend the classes he should take, including chemistry and natural history under Dr Thompson and also Mr McCulloch's lectures on political economy. 'I have attended these lectures and can answer for their great value.' Hall proposes to accompany the young man to and from the rooms three times a week, to give Hall opportunities to talk to him. He recommends that he brush up his deficient maths under a teacher known to Thompson who will be interviewed by Hall. He is also to read Latin and Greek. Hall says that he is pleased 'with his manners and good sense and will introduce him to friends … He dines with me on Thursday when he will meet some of my family and on New Year's Day if he is not otherwise engaged. I hope he will dine with Lady Hunter, my wife's mother. Sir William Arbuthnot wished him to have come to his house on Xmas Day – but he was engaged' (Sir William Arbuthnot was Lord Provost of Edinburgh and related to Hall's wife Margaret). Hall warned Murray's son to stay at home as much as possible for his studies, rather than be drawn into society. Hall assures Murray that Dr Thompson's house is probably the best in Edinburgh, taking real charge of his boarders compared to many others. In January 1827 Hall writes a very tactful letter to Murray, praising his son's good manners and behaviour, but asking that the Murrays – preferably Mrs Murray – write to both Thompson and the boy about 'driving out' on Fridays and Saturdays, (which Hall thinks is quite enough – as does Thompson, who was also taking a keen interest in his welfare). Hall continues: 'he is much liked, and gets many invitations.'[11]

This whole episode shows Hall in a good light, acting as something of a benevolent 'uncle', prepared to put himself out for the welfare of his publisher's son on his first foray from the family home in London. It is quite typical of Hall's generosity and concern (he went on to regularly consult closely with Dr Thomson on the young man's programme of studies). By early April, Hall is able to reassure Murray on his son's progress and that 'he has adhered to the rules about not dining out more than twice weekly', while enjoining Mrs Murray to write to Dr Thomson directly.[12]

However, by the spring of that year, Hall is still awaiting a final verdict on the cookery book, in which he has personally invested so much of his time. He details his preference for a title, even to the extent of suggesting that after the author's name, there might be "of Dundee' – or is the place too small? It might give it too much of a Scotch character perhaps … I have never bestowed so much pains on anything as this preface'. On the question of whether to include a section on household medicines, Hall is of the opinion that this should be omitted as 'it would expose you to the criticism, & snarling & ill will of every practitioner of physic in the country'.[13] Hall spent an inordinate amount of time on the Dalgairn cookbook, but Murray – if he was ever enthusiastic on the subject – clearly cooled. It was eventually published by Robert Cadell. It may have been this failure to engage Murray on this project which prompted Hall to write to him in the summer of 1828 indicating quite pointedly that he had made other arrangements for the publication of any future works of travel, though he hoped that he and Murray would remain good friends.[14]

A year later, Hall had published his controversial narrative of his journeys in North America and the accompanying sketches made with the *camera lucida* under the imprint of Robert Cadell. Murray complimented him on this. Hall replied that he thought this work would be 'more than adequate set-off to the Radicals, here and elsewhere … but in truth, the disapprobation of men who think so differently from me, with respect to the institutions of this Country was a mark of its success', reflecting his increasingly conservative views.

The advertisement for the third edition of Hall's work explains that he had set out to correct wrongful impressions of many of his countrymen (i.e. their anti-American prejudice), 'but had to recant when he was struck 'with the evil consequences of placing all the powers of the state in one branch of the community, to the exclusion of all others … although the democratical part of the body politic, when retained in its right place, is eminently useful … that the right chord has been struck … seems apparent from the outcry raised against the work by those parties in England who are not content to remain in their natural places, but desire to imitate their brother democrats and reformers across the Atlantic … to the utter extirpation of the other estates of the realm – the Monarchy – the Church – and the Aristocracy, etc'. This was the theme of Hall's letter to Cadell on 3 January 1831 when he clearly indicates that he wants to draw the publisher into his way of thinking on politics. Cadell, as a Whig, was the one person he would most like to convert to the 'true faith'. A later letter that month assured Cadell that Hall had 'the best means of having the feelings of the best informed and most influential men of all parties here [London] and I speak of this matter with great confidence.'[15]

On the 1 February 1831, Hall wrote to Cadell:

> What you tell me of your having received orders for 6 of Hall's America is by far the most agreeable thing you have told me for a long time – I am grieving in spirit over the idea of the sale having totally ceased, and after having paid the Author for his last Edition, you must have to dispose of the sheets – have you any hopes of getting rid of the said books? If not, I have a project to get rid of them.[16]

This may have been Hall's idea of getting his books – particularly his *Fragments of Voyages and Travels* – into the schools.

Towards the end of 1829 Hall became embroiled – albeit as a mediator – in a dispute between Byron's biographer Thomas Moore and Murray. The publisher had apparently given the proofs of Moore's work to Hall while the latter was in Paris: he seems at this time to have been sending works to Hall for comment or review. They were then passed to the renowned French publishing house of Galignani. But although Hall was full of praise for the biography, Moore was not happy that these had been passed to Hall, no doubt for his assessment. Both Murray and Moore asked for these proofs to be returned, although Galignani assured them that no improper use would be made of the material (the French publishers were known however for reprinting popular works in cheap version, to the detriment of the original publishers by undercutting the English editions).[17]

Murray acknowledged all the trouble that Hall had taken over this matter, but insisted that the work was his property and that Moore had no power to enter into arrangements with any other publisher, such as Galignani (Murray had already contracted a Madame Bellow to bring out the work in French). The whole matter was settled eventually, but there is some evidence that Hall once again had meddled in an affair without foreseeing the consequences.[18]

In 1802 Archibald Constable (1774–1827) launched the *Edinburgh Review* and in 1812 purchased the copyright of the famous *Encyclopaedia Britannica*. He was an innovative publisher, known for paying his authors handsomely and he himself lived in some style. He was incautious in business affairs and in 1826 became bankrupt, together with his best-selling author Sir Walter Scott, from whom he had bought the copyright of the Waverley Novels (Note 58). It was Constable who said: 'Sir Walter Scott … in his

Notes

58 The bankruptcy in January 1826 of Archibald Constable – who published *inter alia* the works of Scott and Hall – impacted most severely on Scott who had substantial investments in the company, but also included Scott's printer James Ballantyne. Scott was obliged to surrender all his assets in the interests of the creditors.

later years, owed much to the Captain's active friendship. Of acute and wakeful intellect, of wide and varied experience and culture, the interest of Captain Hall was intense in all that concerned Humanity.'[19]

Early in 1825 Constable had mooted to Scott his innovative and very ambitious project to publish a cheap monthly magazine which he reckoned would have sales perhaps 'in the millions'. This was to be called *Constable's Miscellany* with the intention of including in the first issue Hall's Far Eastern voyages, to be released on 1 January 1826. Future issues were proposed to include the travels of Baron Humboldt and the memoirs of the Scottish oriental scholar Alexander Murray. He specially invited articles on 'travel, adventure and remarkable biographies'.

Constable also wanted to put Hall's books on Loo Choo and South America at the forefront of the *Miscellany*. A completely revised third edition of *Loo-choo* was incorporated into the *Miscellany* – the previous editions being published by John Murray. Constable asked Scott if it would be possible to obtain permission to dedicate the entire new publication to King George IV (the King consented on Scott's recommendation).[20] Constable was able to realise his *Miscellany* in 1826–7, which for the first time attempted to popularise quality writing in science, literature and the arts at an acceptable price. He also republished Hall's account of his travels in the Far East in 1826, after Hall became disenchanted with John Murray.

The background to this split with Murray is given in a series of letters from Hall to Robert Cadell prior to his departure for South America. In 1819 he declared that he intended to put his affairs in Constable's hands 'with confidence', 'to take care of my reputation and Interest' This was at a time when Cadell was working for Constable and Co. Robert Cadell (1788–1849) had joined the Edinburgh publisher in 1809 but left after that company's financial crash in 1826 (he had married Constable's daughter who died within a year). Unlike Constable, he was cautious in business matters and lived plainly.

After his financial ruin, Sir Walter Scott – respecting Cadell's business acumen – retained him as his publisher, which proved highly lucrative to Cadell but also rescued Scott's fortunes, largely through the re-publication of the Waverley novels at a popular price. Cadell published Hall's *Fragments of Voyages and Travels* in 1832 and 1834 and the narrative of his travels in North America in 1829 and subsequently (it is worth mentioning that the volume of correspondence from Hall to Cadell in the ten years from 1831 to 1841 runs to around 1,000 items). The *Scotsman* of 23 April 1831 records the praise of the *Literary Gazette* for Hall's *Fragments of Voyages and Travels*, which do 'infinite honour to their author' and the *Edinburgh Literary Journal* opined that 'this is likely to rank in the juvenile library along with Sir Walter Scott's *Tales of a Grandfather*'.

Hall found both Constable and Cadell 'very kind and friendly'. He offered to write about his next voyage to South America. Hall's complaint about Murray seems to be that the publisher had put up the price of the second edition of the book on his travels in the Far East from 7/- to 7/6 without consulting Hall. This was after he 'had already told his friends what the price would be'. Hall did not object so much to price – although he always wanted cheap books for wider readership – but he did object to not being treated in a 'frank, gentlemanly way'. Hall goes on at great length on the point, claiming that Murray had treated as him as a 'nobody', stating that: 'I shall be miserable till I can get out of it'. Matters were not helped when a clerk wrote on Murray's instructions to say that he thought 7/6 was very cheap. Hall let Constable know that he was now in a quandary about whether a third edition should be brought out – even if the second edition should not be sold out and very much wanted Constable's advice.[21]

In a letter of 1 October 1825, Hall says to Scott: 'Constable, the great Leviathan of Book swallowers, has set my pen going again – and I wish very much I could converse with you for five minutes on the subject of this said *Miscellany*, which like a steam engine, is to carry all before it. I am delighted indeed to be in such company – but sometimes a little nervous, too. I shall be most happy to do all I can to assist your part of it.'[22]

On 16 July 1820, writing from HMS *Conway* at Portsmouth, Hall reports that all copies of his Far East travel book had been sold except for 250, and that these too were likely to be snapped up. Therefore there was a good prospect for a third edition. Hall had apparently settled with Murray and – having obtained the copyright to the book – he was resolved not to publish with him again. He now wanted to publish with whomever he pleased, although Murray had apparently hinted that he would like to publish any account of Hall's forthcoming travels in South America.[23] However, Hall drafted an angry letter to Murray which was a lengthy diatribe against the publisher which he first sent to Constable for his comments – the last straw was when Murray had referred to Hall as 'one of his authors'. Hall's *amour propre* was obviously offended by this 'insult'.[24] The correspondence with his publishers certainly reveals Hall as being unduly thin-skinned and sensitive to perceived slights. This may have been because of his awareness of his limited formal education. Despite his several successes, even into the mid 1830s, he is still unsure about his literary talent and betrays his insecurities in long repetitive letters on the subject. However, by the summer of that year he was able to report to Constable that 'all was civil' between himself and Murray, and hoped that he had succeeded in keeping on good terms with his former publisher. At the same time he offered to attempt an article on seamanship and navigation for Constable's *Encyclopaedia for Youth*, but in 1839 (when Hall was 51) when writing to Macvey Napier he said that he might be in a better position to do so if he got a ship for three years to brush up his professional knowledge, having been 16 years ashore. Hall must have known that in this he was being quite unrealistic.[25]

By summer of the following year, Hall is again caught up in the publication of Mrs Dalgairn's cookbook, this time with Constable. He admits he 'is sorry that he ever meddled with it' but cannot now let it drop. He was prepared to write a preface and undertake editing, suggesting that Constable might now be prepared to include it in his *Miscellany*.[26] He was greatly disappointed when Constable eventually turned down this publication. Constable probably regretted this, as it became a best seller that rivalled Mrs Beeton's acclaimed work and ran to no less than 16 editions between 1829 and 1860.[27]

By the late summer Hall had completed the first volume for the *Miscellany*. He approves of Constable writing to the King to obtain a dedication, and proposes that the frontispiece should include a vignette of the King's head 'with a dignified seal' on every copy.[28] Throughout all of this correspondence, Hall offers detailed advice to Constable in his usual way, but seems willing enough to accept his publisher's judgement.

By mid-October, Hall is on another tack. It had been suggested that he write the life of the great navigator Captain James Cook (1728–79), but he is uncertain about this and prefers to bring out a volume of his own global travels culled from some 20 of his journals. In the same letter to Constable he says that he is 'delighted that old Mrs Cook is still alive' and that he will make a point of seeing her when he is next in London – but in the meantime he asks Constable to write to her for any letters. He himself is confident that he could get much original material from Lady Banks – the widow of Sir Joseph Banks who accompanied Cook on his first major voyage – and from Lord Melville, whom he proposes to speak to.[29]

As usual, there are misunderstandings. While Constable is enthusiastic about Hall's proposals, he does not want to be pinned down on terms at this early stage, and disagrees with Hall on remuneration[30] (it is not clear from the correspondence whether the sticking point is the proposal to write up the journals or the Cook biography). Hall's response was clearly unacceptable and he later agrees that he was quite unreasonable and hopes that his letter would be overlooked and destroyed – another example of Hall's impulsiveness and subsequent regret at 'shooting from the hip'.[31] By his own admission, 'he had extravagant notions of his literary value and was now properly humble'. He proposed to set about the book on Cook 'with heart and soul to produce a worthy work' and now wanted to re-establish his relationship with Constable.[32]

By the end of November, Hall is preparing three volumes of his travels and suggests that the payment for this and the Cook biography can await publication – a very different tone from his earlier proposals for payment.[33] However, writing in early December he says: 'I have not seen Mrs Cook nor indeed taken charge as yet of that great job. I hope I may be able to do it – but I have many doubts and fears – although, God knows, I must do something.'[34]

In a postscript to a letter of a letter to Constable on 15 December 1825, Hall says he has seen Lord Melville with regards to 'trying my hand at Cook'. Melville offered 'all that the Admiralty has on the subject … I have not yet seen Mrs Cook but I have found that she is still on the pension list for £22 a year since 1780.'[35] Later, he lets Constable know that he is unwilling to have an announcement of the proposed biography at this stage preferring to 'take a nearer view of the subject before counselling myself to the world on a point on which I am by no means certain of my own self'.[36] In the end, for whatever reason, Hall did not proceed with the project. He may well have been overawed by the magnitude of the task of doing justice to such a national hero.

It was in mid-1825 that Hall became aware of Constable's serious financial difficulties and wrote to him sympathetically, offering to help in any way he could. In his usual nautical terminology, Hall hoped that Constable 'would weather the gale handsomely'.[37] When Constable's newborn publication came out, Hall was ecstatic: 'I have no heart to speak of the dear little Miscellany! Nothing can be more beautiful than it is – if you have any copies to spare, etc. – my whole time and thoughts are at your service.' But by the spring of the following year it became clear that Constable was in deep trouble. Hall had not written for some time because he only had 'commonplaces' to offer at this time.[38] His next undated letter however, indicates that he intends to make a proposal that he trusts will meet Constable's wishes.[39]

This is confirmed in his letter of 28 May when he offers Constable the copyright of the three volumes of his Far East voyages and of his work on South America, hoping that they 'will contribute to the success of the great undertaking of which they will form the commencement' (i.e. the first volumes of Constable's *Miscellany*) – provided that he can be relieved of a previous £100 cash advance and receive 100 copies of the first three volumes of the *Miscellany*.[40] He was in fact making over the rights of his published property to Constable including any profits accruing, which would prove eventually to be a most generous lifeline for the publisher. Archibald Constable was overwhelmed, saying that Hall's action would be 'a consolation throughout the remainder of my days'.

The publication of Hall's narrative on South America was not without its problems. Constable was publishing and he wanted to do Hall proud with a smart and expensive work, which would maintain his reputation for quality. Hall, on the other hand, wanted 'to be humble and to gain favour by the absence of pretension and to win people's good will by ministering to their amusement at small cost'. Hall despaired of agreement and at one point said: 'I am well nigh resolved to drop the whole transaction.'[41] Later, he was to quote a Captain Bowles in support of his view, 'provided that Hall kept out of politics and did not give offence to anyone, in or outside the naval service' and that he would seek the opinion of his brother-in-law Mr Harvey. At the same time he declared that he did not want to do anything which was against Constable's professional publishing experience.[42] By 16 August 1824 Hall was acknowledging the great success of the book, following Constable's original proposals regarding price and format.[43] In a number of ways, this exchange is typical of Hall's relations with all of his publishers.

In his memoirs of his father, Thomas Constable dedicated a whole chapter to Hall. He comments on Hall's generosity of spirit when his father was in severe financial difficulties: 'This noble man, when the sun was shining on his friend, was contented to be just and liberal, but now, his generous nature led him to make such a sacrifice of personal emolument as I believe has been seldom equalled and never surpassed.' His son continued: 'Of all my father's many friends, none was steadier in adversity, or more devoted, than Captain Hall.' Hall was by no means a rich man, and since his retirement from the Navy in 1823, had been obliged to live largely on the half pay of a captain, which was relatively meagre.[44] In fact, Hall's name appears frequently on the lists of subscribers to charitable causes published by *The Scotsman*, usually for a standard sum of £5, which today would be worth as much as £200.

John Gibson Lockhart (1794–1854) was a novelist, biographer and critic – in the latter capacity known for his astringent assessments of Whig writers in his capacity as editor of the prestigious *Quarterly Review* (founded by John Murray the second) between 1825 and 1853. With James Wilson ('Christopher North') he was a leading contributor to *Blackwood's Magazine* in its early days. Hall was first introduced to Lockhart as the prospective son-in-law of Sir Walter Scott and had a close association with him, constantly inveighing him to maintain Tory principles in his editorship of the *Review* (Lockhart received a stream of recommendations from Hall for articles and authors). Apart from his biographies of Robert Burns and Napoleon, Lockhart is best remembered for his seven-volume life of Scott, including a chapter contributed by Hall. Hall was very complimented by this inclusion and in a very long and prolix letter of 24 March 1837 to Lockhart he praises the work extravagantly, claiming that Lockhart 'had been bottling up his genius'.[45]

As early as 1827 Hall had disagreed with Lockhart on the purpose of the *Quarterly Review* and the function of the editor. He had enjoined Lockhart to consider it 'a mighty engine in your hand … this great political and literary guide' – obviously to advance Hall's Tory views and as 'an organ to guide the country to peace and honour' All of this would enhance Lockhart's reputation, 'provided he stood back from the writing, acting as an advisor, in the manner of a captain who delegated appropriate duties to sailors'.[46]

Hall had indicated his willingness to contribute a regular article for the *Quarterly Review*, but on the subject of his favourite hobby-horses – the supremacy of the British constitution; the evil of democracy; the place of church and state; Whigs versus Tories; and others, he lets Lockhart know that he would prefer someone else (obviously someone sharing his sympathies) to write a piece. In a letter to Lockhart he claims: 'Had I not forsworn Party political writing & Pothouse public speaking I think I could almost turn out such an article but I shall be 20,000 times better pleased to see Sir John Walsh at such a task.'[47]

After the resignation of Duke of Wellington in 1831, everything has gone – according to Hall – as he had wished for the Tories politically: the dissolution of Parliament, the 'noble articles in the *Quarterly*, the magnificent debate in the Lords, and the still more magnificent division, etc. etc … you will recall that I always declared that there would not be **one** borough disfranchised – and the result has justified my prophecy' (referring to the late Bill). Hall sees Lockhart as 'one of the leaders in the future action'. He advises that Lockhart 'must not flinch from the cause in thought word or deed. You will deserve (and obtain) the fate of an officer who yaws his ship to avoid coming to the fight … my idea is that your honour and your fortune are completely staked in this affair – you are fully as much bound to the cause of Toryism in Church and State – that is of real Public Spirit – as if you were actually in office – and not at liberty to do as you please', referring to 'the torpor of certain journals at the moment of the Duke's highest need.'[48]

Hall unsurprisingly was a great admirer of the Duke of Wellington. Hall's deceased brother-in-law, Col. De Lancey, had been one of his senior staff officers, while his brother James had painted the national hero's portrait. Hall was in constant touch with another of Wellington's officers, Colonel John Gurwood (then attempting to collate and publish Wellington's dispatches), while Hall encouraged Lockhart to make an article out of Gurwood's work. He also suggested to Macvey Napier – the then editor of the Edinburgh Review – that he employ Gurwood to write a series of articles for that journal, indicating that Napier 'would be doing a great service to the country – you will repay well some portion of the mighty obligation under which the Duke has placed us all'. (Note 59) Hall related how the Duke spent a whole day at his country house reading aloud to his guests his own dispatches from Gurwood's book. He also let Lockhart know of the difficulty he had in getting the modest Gurwood to write up his own experience of the Peninsular War, where he had distinguished himself by his bravery in the course of capturing the Governor of Cuidad Rodrigo (Note 60).[49]

Notes

59 Despite their political differences, Macvey Napier – the editor of the *Encylopædia Britannica* – published a number of reviews by Hall for the prestigious *Edinburgh Review*, including some of the works by Sir John Barrow, Second Secretary of the Admiralty for many years.

60 Colonel John Gurwood (1790–1845) exhausted himself over the last seven years of his life, struggling with the writing of these dispatches. Challenged on his behaviour at Ciudad Rodrigo, he committed suicide in 1845.

In one of the early reviews of Hall's book on his travels in North America, the *Quarterly Review* is very sympathetic to Hall's ultra-conservative views, providing lengthy quotes from Hall's narrative.[50] However, Hall was unrepentant when asked by Lockhart to amend his draft of an article on North America for the Review, which Hall said he could reject if he wished: 'I will not father any article on that subject, at all events, at which there is any cringing to the democrats on either side of the Atlantic.' By this time (1831) Hall had become an even more dyed-in-the-wool Tory than before, constantly nagging Lockhart to support this cause as editor of the *Review*.[51]

Following his departure from Hainfeld after the death of Countess Purgstall, Hall became embroiled in an attenuated dispute with Lockhart concerning the last letter that Sir Walter Scott wrote to the lady. She had been quite distressed after the death of her beloved son and – having sent to Scott a memorial book celebrating his and her husband's life – not to have had a reply from him. In fact Scott had replied but the letter apparently never reached her – but she was delighted to hear of its existence and pressed for a copy to be sent to her, while Hall was in residence at Hainfeld. Hall also very much wanted it to be included in his narrative. That letter is generally regarded as one of the most intimate and moving that Scott ever wrote and is included in Appendix 1. In a series of letters to Lockhart from Paris between 1 February and 25 March 1836, Hall pleaded his case:

> I … hope that you will not consider me indelicate, or importunate, in begging you to reconsider the subject of Sir W.S.'s letter to Mme. Purgstall … I have nothing to show, legally speaking, in support of this assertion that the old lady would have given me the letter, but I could show you many things, under her own hand which, if it were necessary, would make out a case 'a fortiori' for I believe she would have given me anything in the Schloss – or even the Schloss itself, had we been inclined to ask for it!

Hall assures Lockhart that he did not ask to make use of the letter if he thought that in any way it would be detrimental to Lockhart's own publication (his *Life of Scott*). Hall asserts that he thinks it would show certain important links in Walter Scott's life, provided it were to appear in Hall's work first – especially as it would appear alongside Hall's anecdotes on Scott which he intended and would therefore enhance his biography. He had been given the opportunity – by his experience at the Schloss – of welding certain links together. Hall then states that if he is wrong in asserting his claim – if Lockhart's *Life* were to be published before *Schloss*, or had he received the letter when requested – he would have cheerfully given Lockhart permission to use it.

He goes on at great length on this point saying that it will make no difference to Lockhart's book if it comes from the original letter or Hall's own published work – and if permission were not given, 'it will castrate my poor *Schloss*, for its most important chapter by far is entitled *The Countess and Sir Walter Scott* in which I give all I can recollect of the early intercourse between them'. Hall goes on to say that it is important to the book as a whole to give evidence of their intimate friendship, 'as is implied by this most beautiful letter'; and: 'It would be preposterous in me, indeed, for one moment to expect that you & Mr Cadell should consent to anything which should hurt your mighty work, which is to last for a long time, in order to benefit such a … production of mine at its very best.'[52]

Later that month, Hall again wrote to Lockhart in the same vein. Finally, his persistence was rewarded, as evident when he writes to Lockhart on 25 March:

[Regarding] your copy of Sir Walter Scott's letter to Mme Purgstall – and I take the opportunity – sincerely I am very much obliged to you. I have to thank you through Mr Harvey respecting the Cranstoun and Stewart family … No one, but ourselves is aware of the terms upon which our old Countess was with her old family and we do not mean to speak of this point to anyone. For the rest, as there is not one word in my *Schloss* which can give offence to any member of her family – or which is not creditable to the Countess … Pray say nothing of all this. I hope you get the new notes about Balzac.[53]

From Paris on 18 April 1836, Hall writes: 'My *Schloss* is in the press – and I hope will amuse you. It has cost me some trouble – more than any other production of my slow moving pen.' Later, in a letter from 132 George Street, Edinburgh, to Lockhart, Hall again refers to this permission for the Scott letter to be included in his narrative:

'I hope you will be satisfied that any sense of your attention in giving me Sir W.S.'s letter to buoy my poor *Schloss* was hearty … and its having appeared in a work rapidly passing into oblivion, will be no sort of objection (on the contrary) to its obtaining a place in the most popular and enduring work of the age' (Lockhart's *Life of Scott*).[54]

But in fact, his account did give offence to at least one member of the family – Henry Cranstoun – who based his complaint on the following review in the *Quarterly Review* – whose editor was none other than Lockhart and who gave the book a lengthy treatment:[55]

The idea of attaching an English gentleman and his family, picked up at random, without previous connexion or even acquaintance, to her bedside for the rest of her existence, is so extravagant that it seems to confirm a suspicion, which many other circumstances of her conduct excite, that the poor lady's *eccentricity* was sometimes so great as to amount to absolute aberration, and yet this extravagant project she accomplished. Captain Hall, for some time unconscious of the monomania of his hostess, and of the toils she was spreading around him, sets about making himself and his family *comfortable* in their new habitation.[56]

The reviewer also comments on how agreeable Hall must have been with his experience and knowledge of the world, but also accused the lady of 'a degree of selfishness in detaining Hall to thwart the priests who might re-arrange her funeral' and suggested Hall created an 'artful and elaborate fiction, rather than a narrative of contemporary events'. The reviewer questions whether the friends of the Countess might not regret Hall's exposure – acknowledging Hall's usual frankness – even if many are averse to anything in print about domestic affairs. In this he was prescient, given that this review elicited a furious response from Cranstoun – who spread himself over three pages in a subsequent published letter to *Blackwood's Magazine* in Edinburgh.[57]

Cranstoun accused Hall of implying that the Countess was left destitute in a foreign country, neglected by her family. Cranstoun pointed out in some detail that his brother George together with his niece, had paid a visit to the Countess lasting some months, when her son was still living in 1815. When news of his death was received in 1816, Cranstoun immediately travelled day and night at the worst season of the year, in a journey of 1,700 miles in 17 days to be by her side, bringing with him ample funds to pay off all demands and remaining at Hainfeld for two months. At the Countess' request, Lord and Lady Ashburton (Note 61) together with his wife, her sister and brother, paid an extended visit of seven months.

In Cranstoun's words, 'Lady Ashburton was so fondly attached to her aunt, that she determined to pass a whole year in her society after the rest of the party left Lower Styria'. Cranstoun himself paid a third visit to bring Lady Ashburton back to England. Before they left, they entreated the Countess to return with them, to no avail. Cranstoun claimed he simply could not understand Hall's motives in misrepresenting the situation, which he must have known about. He charges Hall with implying that Dugald Stewart had a hand in securing a wealthy husband for the then Jane Cranstoun, on a distorted interpretation of Hall's phraseology (Note 62).

Hall made the point that as the narrative was concerned solely with his stay at Hainfeld, he deliberately avoided mention of family connections – such as the visit of her brothers, which he thought would be appreciated by the family and he be given credit for this. The brothers (George and Henry) had apparently specifically chosen to visit the Countess to support her at the time of her son's death, when they also provided financial assistance. On reading Cranstoun's criticism, Hall had promptly inserted a new page in unsold copies of the book by way of explanation and immediately arranged for the same correction to be inserted in the second edition.[58]

Hall's justification was supported by the redoubtable Mrs Anne Grant of Laggan, who in a letter of 10 December 1836 to Mrs Hook of Edinburgh opined:

> You have, I take it for granted, read Captain Hall's account of his residence in Styria, and of the Countess Purgstall, whose character and sufferings create a deeper interest than those of any heroine of romance. All the relations of the hard-fated Countess are clamorous against the Captain for this publication. For this I can see no reason: there is nothing to diminish the Countess's high character, except it be that her grief, like her love, was unlimited … I am glad, however, that the Captain remained to witness the conclusion of this tragic scene.[59]

In a note in his book about Sir Walter Scott, Sir H.J.C. Grierson claims that he too did not know why Hall's narrative appears to have provoked some resentment, and that according to Lockhart – on the authority of Lady Davy – that Hall was to be 'cut' (i.e. 'sent to Coventry') by London society.[60] Walter Scott, in a letter to Hall said that

Notes

61   The young Lord Ashburton (1782–1823) was the second baron, Richard Barré, and had been sent from London to Edinburgh University, where he was put under the care of the Stewart family with whom he resided. After his death in 1832 he left the substantial sum of £8,000 to Countess Purgstall – his aunt by marriage.

62   Hall responded in the January issue of the Magazine, neatly sidestepping a whole number of points raised by Cranstoun as being the responsibility of the reviewer, not himself, but also dealing with two substantive issues. He admitted to wrongly ascribing financial assistance from Lord Ashburton at the time of the death of the Countess' son – as a result of misinformation from the Countess herself.

Lockhart himself must not scruple in his work about offending people, claiming that the public now demand more of domestic matters than they previously did (i.e. of the intimate workings of households). He told Lockhart to be bold, even if he is abused by the idle and thin skinned.

In the end the reviewer is decidedly complimentary:

Whatever subject [Hall] undertakes to write upon, he makes it as amusing as a fairy tale … his narrative we must presume, as accurate in matter of fact as one of his log books – is by the accident which produced it, the out-of-the way circumstances, etc, etc much more like a novel than an episode in a continental tour … in Captain Hall's hands nothing is commonplace. His views of any subject are at once simple and shrewd, original yet unaffected … but to these qualities Captain Hall adds another, which though not of a literary kind, has contributed very much to his literary success. He seems to have received from nature, and to have strengthened by the habits of his professional life, a busy, inquisitive, and if we may use the expression, *venturesome* turn of mind, which leads him to seize opportunities, and to pursue prospects, upon which men of less active or more reserved dispositions, would have hesitated to venture. Not one, perhaps, of fifty travellers, to whom the accident which produced Captain Hall's visit to Styria should have presented itself, would have ventured to avail himself of it.[61]

A review by Edgar Alan Poe – usually a critical reviewer – said that: 'The entire volume, has many charms of matter, and more particularly of manner. Captain Hall is no ordinary writer. This justice must be done to him.'[62]

Apart from the controversy over *A Winter in Styria*, Hall's works generally received good reviews – those of Hall's *Fragments of Voyages and Travels* were uniformly complimentary. The *United Services Journal* carried an unusually long review of the second series, with extended quotations: 'His *Fragments* form, in fact, a succession of lights and shades without any apparent effort to produce that effect … sound instruction in an entertaining guise … [and] quiet humour.' It even carried a long excerpt on Hall's advocacy of captains carrying enough fresh water to allow for the washing out of salt from sailors' shirts for their comfort, indicating Hall's emphasis on kindness in command. *The Scotsman* of 23 April 1831 records the praise of the *Literary Gazette* for Hall's *Fragments of Voyages and Travels*, which do 'infinite honour to their author', while the *Edinburgh Literary Journal* was of the opinion that 'this is likely to rank in the juvenile library along with Sir Walter Scott's *Tales of a Grandfather.*' *The Quarterly Review* (XCIII) of March 1832 claimed that *Fragments* was a 'performance unique in literature' and the *Monthly Review* in April 1832 stated that whereby 'a father may have given his son an excellent education … he cannot give him a more valuable present than those FRAGMENTS – he should make them the object of his study by day and by night.'

Dr. Coplestone, the Bishop of Wandaff – described as 'one of the most eminent scholars of the age' – said:

Basil Hall's style appears to me to be the very model of correct and perspicuous writing, combining elegance and ease with a terse mode of expression. His skill in describing external objects, and especially any artificial and mechanical process, is unrivalled. He knows how to finish his picture, and knows where to leave off. The reader sees, as it were, whatever he describes; and such is the felicity of his language, that it impresses the matter indelibly on the memory, as having afforded not only pleasure, but instruction.[63]

A number of Hall's works were translated into French, Spanish and German and he was awarded an honorary L.L.D by Oxford University on 11 June 1831, presumably on the basis of his writing. Professor J.D. Forbes records in a letter of 17 June to his sister Jane Forbes: 'among those most enthusiastically received [with applause] were Washington Irving (Note 63) and Basil Hall LLD! Now say a word against him at your peril. Never was anyone so gay as he in his uniform surmounted by the scarlet gown.'[64]

By 1831 Hall seems to have become something of a writing recluse, as he says to his old friend Mrs Hunter, describing himself as 'a crusty old author negligent and indolent … I have not enough strength to go into company and play – tell long stories – make people laugh – so I sit in my chair, bawl for pen and ink, turn up some of these old Journals which the General has spoken of – write a book, send it to the press and thus do what I can, by the proxy of types and printers' devils what I have no longer health for to do in my own individual furrow.'

References

1. Smiles, *passim*
2. Hall to Murray, 16 November 1817, NLS MSS Acc. 40504/4055
3. *Ibid.*, 2 March 1819
4. *Ibid.*, 18 June 1819
5. *Ibid.*, 16 August 1825
6. *Ibid.*, 16 January 1820
7. *Ibid.*, January 27 1820
8. *Ibid.*, February 7 1820
9. *Ibid.*, 21 January 1824
10. *Ibid.*, correspondence Nov–Dec 1826
11. *Ibid.*, January 1827
12. *Ibid.*, 3 April 1827
13. *Ibid.*, 13 April 1827
14. *Ibid.*, 25 August 1828
15. Hall to Cadell, January 1831, NLS MSS Acc. 21008, ff.1–4
16. *Ibid.*, 1 February 1831, ff.14–18
17. Hall to Thomas Moore, 10 December 1829, NLS MSS Acc 4054/4055
18. *Ibid.*, Murray to Hall, December 22 1829
19. Constable, Vol. III, 471–472
20. Grierson (1932–7), Vol. IX, 320–7 in Johnson (1970), 942
21. Hall to Archibald Constable, n.d. NLS MS Acc 7200 f.9
22. Constable, Vol. III, 487–489 & Hall to Walter Scott, Constable Letter-Book 1829–36, NLS MS 792
23. Hall to Murray, NLS MS Acc.7200 f.9 & 13
24. *Ibid.*, January 1820, f.19
25. Hall to Constable, 16 August 1824, NLS MSS 7200, f.24 & Basil Hall to Macvey Napier, 30 April 1839
26. *Ibid.*, 26 June–16 August 1825, ff.41–42 and 27 August 1825, ff.50–51
27. *Ibid.*, 1 December 1825, ff.88–89
28. *Ibid.*, 28 September 1825, ff.52–54 & 1 October1825, f.55
29. *Ibid.*, 24 October 1825, ff.64–5
30. *Ibid.*, 10 November 1825, f.66–9
31. *Ibid.*, 12 November 1825, ff.70–2
32. *Ibid.*, 13 November 1825, ff.74–77
33. *Ibid.*, 26 November 1825, f.84
34. *Ibid.*, 1 December 1825, ff.88–89
35. *Ibid.*, 15 December 1825, ff.92–95
36. *Ibid.*, n.d. f.99
37. *Ibid.*, n.d. f.107
38. *Ibid.*, 9 March 1826, f.108
39. *Ibid.*, n.d. f.109
40. *Ibid.*, 28 May 1826, f.110
41. *Ibid.*, n.d.,1823, f.22

63 Washington Irving (1783–1859) was a hugely successful American writer and historian, famous mainly for his short stories and much admired by Scott, Byron and Dickens.

42. *Ibid.*, n.d., 1823, f.23
43. *Ibid.*, 16 August 1824, f.24
44. Constable, 471–499
45. Hall to Lockhart, 24 March 1837, NLS MSS 932, *Letters of Lockhart* Vol. X, f.51.
46. *Ibid.*, 31 March 1827, f.43
47. *Ibid.*, n.d., f.45
48. *Ibid.*, n.d., 1831, f.48
49. *Ibid.*, 20 September 1832 & Basil Hall to Macvey Napier, 18 May 1830
50. *Quarterly Review*, Vol. 41, 440
51. Hall to Lockhart, n.d. NLS MSS, 932 *Letters to Lockhart* Vol. X
52. *Ibid.*, f.57
53. *Ibid.*, f.59
54. *Ibid.*, f.64
55. *Quarterly Review,* 1836, Vol. 57, 110–132
56. *Ibid.*, 119
57. *Blackwood's Edinburgh Magazine*, December 1836,Vol. XL, 842–844
58. *Ibid.*, January 1837, Vol. XLI, 31–32
59. Grant, 1845, 308–9
60. Grierson, 1938, 33N
61. *Quarterly Review*, 1836, Vol. 57, 110–122
62. *Southern Literary Messenger*, Vol. 2, Issue 11, Oct 1936, 727
63. *Journal of Royal Geographic Society*, 1845, Vol.15, xlii. John Murray
64. University of St. Andrews JFOR/1/297 msdep7 – incoming letters 1831, no.23, 17 June 1831

'My Dear Dickens...'

A friendship between Hall and Dickens appeared to have started about 1839, some five years before Hall's death and in the same year in which Hall was present at a *levée* hosted by Queen Victoria at St. James's Palace on March 17 1838.[1] This correspondence does not appear – certainly in the form of letters – to have continued beyond 1841, probably because of Hall's mental instability. During this time, however there was an intense exchange of correspondence – although the length and fulsomeness of Hall's letters compared to the relatively short replies of Dickens – suggests that this might have been a somewhat unequal relationship. But this correspondence is important in revealing much about Hall, his family, and his approach to writing in the latter years of his life. For this reason, his letters are quoted at some length here (Note 64).

To Basil Hall, 3 December 1839. Dickens acknowledges receipt of *Schloss Hainfeld* – and gives assurance that although he does not read all books that arrive, he will certainly read this. Mrs Dickens wishes to become acquainted with Mrs Hall and Dickens sends in particular his good wishes to Basil's eldest son, Basil Sidmouth de Ros Hall.[2]

To Basil Hall, 28 December 1840. Thanking Hall for a copy of *Patchwork* Dickens says: 'I have been pursuing the fortunes of the child in which you took so much interest, ever since its receipt, and have only had time to cut it, to read the preface, and to devour (very gluttonously) the paper called the Gallows and the Guillotine, which struck me very much indeed. It is a great piece of description.' Dickens then gives his views on public executions (Note 65) and continues:

> What can I say to you in acknowledgement of your high commendation of the tale I am drawing to a close – with no common regret and pain I do assure you – for I am loath to finish it – and of the cheering encouragement you give me. It would be idle to tell you that such expressions of interest from thinking and gifted men are a source of the purest happiness and delight. You know that, I am sure, and I cannot thank you enough for your generous applause.

Notes

64 Volumes I & II of *Letters* (1969) refer frequently to the collection of Dickens correspondence, but do not quote folio numbers. Where the latter are given, this refers to this collection accessed directly by the author.

65 Dickens later became a campaigner against these. Both he and Hall shared a humanitarian interest in criminal punishment and prison conditions, which Hall studied in some depth during his travels in North America.

Hall had this bust of himself in 1840 made by the society sculptor Samuel Joseph, as a gift to Charles Dickens. Courtesy of Pollock House, Glasgow.

Dickens closes with the hope that Hall will accept with his compliments, copies of '*Master Humphrey*' (*Master Humphrey's Clock*) as the episodic parts are issued.[3] Hall was a great admirer of Dickens' work and in his letters wrote effusive panegyrics on the weekly instalments of his novels. He noted any incidents of pathos as potential material for Dickens, and wrote him long descriptions of them. The reference to executions was a comparison of the English and French methods of execution.

Hall had witnessed both the execution by hanging of Thistlewood and his associates in the Cato Street Conspiracy of 1820 and of a French murderer who was guillotined. Replying to this letter on 10 January 1841, Hall wrote: 'In my gallows chapter – which I inserted *solely* from the encouragement which some parts of your writings gave me to be bold – I added the letter about the boy (Note 66) expressly in the hope that it would touch you – & rejoice greatly that it did.'

Hall's letter to Dickens went on: 'In one of my Chapters called the End of Life (Note 67) … also I ventured, here and there, on a touch in your vein – but as I have a great horror of the crime of imitation I hope I have not betrayed my secret to any eye but yours. Human nature, it is true is so wide that there is room for all of us – but you must know right well what a pack of harriers your success has set yelping at your tail.'[4]

What is clear from these letters and those which follow is a burgeoning literary association between the two writers, albeit that their subjects – with the exception of Dickens' later travel writing – are quite different. Hall acknowledges that he had learnt

Notes

66 The letter in question was a poignant one from the condemned leader of the conspiracy – on the night before his execution – to his young son, exhorting him to stand upright in the world.

67 'The End of Life' is the sad account of the death of a destitute Swiss lady whom Hall made considerable efforts to assist.

much from Dickens' 'exquisite' writing. Subsequent correspondence indicates that this develops into a more familiar and personal relationship.

On 10 January 1841 Hall sent Dickens a copy (offering to send others if he was willing to distribute them) of a letter he had written to the *Hampshire Telegraph* appealing for contributions for the widow and eight children of Captain Hewett, lost on the HMS *Fairy* while surveying in the North Sea. His letter, Hall said, was meant 'to appeal rather to the reason than to the heart', but he had introduced certain 'sundry points' (Dickens sent a subscription of three guineas).

In the same letter, Hall says:

> I wish I could give you some sort of idea of the kind and degree of interest which your delicious 'Hummy' as the children call it, excites in my family – I do not know which are most pleased – the old or the young – but the avidity to read each new number is the same in all. It is generally read aloud in the family every Saturday evening by Mrs Hall who does it great justice … so happy a group as is found when I come out of the town with the Clock (Note 68) in my pocket. During the week all sorts of speculations are afloat among us as to what is to happen next with our favourite characters. They (the characters) have all as real an identity in our imaginations as any living persons … and you would be delighted to see … of their being imaginary creations which fill the minds of the children … An idea has got about that you do not like to be spoken to about your works. But I cannot tell you how deep an impression your darling Nell has made on Mrs Hall and on our eldest daughter now nearly 15, though not what is called delicate, is still a tender plant. She has a mind and feelings far beyond her years – and is just such a refreshing – considerate – kind – high principled … as you make yours. I think you saw her, for a moment, but you could not know anything of her – nonetheless, by that intuitive sympathy which gives to the eyes of genius, a sort of telescopic, or microscopic, (take it either way you please) power of divining character. Just as I wrote the last line my second daughter, funny girlie as ever … came into the room and I asked her which of your characters she liked best – after pausing a little, she said "Oh, Nell's, being so much above the situation – is what interests me most. – next to her, I like the small servant." Hall goes on to praise other characters.

He refers to perusal of Magdalene's narrative bringing back memories of himself and his sister as youngsters playing on the gravel walks around Dunglass – and then of her growing up – and himself returning from the coast of Spain, in the War, and finding her and her sister ('my greatest friends in these days') 'trigged up in the Spanish hats in national sympathy for the patriots'. He refers to 'poor de Lancey who came with him from Corunna'. Hall then mentions how, less than 24 hours before de Lancey's marriage to Hall's sister Magdalene, de Lancey had mentioned casually that he had shared a cabin with an officer called Hall, and only when the latter's first name was recalled, did everyone in astonishment, recognise that this was indeed Basil who had rescued him.

Notes

68 The 'Clock' was *Master Humphrey's Clock* – the headline under which Dickens wrote his *Old Curiosity Shop* in instalments.

Hall had ended his letter of 10 January: 'Hoping that you are not serious in proposing to stop the Clock in a few numbers – pray wind it up & let us have 100 more such.'[5] Dickens had responded on 15 January by saying: 'the clock does not stop, and was never intended to. It goes on but with a new story.'

On 15 January, not having had an answer to his letter of the 10, Hall wrote again from Portsmouth (where he was then residing with his family) – his letter apparently crossing with that of Dickens above. He reported, in considerable detail, that the subscription for Mrs Hewett was going well, described a 'singularly poetical & touching' dream his elder daughter had had about a midshipman lost on the *Fairy*, and suggested that Dickens 'might immortalise it by giving it as a dream of poor Nell's'. Hall then asks that should Dickens use this, not to mention his daughter's name.[6] The Hewett case seems to be characteristic of Hall in his many well-meaning efforts to help others in distress, but the relaying of his daughter's dream is also symptomatic of his somewhat ingenuous suggestions to Dickens of incidents of pathos the latter might use: it would be understandable if Dickens was embarrassed by these, especially as Hall's *metier* was not novel writing.

In *The Old Curiosity Shop* Dickens told Hall that he was experiencing great distress in approaching the discovery that his character Kit was to make: 'Having described to Catermole (Note 69) how Nell was to appear before her winter burial, and her grandfather, waiting in the church, after it', he added that he was breaking his heart over the story and could not bear to finish it. He was doing so, 'with no common regret and pain'.[7] On the 14 January 1841 he wrote again to Basil Hall on the same subject, saying: 'I have been breaking my heart with such constancy over the Curiosity Shop, that I have not been able to write since I received your welcome letter.'[8]

This suggests that their relationship had become a relatively intimate one, confirmed by Hall's letter of 14 April, when he reports that the cast of his (Hall's) bust is now ready 'for any niche you may find – I shall feel most gratified' (in a shorthand reply, Dickens thought the likeness '*amazing*') (Note 70). In the same letter, Hall says:

> Your attention to me in the matter of your own bust, I must again say thank you for. In my position and in society (which, certainly is a most agreeable one) exposes me, occasionally to some situations, and gives me means of testing the character of others. I meet some officers who, because I chance to be on half pay and in plain clothes, treat me as of no rank – while others are to the full as respectful as if I were in command of a line of battleship at Spithead, with a couple of 'snakes' on my shoulders … In like manner, I have frequently occasion to apply to such an officer for favours – not for myself, indeed (for I happen to want nothing) but for old shipmates and others, who fancy I have influence. On these occasions, I find the most remarkable differences – sometimes an officer says 'Capt. Hall – we can't refuse anything which you are pleased to ask – it shall be done.' Others say 'Why – really we are so terribly faced, especially by

Notes

69   George Catermole was an historical painter who, in addition to illustrating Dickens' work, illustrated Sir Walter Scott's *Waverley* novels.

70   A bust of Hall – sculpted by Samuel Joseph – can be seen in Pollock House, Glasgow, from the Sir William Stirling Maxwell Collection. It was shown at the Summer Exhibition of the Royal Academy in 1840.

unsuitable requests – not, my dear Sir, that yours is so' that they are forced to make a rule of refusings, etc. etc. So that – taking all the shades of official and private character into account – I have many painful snubs. Other officers I meet with such ready kindnesses … in the intervening period, between making a request, and getting the answer, is always a painful one – because it may bring some dose of humiliation with it. I have seldom accordingly felt more anxious than I said for *your* answer to my requests about the busts, I could not have known that you would at once see through the case, and detect that my proximate object was a job for Samuel – I felt uncertain how far your goodwill for me, personally, or your favourable consideration of my lucubrations, printwise, might induce you to offer the great mortification of a rebuff. In the first place I felt honestly conscious that I made no false pretence in expressing a hearty wish, on my own account, and that of my family, to create your likeness – and in the next, I saw, or fancied I saw abundant evidence in your writings of that kind of generous consideration which would prevent you from putting me in any kind of awkward predicament. I was therefore scarcely moved when I read in a letter of a person … who pretends to know you better than I did – 'Depend upon it, Dickens will refuse!'

The last Barnaby has in it some truly Shakespearean touches. This, by the way, is a remark stolen from my wife – when she was reading to us'.[9]

Samuel Joseph (1791–1850) was a famous sculptor whose eccentricity of style precluded him from general popularity, despite the number of famous people he had sculpted, including Hall himself. Hall had written to Dickens on 29 March: 'I have a favour to ask of you … I wish you to allow your Bust to be done for me, by my friend Mr Joseph the Sculptor.' He explained that Joseph was in financial difficulties – yet another example of Hall helping 'lame dogs'. Dickens agreed, and Hall wrote 'Thanks, noble Sir, for your prompt acquiescence'. Although Dickens sat for this, and a clay model that Dickens admired was completed, Hall did not buy it – presumably because of the breakdown in his health. Dickens also declined to buy it and in July 1848 Samuel was still seeking a purchaser. He died bankrupt in 1850. The model was later destroyed.[10]

To Basil Hall, 27 January 1841, Dickens wrote:

I am sorry to say that I dare not go out in the morning (being very busy) until next Tuesday, sorely tempted as I am to be undutiful for the sake of Miss Edgeworth and declining the invitation said: 'If I were not resolute in shutting myself up now and then, either to write or think as the case may be, there would soon be no Clock. If the Queen were to send for me at such times, I wouldn't go to her'.[11]

Hall had written to Dickens that morning saying that Maria Edgeworth would much like to meet him. Hall's letter ended: 'I take it quite for granted, you see, that you will be pleased to make the acquaintance of so distinguished a person who, I assure you, appreciates your talents fully.'[12] Although the latter is true generally, Maria Edgeworth did not, for example, think much of Dickens'American travel narrative.

Hall, obviously annoyed by Dickens' declining the invitation, had replied the same day: 'I shrewdly suspect my friend, that you have a great fancy for wagging your tail, & that this is the explanation of your inability to go out roaring in the woods! No matter

– that is your affair – not mine – and I only hope that you will forgive me for having proposed the thing. A mere accident prevented me from seeing Lord Byron & possibly you may regret some day that you have cut old Maria Edgeworth. Perhaps, however, I am wrong after all – if so – pardon my suspicions.'[13]

Dickens wrote to Hall on the 28 January explaining in some detail the pressures he was under and that he had offered the one day in the week when he took a holiday to meet Hall and Maria Edgeworth.

On 16 March 1841 Dickens wrote in the most emotional terms after his reading of Magdalene's narrative of her experiences at Waterloo (as related in a previous chapter). By an extraordinary coincidence, Hall had not only picked up de Lancey from a boat adrift after the Battle of Corunna (and prior to his meeting Hall's sister for the first time), but had also brought back from India her second future husband, Captain Henry Harvey on his ship. However, Magdalene died in 1821, barely two years after this second marriage.

In his letter of 13 February 1841, Hall described the reception of *Master Humphrey* No. 44:

> It was … brought in triumph to the drawing room, where in two minutes, all the family were assembled – all work left off – & every mind & heart bent on the fate of poor Nell & the old man. The effect was such as you might expect – I mean the first effect – but you will hardly anticipate the result – though indeed, though you have too much of old Shakespeare's kidney about you to be surprised at the apparent incongruities of human feelings – all the party were in deep affliction – weeping and sobbing as if their hearts were breaking, when first one ludicrous incident, & then another, gave a fresh direction to their emotions. A Lady, a neighbour & a great friend of ours, hearing the shout which announced the arrival of the Clock, had come in and joined the 'Niobe' group. But it chanced that she had left her pocket handkerchief at home – & after swabbing away with her sleeves for some time, she was obliged to borrow the end of my eldest girl's handkerchief & there they were, tugging at the opposite ends of it, when the door opened – and in walked Sir Edward Codrington's flag captain! – No order had been given (as usual when a number of the Clock arrived) – and so in came Capt. Montague. The contrast between his merry face, & astonished look – & the speechless grief of the weeping circle, was so great, that – after a after a pause of three seconds – they all burst out laughing!

Hall then goes on to praise certain of Dickens' passages extravagantly.[14] Apart from its humour, this description with others, shows Hall to be a quite domestic man by this stage, with a deep feeling for his family.

Dickens, in his reply of 19 February 1841, said: 'I quite understand how you all laughed when the friend came in, and am glad you did so, because I know how truthful and heartfelt the crying must have been that went before. My love to the whole audience.' Dickens then goes on to describe the happy state of his family, including the recently born youngest son in affectionate terms – and his worry that it all makes him feel a little sad: 'I am expecting every day to be gray, and have very nearly persuaded myself that I am gouty.'[15]

In his letter of 12 March 1841 Hall says that: 'Barnaby is admirable – quite equal respects superior to anything you have done before – Shakespearean in its conception and WalterScottish in its expression. The family reads the 'Clock' on the day it arrives, by regular appointment. We all say – with the Prophet – "Oh, King (of writers) live for ever". He told Dickens that he was 'engaged in a new work, some parts of which will tickle you'.[16] He subsequently wrote (Hall to Dickens 19 March 1841) that its subject was Portsmouth, where he was then residing with his family, and he had 'already sketched out more than a dozen chapters on the Dockyard alone'. Hall never wrote this book and was incarcerated in the Haslar Hospital for two years prior to his death in 1844. This letter of the 19 March is incidentally the first in which Hall changes from the formal 'My Dear Sir' to 'My Dear Dickens', his opening being:

> My Dear Dickens – With all my heart – but I cannot allow you to take the priority in this matter [referring to Dickens feeling the junior – at least in age] … (by the by, do you know the cockpit translation of this saying – "Seniores priores" – "age before honesty" which I have made use of drolly several times?) Do you remember a note I wrote to you about Miss Edgeworth which I commenced with My Dear – then said I had almost written Dickens, etc., etc? But to come to more serious matters, I may remark that of all the opinions I have heard on my sister's narrative, none have appeared to me so just and forcible.

This letter also describes his family's reaction to the death of Dickens' raven and Hall's own pain at the death of a pet crow 40 years ago and his remorse at having killed a small bird as a boy.

Hall wrote to Dickens from Portsmouth on 1 April 1841:

> And this, my friend, brings me to the last paragraph of your note and which you say that my humility makes you weary. I am sorry for that – and yet I see perfectly how it is so. The truth is, that, I, as well as, I suppose, any other man who has worked in earnest, & found the exact length of his tether, & knows what he can do – and has often felt what it is to try hard to reach a point of excellence which he … cannot reach, must, of reality occasionally feel how insignificant he is effectively [?] – compared to what he would wish to be – or what he finds the world rates him at … God knows I am the last to complain of the public, who have treated me with great favour – & yet (this is a whisper, mind!) I do honestly confess to a twinge of genuine jealousy, one day, when I visited Bradbury and Evans's printing Office, and asked what was that enormous pile of sheets. 'Oh, Sir,' said the fellow 'there lies sixty thousand copies of the next no. of Humphrey's Clock'! I turned me about and said ' What's that small bundle?' 'Oh, Sir' said the dog, grinning from ear to ear, 'That is one thousand of your new book!' I could have cuffed the imp.

Hall goes on in this vein, lauding Dickens' genius and affectionate sympathy, continuing: 'Your letter made my young party squeal with laughing, and they are all enchanted with the prospect of seeing you … in their own house. I am especially rejoiced that you approve of my 'Seaport' notion' (this refers to his proposal to write something based on his knowledge of Portsmouth).

The death of Hall's youngest son – Frederick Richard, aged 4 – was announced in *The Times* of 25 May 1841. On 26 May, Dickens wrote:

My Dear Hall, I saw the paper yesterday, and had sorrowful thoughts of you.

The traveller from this World to the next, found the Infant Child he had lost many years before, wreathing him a bower in Heaven.

Dickens then goes on to try to comfort Hall with notions of the lost son as an angel, calling Hall his father on Earth.[17]

Hall responded on the 27 June 1841:

The truth is – that during the whole of the last fortnight – by far the most anxious and interesting – albeit the most melancholy of my life – *you* have been mixed up with the whole proceedings in the most singular manner … and my wish is – or has been – to give you some notion of this. But I now much fear that I shall not be able to do so … I find that the most vivid images, and scenes such deeply engraved … cutting almost through to the metal of my nature – have faded almost away – and I fail to grasp them when I seek to record them. At every turn, these amazing incidents I caught myself saying 'Oh here is a point for Dickens' – 'how well he would value this!' till at length, over moments of the deepest distress, took a personal sort of character in communion with you, and I felt then and since, that if I could only contrive to give you even a faint sketch of what happened and what I thought and felt, it would be a source of high interest to you. There was fever, no doubt, in all this – but I suppose it was true to nature, or life fit for your greatest pen. I fear much, however, I shall not be able to accomplish my purpose – for three reasons – first, and chiefly, I am in such distress in consequence of this loss, that I feel weakened in powers of expression and description. Second, I cannot rise at all to the purpose until I have rest at night – and my remaining children are all still ill with the hooping cough. I am exhausted for want of sleep – I feel even the most remarkable passages gliding away from my memory in such a way but I question if I shall now be able to catch hold of their traces.[18]

Hall goes on at length about how Dickens might view his experience and his own inability, through grief, to describe it.[19] There is something slightly macabre in this, as if Hall is actually thinking of writing (or getting Dickens to write) on this experience. There can be little doubt about Hall's genuine anguish and his acknowledgement of the effects of a 'fever' of grief, while simultaneously he sees his feeling as potential copy.

In a letter of 17 June 1848 to D.M. Moir of Mussleburgh, Dickens said in reference to the effect of the death of Little Nell and its comfort to others who had suffered a similar loss: 'Poor Basil Hall lost a little boy for whom he had a great love – I think his insanity began about that time – and he wrote out all the secret grief and trial of his heart to me, wherever he went afterwards. Always referring to the same book.'[20]

On 28 June, Hall wrote at considerable length (marked 'Private') from Cheltenham:

My Dear Dickens, Whenever I take up my pen to write to you, such a multitude of things come forward for an explanation – I often do not know where to begin – and am sometimes found away altogether from my paper by an apprehension of over-taxing your favour.

Hall then asks Dickens if he would meet with him to talk over Hall's response to an invitation to write for *Chambers' Edinburgh Journal*. It apparently sold 70,000 copies a week and would 'augment his miserable half pay'. Hall indicated that he had 81 volumes of his old journal that he could 'mine'. It would seem here as if Hall is pleading poverty, but it did not dissuade him for example, from embarking shortly afterwards on what was proposed as an extended (and expensive) tour of Europe and the Middle East. It does seem odd – coming from a celebrated author – that he should have felt it necessary to go to such lengths in seeking Dickens' advice on a relatively minor literary matter. He then unburdens himself on his recent loss:

I forgot when I spoke to you last about my domestic affairs. But I find in my portfolio, the commencement of a letter to you dated 29 May and it seems to sustain a small point or two I shall keep for you. After my poor dear little Freddie's death we decided to take a trip for the benefit of the remaining children who are still suffering fearfully under the whooping cough – a terrible disaster when it falls so heavily on delicate people. I carried all my party to Freddie's grave in Kingston Churchyard, at the north side, which from a popular prejudice, has been left almost entirely untenanted. We went together … the poor manny was placed by my own hands in his little grave – for I did not allow an undertaker or a servant, or anyone but ourselves to touch his body or to dress him, but he was left smiling, and as if asleep in his bed – to be placed in his coffin – and there too he lay – the image of peaceful rest – and covered from head to foot with flowers … the night of his funeral, when I went to his room, very early, to shut down the coffin lid. The sun shone full upon his face as he lay – the flowers scarcely withered in his wee bit hand [Hall has retained this Scots expression] and he looked to me yet alive. I thought it would break my heart to take my last look and for an hour I knelt by his side before I could muster courage to close him up for ever. No – no – I hope not for ever, your charming idea my friend, of the angels playing about and talking of their earthly Papas has often helped to assuage my grief … but this will never do! If I begin all graphics [?] in a letter to you on a topic so fertile, I shall never have done – and I wish to get this letter off. I shall merely mention that in the evening after Freddie's funeral and the day before our departure … we all went to the grave which by the prompt, and I will say, kind, attention of the sexton, we saw very nicely done up … in consequence of my requests that the larger bit of green sward, which had been carried unruffled, to the spot, and the daisies were still growing on it, We each planted one – and those I believe are still extant. You would have been interested to see us all standing around telling stories of our poor little friend, and even, almost laughing, certainly smiling – and all with cheerful recollections of him who was taken away. But it is not when wounds are fresh that they pain strongly, as you know. Well, our two girls and remaining boy are still so ill with the whooping cough that change of air was thought necessary – so we went to Winchester on 27 May – but oh, Sure! Such a horrid night! I shall never forget it – I thought all three would have been suffocated in turn. That was on Thursday. On Saturday we went on to Salisbury – a little better. And thence to Amesbury – to Stonehenge where we remained Sunday – rather better. After we went to Deptford Inn and so on to Bath, where we saw a skilful doctor who gave us both medicine and comfort … but I cannot avoid telling you of the melancholy effect on the girls. It deprived them not only of their looks, but of their spirits and made them look like dead people – walking in the motions of life without the soul!

Hall describes other journeys – and eventually:

[At Malvern] the air is delicious and there by the help of donkey riding and quiet walking in the absence of all excitement and the best water in the world – we gradually got better and after a fortnight's stay we were once again in such strength and spirits that we enjoyed a visit to the porcelain works at Worcester and began to return to the world.

At Cheltenham, the family were stimulated by all the frenetic activity associated with the election, when Hall commented: 'I can see that the children half hope to have a dead cat or a rotten egg come their way.' But he also worries about the risk the family runs from another winter in England, 'so we propose to carry them off to Malta this autumn'. Hall continues:

I confess that it could be a momentary effort to break up my happy home at Southsea – again to become a wanderer across the face of the earth – but this is only a transient feeling – and foresee much enjoyment in it. We shall probably when the spring arrives go onto the Ionian Islands, Greece and Egypt and Constantinople and so perhaps return by … Moscow and Petersburg and then make a circuit of the Baltic (Note 71).'[21]

Dickens was in Scotland when Hall was to be in London, so they did not meet. One more letter from Hall has survived in the Huntington Library, written on H.M.S. *Indus*, off Algiers on 3 September. It was headed 'Entre nous if you please', to ask if an enclosed small sketch he had made of Mount Etna might be acceptable for Catherine Dickens' (Dickens' wife) album. No answers from Dickens to Hall's last four letters are known.

Dickens did return 'a devil of a long letter' Hall had written him from Trafalgar, because he wanted it for his Journal which he had decided in future to write for publication. Hall described his family as 'half dead with anxiety to know how Mr Haredale is to deal with the murderer whom he succeeded in getting down'. According to D.H. Paroussien when commenting on the letter method of compiling a travel narrative used in Dickens' *Pictures from Italy*, 'the letter method had proved reliable by no less an experienced traveller than Captain Basil Hall, who had introduced Dickens to this technique'. It was upon Hall's recommendations that Dickens used the method in the composition of his *American Notes*, and having apparently found it satisfactory was prepared to use it again. Hall and Dickens had been friends since 1839 and both showed an enthusiasm for travel literature.[22]

In his letter of September 3 1841 Hall said:

Heretofore, I have written my Journals chiefly for my friends – or for myself – and when I came to make out of them a book of travels, I had to select much purely as it seemed

Notes

71 There are virtually no records of these travels – probably because they were truncated due to Hall's illness – but in a letter of 12 April 1842 to the Egyptologist Sir John Gardner Wilkinson, Hall reports on his calculations of latitudes etc. 'from the top of old Cheops' (Bodleian Library Manuscripts and Special Collections, Oxford).

suitable for the public eye. This, however, was a difficult and rather dangerous task – dangerous, I mean, to the unity of the texture in the work and very often fatal to that sustained interest without which such a book of travels is the dullest of dull reading. Besides, I have often had reason to fear that in thus taking detached facts of a Journal, much of the simplicity of truth was lost. The whole, indeed, might be written in perfectly good faith but when sundry omissions come to be made, it often struck me that a false impression might remain.[23]

In his writing Hall was convinced of the need to record incidents and conversations immediately (which in company was sometimes looked on with askance), but he also admitted to Dickens that he had revised his South American work no less than seven times. In that narrative he also went so far as to getting his brothers to rank his draft paragraphs on a scale of one to ten for public interest, and to excise accordingly.

References

1. The Scotsman, 21 March 1838
2. House, Tillotson, & Storey, Vol. I, 609, n.1.
3. *Ibid.*, Vol. II, 173, n.4
4. Huntington Library MSS 18497 (n.4)
5. Huntington Library MSS 18497
6. *Ibid.*, 15 January 1841
7. Brennan, lxiv, n.6
8. House, Tillotson & Storey, 179n
9. Huntington Library MSS 18506
10. House, Tillotson & Storey, 445n. & Vol. II, 445 n.3
11. *Ibid*, 197 & Vol. II, 196–7, n.3
12. Huntington Library MSS 18501/2
13. *Ibid.*
14. *Ibid.*
15. House, Tillotson & Storey, 215–5 & Vol. II, 215–6
16. Huntington Library MSS18503/4
17. House, Tillotson, & Storey, 285 & Vol. II, 285
18. Huntington Library, MSS 18507 & House, Tillotson, & Storey Vol. II, 285, n.4
19. House, Tillotson & Storey, Vol. II, 286
20. *Ibid.*, Vol. 5, 1847–49, 341–342
21. Huntington Library MSS 18509
22. Paroussien, Vol. 22, 60
23. Huntington Library MSS HM18510

To Discover which Methods are Best

On 12 June 1819, writing from Dunglass to the Marchioness of Londonderry – who had obviously enquired what he intended to do with his time 'in this unproductive time of Peace!' – Hall stated that:

For a long time I have given up the hope – but the wish to engage in any other line of life than this. The joys of life seem to be unsettled, and independent of situation and circumstance. But the chances of happiness may be fairly said to be as good in any one line as in any other and better if sought for in companionship with duty, and connected with a just, and disinterested ambition. Such being the state into which my thoughts have subsided, I have taken my resolution to make my business and amusements … as much as possible, towards an acquisition of professional knowledge.

Hall had obviously become disenchanted with travelling for its own sake and treading well-worn paths.

I travelled, as I told you in a former letter, over a considerable part of the Continent last year … I found that most people had done the same, and without having some knowledge of what was talked of, little was to be gained … I had seen enough of London society last spring to last me for a considerable time. Then how to dispose of my time became the question.

Hall must have been quite close to Lady Londonderry to reveal his plans in some detail and his justification for these, largely related to the lack of any naval post at this time.

At length I decided on coming to the country as soon as the College winter session was closed. Here I have fitted up an Observatory to which I have brought all the instruments which I was in the habit of using at sea, together with some others which this quiet mode of living has put within my reach. I have got all sorts of Books on Navigation & Astronomy and have access to an excellent library – so that I may vary the topics when the principal one becomes fatiguing. As I have plenty of leisure, I can vary the experiments in all sorts of ways – by this means I hope to discern what methods are the most exact and the most ready, when the time will come when that leisure is wanting. It is the business of nautical astronomy to discover the geographical [situation] of any spot – that is its Latitude and Longitude – supposed not to be accurately known.[1]

Hall subsequently became a Commissioner of the Board of Longitude and came to be regarded as something of an expert on navigation and navigational instruments. In 1838 his advice was requested on the purchase of instruments for a US government expedition to explore Pacific Island and the Antarctic. Hall was keenly interested in the development of accurate naval chronometers for proper navigation. He reported on the disastrous loss of the troopship *Arniston* off the South African coast in 1815 as being due to the lack of a modern chronometer, and wrote a paper on the use and care of chronometers at sea for the *United Service Journal*.[2]

He expanded of his long-term objectives:

> It is of great consequence to be able to make this out quickly and accurately, and the methods are various. Now, what I am engaged in here, is in some respects the reverse of this, because the situation upon which I perform my operations is very accurately known. But you will observe that owing to this circumstance, I have the means of pulling every observation to a sure test – and thus to discover which methods are the best. This is my principal object, but you will readily conceive that around it will flow a number of analogous circumstances more or less connected with this branch of my profession. My expectation is – or rather my hope – that I may by & by be employed in some service where this kind of knowledge might come into real use. If the Peace lasts, this I think not improbable – and if a war breaks out, one has other things to attend to in the first instance … I hope I shall have perseverance to go on.[3]

Hall was an untrained scientist (the term was unknown until the early 1830s) and he was one of the last of the 'amateurs' who could indulge in a wide variety of scientific and technological interests and still make a worthwhile contribution in an age when specialisms were relatively undeveloped. His *forte* lay in meticulous observation and recording of phenomena, converting these to some practical applications, especially in seamanship. Despite having spent all his sea-going life under sail, he was a strong advocate of steam power and any innovations (such as the replacement of hemp ropes by iron cables) which he thought were an improvement. He was however acutely aware of his lack of theoretical training in areas such as mathematics, which the classes he took under Professor J.D. Forbes (Note 72) clearly exposed. In a letter to the noted astronomer Sir John Herschel, Hall said that at his lectures, 'he felt like a flea' and commenting on Forbes' extreme youth while confirming Herschel's good judgement in proposing Forbes as Professor.[4]

Towards the end of 1836 Forbes gave these lectures in natural philosophy at Edinburgh University and Hall wrote a number of letters about them to his mentor. Several of these are written from Ashiesteel, a grand house on the banks of the Tweed in Selkirkshire – the home of Major General Sir James Russell – which Hall described

---

Notes

72   James David Forbes (1809–68) was the professor of natural philosophy at Edinburgh University between 1832 and 1860 and was subsequently Principal of the United College of St. Andrews. He made significant contributions to the science of heat, vulcanology and glaciology, which took him on a number of high-altitude travels in Europe.

as 'his nest in the hills' (Sir Walter Scott had lived in it for ten years prior to the building of Abbotsford).

Hall was impressed by the classes and the manner of delivery (as he wrote to Forbes), but admitted that he was 'an idle fellow' who preferred to omit the theoretical proofs – especially in the astronomy classes which involved advanced geometry and algebra – and was quite prepared to accept the facts as given. If this seems surprising for a scientifically-inclined naval navigator, it will be recalled that Hall's formal education was limited and his nautical experience would have been strictly practical rather than theoretical. Hall was some 20 years older than his erudite tutor, so that he felt justified in exhorting Forbes to advise his students to 'avoid the deep remorse of neglected opportunities' presumably prompted by Hall's own experience. He also offered Forbes the use of his several astronomical instruments, which at that time were lodged at the Edinburgh Royal Observatory by 'the young men of the Physical Society' in the natural philosophy class.[5]

One letter in the Forbes Collection is of some interest, being the only one found from Hall's father Sir James to his son. On 6 February 1837 Hall gave it to Forbes. Dated 13 November 1815, Sir James says that on opening a number of boxes sent by Hall from his Far Eastern travels, he found a bower made of bamboo 'having all the peculiar character of the Gothic [architecture] … also an enormous pair of fans … and a multitude of utensils', but that Sir James 'needed to read the journals to make sense of these artefacts'. Sir James also makes reference to a parcel of papers on Table Mountain – on which his son was to write a geological paper. Hall appears to have worked with his father on a number of scientific projects and in 1835 – after his father's death – wrote a paper on an invention by his father to regulate high temperatures.[6]

In his important work on the theory of glaciers, Forbes was very complimentary about Hall's observations and his analogies with the movement of lava flows. Claiming that 'in more than one part of his writings, he had suggested the picturesque analogy of volcanoes and icy mountains'.[7] Writing of Vesuvius, Hall 'uses these remarkable expressions while describing an eruption of lava', likening them to frozen rivers. Later Forbes goes on to say 'this remarkable passage worded with the usual scrupulous care of the author … show[s] that he has arrived at more correct notions on this subject than any of his contemporaries; notions which required careful observation to give them the force of demonstration'.[8]

He credits Hall with suggesting the plasticity of glaciers, which allowed the centre of the ice mass to move faster than the sides.[9] These comments, coming from this distinguished source, confirm that amateur though he was, Hall was capable of a genuine scientific approach to his observations and of making insightful deductions on these. The writings referred to by Forbes include Hall's last work *Patchwork* (Vol. iii, 1841). In the same collection of correspondence there is a letter of 20 June 1836 from the very eminent Alexander von Humboldt (1769–1859) introducing Hall to Henrich Wilhelm Dove (1803–1879), a Prussian physicist and pioneer in climatology.[10] Hall's interest in science – stimulated by his father – started at a young age. There is a reference to his developing interest in geology in Sir James Hall's letter to Marc-August Pictet (Note 73) when Hall would have been about 21:

Notes

73   Marc-August Pictet (1752–1825) was a polymathic Swiss naturalist with a special interest in Swiss mountain geology who. He visited Edinburgh in the course of a three-month journey through Britain.

Hall made his early geological collections around Arthur's Seat, Edinburgh. Ewbanks's Picturesque Views of Edinburgh, Engr. W.H. Lizars, Edinburgh City Libraries.

Basil is your old acquaintance and already lies under obligations to you. You may remember him carrying a bag full of specimens in our excursion along the foot of Salisbury Crags [Arthur's Seat in Edinburgh]. That excursion contributed very much along with the observations which he heard on that occasion and in which you took so large a share, in raising in his mind an ardent passion for geology, which have led him to make a number of very interesting observations in his various cruises … my son has taken advantage of every opportunity which chance has thrown in his way of gaining information in the mathematical and chemical sciences.[11]

One of Hall's most significant geological discoveries was when he found the granite-hornstone contact in the Platteklip Gorge on Table Mountain. This he communicated to his father's old colleague, Professor Playfair. The professor was a staunch supporter of the Huttonian theory of the earth's origins, and together with the examination of the rocks of Glen Tilt in Perthshire, Hall's discovery – according to the Geological Society of South Africa – 'contributed in no small measure to the termination of the Werner-Hutton controversy and the laying of an important foundation stone in the progress of the sciences of petrology'.[12] Playfair prepared Hall's discoveries for publication in 1815 while Hall sent many geological specimens from his global travels to the Royal Society of Edinburgh.

Hall had a long association with the distinguished Scots geologist, Charles Lyell (Note 74). In a letter to his mother in late 1824, Lyell described a visit to Dunglass where he found Sir James Hall 'far past his prime … but luckily Captain Basil Hall … was there, whom I have often met in town. He is one of the most gentlemanlike and clever man I

Notes

74 Sir Charles Lyell (1797–1785). Although initially trained as a lawyer, Lyell became one of the most distinguished geologists of the 19th Century, being elected as Secretary to the Geological Society of London in 1823 and as a Fellow of the Royal Society in 1824. In 1831 he was appointed Professor of Geology at King's College, London. He is known particularly for his main work *Principles of Geology* (1830), in which he emphasised that historically the geological phenomena could be explained by modern causes (ODNB Vol. 34 852–856 Martin Udwick).

have ever met with. We made some great expeditions to St. Abb's Head and other parts of the coast with Sir James and his son'.[13] For his part, Hall much admired the tactful and sensitive way in which Lyell had approached the controversial issues bearing on traditional religious beliefs in his great opus *Principles of Geology* – to which Hall also contributed a number of drawings.

In this connection it is interesting that Hall also had some association with Charles Darwin. Hall was asked in 1838 by Captain Robert Fitzroy to provide a review on the narrative of the *Voyage of the Beagle*.[14] Darwin had been much influenced by Lyell's *Principles* – they were later to become lifelong friends – and much of the narrative is concerned with geology and the oceanic origins of the South American continent (the voyage and its results were to lay the foundations of Darwin's later seminal work *The Origin of Species*). Unsurprisingly, Hall's review focuses on this aspect, but the work is less a critical assessment that a re-iteration of what is in the narrative itself. He does however pay credit to the scientific achievements of the voyage and to the character of Fitzroy, perhaps predictably since the latter was a strong Tory with an aristocratic background.[15] But Fitzroy complained in a postscript to his letter to Darwin of 20 March 1839 that 'there is something very vacillating & unsatisfactory about Basil Hall – and his review – he has been very shilly-shally and contradictory'.

In a letter to Macvey Napier – the editor of the *Edinburgh Review* – Hall said: 'You will find Fitzroy's book full of curious matter – this is in fact three distinct books … each of which might really furnish an article, especially Darwin's which is full of curious and bold views, written in a fine vein of manly philosophy' – whatever that means.[16] A year later Darwin wrote to Hall, referring to Hall's exploration of Loo-choo and specifically the location of Sulphur Island. Subsequently, Hall urged Darwin to bring out a cheaper edition of his Journal.[17]

Hall had a lifelong interest in astronomy, especially in how it related to navigation. He served on the Committee of the Astronomical Society of London, which in 1833 prepared a Report to the Admiralty on improvements to the Nautical Almanac.

This interest in the relation of geographical subjects and their positioning led Hall to experiment with an invariable pendulum while he was in South America. The results were conveyed in a letter to the celebrated naval instrument maker Captain Henry Kater (Note 75) and published in the *Philosophical Transactions* for 1823. Kater had carried out similar experiments in Britain – which involved measuring the vibrations of the pendulum in relation to the sun and stars – in order to provide a physical basis for a standard of length, and to thereby improve understanding of the shape of the earth (Hall's friend Captain Edward Sabine had made similar observations on Melville Island).

Hall measured these vibrations – most notably at the Galapagos Islands, but also at San Blas in Mexico and at Rio de Janeiro – and encouraged by Sir Thomas Hardy (his Commander in Chief) and very ably assisted by Henry Foster (Master's Mate on Hall's

Notes

75 Henry Kater (1797–1835) was particularly known for his improvements to measuring instruments, leading to the introduction of imperial standards – on which he advised the Board of Longitude and which led to the Weights and Measures Act of 1824. He later became much involved in measuring the difference in longitude between the Paris and Greenwich Observatories (like Hall, he was in frequent contact with Mary Somerville, William Hyde Wollaston and Maria Edgeworth).

vessel, the *Conway*). It must have been a tedious business, but Hall attacked it with characteristic determination and precision. Typically, Hall described the immediate environment around his observatory on the Galapagos very minutely, including the often-adverse weather conditions and the meticulous setting up of the instruments. His conclusions were important in confirming Kater's methods and earlier results.

Hall had intermittent correspondence with William Whewell (1794–1866) – a renowned polymath of his time, whose interests embraced physics, geology, astronomy and the philosophy of science. Whewell helped the astronomer Sir John Hershel to revise the basis of mathematics and it is claimed that Whewell invented the modern term 'scientist'. Professor J.D. Forbes said of him that he was 'a man of the most profound and varied knowledge, of the highest powers of conversation and of great bodily and mental activity'.[18] Hall appears to have corresponded intermittently with him from 1826 to 1842. There are several letters from Hall to Whewell from 1826 to 1841, which concerned the fate of the pendulums that Hall used in South America. These were apparently expensive items, together with their special cases, which Hall requested be returned from the Board of Longitude (Hall hoped to be able to afford a pendulum of his own in due course). At the same time, he offers to send the results of his experiments at Greenwich – he emphasised that these required to be repeated many times over. In this letter, Hall humbly accepts his lack of mathematical knowledge: 'a mere servile follower of those who have leisure and knowledge to devise Experiments'; a frequent refrain of Hall's.

Whewell addressed the Geological Society of London in 1830 and in doing so made reference to Hall's work – an address which Hall greatly approved of, not least the complimentary remarks that Whewell had made regarding Hall's father and supporting his argument for pressing mathematics into the service of geology.[19] In 1839, at Whewell's request, Hall provided some information (little as it was at that time) on the hydrography and tidal regime around the Philippine Islands. As late as January 1842 from Malta, Hall is commenting on the tides there and mentioning that he is asking Captain Beaufort to provide a suitable barometer for the able Assistant Dockyard Engineer (one Grant Dalrymple) to make more accurate measurements – Hall again, typically 'fixing' things through his network of connections.

In the report of the Astronomical Society of 1821, having offered to carry out research in the South Seas, Hall was given precise instructions that included to fix the conjunction of planets, moon and fixed stars and their differences of ascension and declination; to look for comets, solar eclipses or transits of mercury; to watch the position of Mars and Venus; and to regularly observe the tides. He did not himself carry out this work, but in a comprehensive memorandum to the Royal Geographical Society, he identified a wide range of appropriate topics.

In 1826 the Secretary to the Admiralty, John Barrow, had began enquiries on the possible follow up to a scientific voyage undertaken by Lieutenant Foster (who had rendered invaluable assistance to Hall's scientific work in the course of his mission to South America in 1823). On Barrow's behalf, Dr William Wollaston (Note 76) had

Notes

76 William Hyde Wollaston (1766–1828) was primarily a chemist but with an interest in physics and related subjects. Noted for discovering two chemical elements and developing a way to process platinum ore, he was also an inventor of camera lenses and revived interest in the *camera lucida*. He was Secretary and briefly President of the Royal Society.

asked Hall (among others) to make suggestions on the *desiderata* of such 'voyages of discovery'.

Typically, Hall went about the task with gusto, producing a lengthy statement on 6 March 1826, which Wollaston forwarded to Barrow. Hall's approach was nothing if not comprehensive and systematic. It covered everything from practical navigation and experiments to improve nautical and astronomical tables, to general scientific observations and anthropological records. He was particularly enthusiastic about improvements in longitudinal and latitudinal accuracy, and discoursed on the need to establish the resources of ports around the globe for supplies to both merchant and naval vessels.

More than anything else, he proposed the extension of observations using the invariable pendulum – which he had used in South America – to many other stations to determine the 'figure of the Earth' and on the comparison of the value of different navigational and scientific instruments. His suggestions embraced the measurement of currents, tides, winds and the effects of magnetism. There is no record of how this was received, but his reply to Wollaston is a reflection both of his range of practical experience and interest in this field and of his serious attention to the request – with a particular concern that the information gathered should be widely accessible.[20]

When Professor Forbes visited London in the period between 19 April and 22 June 1831, he met many of the most eminent scientists of the day – a number of them known to Hall, whom he also saw in the city, as well as his brother James. In his journal, he provided intimate cameos of their characteristics, such as the mathematician and astronomer Mary Somerville:

> Mrs Somerville had 'piercing' eyes and was 'simple and pleasing, abstaining from scientific subjects with which she is so well acquainted, but in being ready to talk on them all when introduced, with the naïveté of a child, and the utmost apparent unconsciousness of the rarity of such knowledge as she possesses – so that it requires a moment's reflection to be aware that one is hearing something very extraordinary from the mouth of a woman.[21]

Mary Somerville.

Hall became familiar with the Somervilles – as indicated by their correspondence over more than 20 years from 1823 onwards. Although Hall was never in the same scientific league as Mary, she seemed to respect his writing experience and would send drafts of her work to him for comment. At one point he admits after reading her latest work (probably her translation of Laplace's *Celestial Mechanics*) that, 'I am no mathematician at all and could not solve a quadratic equation or any other' and that much of the work takes him out of his depth, but hopes that the work will appear in public, emphasising as always the need for a small, cheap work. As a broadly-based geographer Mary was quite familiar with Hall's work with the pendulum. The good wishes sent to Mary from Hall's mother and Fanny indicates that the families also knew one another.[22]

Mary Somerville was a friend of William Wollaston – to whom Hall had sent several of his journals for the purpose of him passing them on to her. Hall was thoroughly upset to find that some these had not reached her. Fearing their disappearance, he was greatly relieved when they were later found.[23] Later, he was greatly distressed to hear from her of his long-standing friend's complete loss of memory, reminding him of his father's similar experience.[24]

Hall also corresponded with Mary's husband, Dr William Somerville – on one occasion hoping that he will look at a copy of his 'little Bookie' (*Fragments*), which Hall had sent to Mary. When the Halls are invited to dinner, he asks Mary that he be given simply 'a dish of plain boiled rice, as she had done previously … my regimen being as strict or stricter than ever', suggesting that Hall might have suffered from a stomach ulcer: he was known for his abstemiousness at table. The Halls evidently reciprocated the Somervilles' hospitality in Edinburgh, when Hall promised 'not to teaze you any more with my politics – irritating topics at any time, doubly so when under the influence of toothache'.[25] The families were in fact on sufficiently intimate terms for Hall to ask the Somervilles – then staying in Rome – to receive a cousin, Lt. Douglas Halkett, *en route* from India and to show him around (the Halls were residing at Malta, mainly to avoid an English winter after the desperate bout of whooping cough experienced by their surviving children). Typically, Hall offered to help with any sketches for the major new work which Mary was then engaged on.[26]

In a letter to Sir John Herschel (Note 77), Hall declared that of all his pursuits, astronomy was the most important. Certainly his continuous and detailed correspondence with the acclaimed astronomer from 1821 till the 1840s is evidence of this. The letters indicate clearly that the two families became quite intimate, with Margaret Hall supplying the domestic detail in her letters to Lady Herschel, while Basil focussed on the technical aspects. An early letter from Valparaiso from Hall apologises for the inadequacy of his description of the comet which Hall observed there, despite his detailed notes on the sighting. In the same letter, Hall is even more humble on his lack of attention to astronomy – in company with many others in his profession, during long years and many opportunities in the navy.[27]

Hall provided Herschel with a summary of his travels in South America, but focuses on what he thought the astronomer would be most interested in. This was his remark-

Notes

77 Sir John Frederick William Herschel (1792–1871). The son of the internationally renowned astronomer William Herschel, John Herschel was a polymath who became a physical scientist – described as the most eminent in Britain – and who reformed British mathematics. Together with his father he constructed the first large reflecting telescopes and made important contributions to the development of photography. Elected a Fellow of the Royal Society in 1824, he went to garner other scientific honours, twice gaining the Copley Medal and becoming President of the Astronomical Society in 1827. He spent four years in South Africa making important observations on the return of Halley's Comet in 1835 (ODNB Vol. 26, 825–31, Michael J. Crowe).

Sir John Herschel. Illustrated London News.

able navigation – out of sight of land for three months and over thousands of miles – to find the entrance to Rio de Janeiro in a mist and without a good chronometer, but using a variety of instruments and taking many 'lunars' (a method for determining longitude at sea by lunar distances). In the process he ascertained the longitude of the city within five miles.[28]

Hall felt obliged to apologise for the lack of astronomical observations, apart from the Valparaiso sighting and his pendulum experiments in the Galapagos Islands during his time in South America, against the expectations of the Astronomical Society. He explained that his manifold duties at a time of great political turbulence on the continent pre-empted this, which was undoubtedly true. He hoped however that this would not preclude further commissions of a scientific nature. He confides to Herschel that it had always been his intention to engage in such scientific work – hitherto frustrated by the constraints of naval employment – preferably in private travel that would allow him to be accompanied by his family. Later he fantasises about such a plan, involving circumnavigating the globe over a period of two years and all the places on his imagined itinerary.[29] By 1830 Hall is asking that his wife be presented to Lady Herschel and he wishes soon 'to become a fixed member of your London circle'.

Herschel appreciated comments from Hall on his last book, but also took the opportunity in a letter of June 1831 to describe how his giant 40-foot telescope was affected by very low temperatures (so low that his walnut trees were killed by frost up to 50 feet high).[30] He had invited a Thomas Henderson of Edinburgh (at Hall's suggestion) to view the telescope at Slough which was still very much in use. Henderson was then proposing the new Edinburgh Observatory, but Hall warned Herschel not to expect a man of any great knowledge or manners. However the apparently very shy Henderson became the first Astronomer Royal for Scotland in 1834, serving for ten years in that position – another example of Hall quite disinterestedly promoting someone he thought ought to be helped.

By 1832 Hershel had determined to visit South Africa to research the southern constellations, which resulted in the well-meaning Hall getting into a typical difficulty.

In a long letter the First Lord of the Admiralty, Sir James Graham, indicated to Hall that the Government was very much minded to nominate Herschel as Astronomer Royal. Hall replied that a greater compliment would be to offer Herschel and his family a free passage to the Cape aboard one of his Majesty's ships. Graham saw no difficulty about this, whenever a vessel was sailing in that direction, and Hall asked that Herschel relay his response through him.[31]

To Hall's consternation, Herschel replied that although he was very appreciative of the Admiralty's offer, he did not want any official involvement, since his work was solely for pleasure and that he would prefer the comforts of a standard passenger ship, while acknowledging that the issue of transporting his large instruments – including a 20-foot telescope – might cause him to abandon the project.[32] When this was relayed to Graham he saw no difficulty, since Herschel's project was entirely for the advancement of science (and incidentally to the benefit of H.M. Navy) carrying no official obligation on the astronomer. Hall was forced to indicate that Herschel should speak directly to Graham on the matter, but clearly feels himself to have got unwittingly into a diplomatic 'scrape'.[33]

For his work abroad, the ever-helpful Hall sent Herschel his old sextant that he had used over the last 25 years, with the necessary instructions and other materials, together with plans for fixing the telescope mirrors (prepared by Hall's carpenter), while Mrs Hall responded to a request by Lady Herschel, asking advice on the practicalities of voyaging.[34]

Writing from Hainfeld in Styria, Hall claims to be 'quite happily cut off from the rest of Europe' but also longs to hear of Herschel's progress in South Africa, expressing the wish that he will employ Hall in any way. He has learnt to read German, while admitting it is the most difficult of the six or seven languages he has attempted – Mrs Hall was apparently much more fluent in the language (Hall makes the interesting comment that he could now live happily anywhere). Referring to a popular scientific publication which Herschel might undertake, Hall reveals that 'I have been able to save upwards of £1,500 [i.e. £65,000 today] out of the profits of my books' – while Herschel might be able to add another zero to that sum.[35]

From Berlin, Hall lets Herschel know that he has met many eminent German astronomers – one of whom had developed a quite new way of using the pendulum (which Hall described in detail) and also a huge map of the moon that was to be published by Barth of Leipzig, the text of which Hall thought he might be able to translate for the benefit of British readers. In the same very long and technical letter to Herschel, Hall describes his invention for stopping and releasing a carriage without getting out of the conveyance. Meantime, Mrs Hall was writing frequently to Lady Herschel on domestic matters.[36] In the following year, Hall gives detailed advice to Herschel on his voyage to the Cape via Rio, including the recommendation to make a duplicate of all his observations, should he 'go to the bottom'.[37]

At the end of 1839, Hall is overjoyed to hear that Herschel is returning home from South Africa and takes the opportunity to send a long list of his observations on an eclipse of the moon from the Edinburgh Observatory.[38] He adds a postscript to a letter from his wife to Lady Herschel, indicating how sorry he is to learn that the famous telescope built by Herschel's father at Slough is to be dismantled before Hall had the opportunity to sketch it, and will now have to make do with the remains.

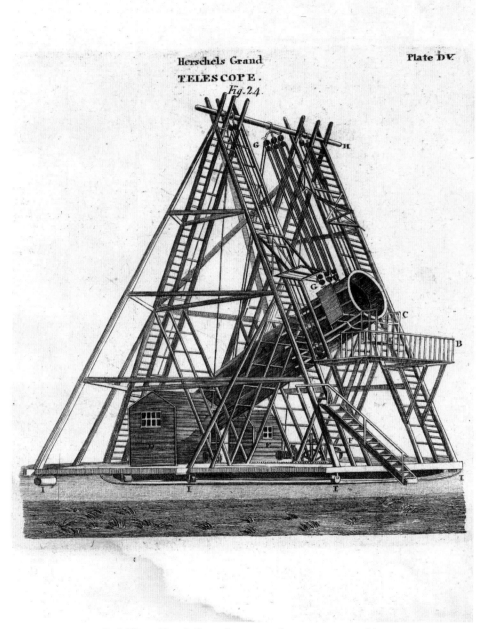

*Sir William Herschel's revolutionary telescope – examined by
Hall – was one of the technical wonders of the age.*

In the last undated letter in 1840, Hall reveals that he had had attacks of rheumatism when he was 'moping' at Rome without any particular object in view, envying Herschel's focus on his work, whilst feeling that he 'had written himself out'. He lets Herschel know that he 'loved astronomy the most of his pursuits'.

Anything to do with nautical technology was grist to Hall's mill (Note 78). One of the great naval calamities of the 18th Century was the sinking of the *Royal George* while she was undergoing repairs in 1782. Eight hundred lives (including 250 visiting women and children) and her commander Admiral Kempenfelt, were lost. As the wreck was becoming an obstruction to the anchorage Colonel Sir Charles Pasley of the Royal Engineers was authorised in 1839 to clear the wreckage, using underwater gunpowder and electricity, which he had experimented with. Enormous submarine charges of powder in oak barrels lined with lead – each containing 2,000 lbs of powder – were used very successfully to completely destroy the wreck. The barrels had to be welded shut – an operation which was potentially suicidal. It was the first time that underwater explosives had been used for such an operation. It lasting some three years and was regarded as a breakthrough in the history of diving.

Typically, Hall got in on the act, although it is not clear how. In a series of letters in August and September 1839 he provided a number of very detailed reports on the progress of the operation to the Admiralty's Hydrographer, Captain Francis Beaufort (Note 79), with the implication that he was present in some official capacity. At one point he reports that some soldiers are to be instructed to go to the bottom as a trial – in Hall's words, 'to put the helmet divers to their mettle as they are rather inactive, and begin to give themselves airs' (given the extreme danger of their work, this might be forgiven). According to Hall, on 26 August Colonel Pasley himself went down twice in a diving bell, despite adverse tidal conditions. Beaufort had apparently asked Hall to investigate underwater tidal conditions, to which Hall had responded positively, saying: 'should I ever again get the command of a ship ... I intend, if I can afford it, to have a helmet of my own to work with.' The helmeted divers themselves were apparently very fearful of descending 'at the least run of tide'.

Hall wanted to investigate the tidal conditions at Spithead, but complains: 'I wish I had a ship here – for I feel bitterly the want of a boat of my own to row about in at leisure – when and where I should choose. I borrow one occasionally, but it is unpleasant work.' After a series of failures with smaller charges, Hall describes a successful explosion which threatened the breaking of the timbers of the lighter on which he and Pasley were standing and which Hall likened to a 'tolerably severe galvanic shock ... It appeared to me as if I should have been lifted off the windlass on which I was standing

Notes

78   Hall became something of an authority on several aspects of civil engineering, and published a series of papers in the *United Services Journal* on his observations derived from his North American experience – including for example a patent slipway, which he presented as evidence to a House of Commons Select Committee.

79   Sir Francis Beaufort (1774–1857). A naval captain who shared many interests in common with Hall, especially nautical charting. He eventually became a most distinguished head of the Hydrographical Office in 1829 – a post he held for 25 years. His name is commemorated in the wind scale, which he standardised. He was given the task of finding a suitable naturalist to accompany the *Beagle* voyage and confirmed Darwin's suitability.

… A feeling of awe and surprise came over some minds … as if a huge submarine giant had struck the keel with an immense hammer, upwards … I shall not soon forget it.' Hall waxes lyrical about the effects of this undeniably awesome event, while the newspapers gave colourful accounts.

Hall co-authored a paper in 1839 describing the capstan recovered from the sunken vessel and his own experience of diving in a primitive diving bell nearly 20 years earlier (Note 80). In August 1820 on the point of departure for South America, he was offered this opportunity at Spithead and with a Captain Elliot descended almost 30 feet. He describes an almost unbearable pain in his ears, while he and Elliot suffered bleeding from ears, nose and throat for a week afterwards. In his article in *Chambers' Edinburgh Journal*, Hall mentions that it cannot be given to many to be at the bottom of the sea and at the top of one of the highest mountains within the space of a fortnight – following his expedition with Elliot to the top of the volcanic peak of Teide on Teneriffe at some 3,718 metres[39] (at one point his father is recorded as having expressed relief that his son did not in fact make an ascent in the opposite direction in a hot air balloon).[40]

Closer to his primary interest, he wrote an early paper *On the Proper Method of Laying Down a Ship's Track on Sea Charts, with some remarks on the importance of Time-keepers in Navigation* for *Brewster's Philosophical Journal*. Also in reports of the Royal Societies of both Edinburgh and London, Hall published papers on such varied topics as the comet seen at Valparaiso and the operation of the new Dundee Ferry (in 1826 Hall supported Alexander Greenhill in his attempts to promote a ferry service across the Forth, against some opposition, starting from Leith – it was not until the year of Hall's death in 1844 that such a service was established). In addition, Hall's advice to the Admiralty on a system of steering for the new steam warships from a raised platform on at the bow was adopted and was extensively reported in the *United Services Journal*.[41] The same journal carried his article on the efficiency and reliability of Massey's Patent Sounding Machine.[42]

Hall took a keen interest in the design of lighthouses, especially the efficiency of the light itself. He was in touch with several others similarly involved – such as his old friend Captain Beaufort – from the late 1820s onwards. Hall was familiar with the work of other experts such as Augustin Jean Fresnel and Alan Stevenson (the eldest son of the celebrated lighthouse builder, Robert Stevenson). One of the most assiduous innovators in the development of lighting technology was Thomas Drummond (Note 81). His 'Drummond Light' – set up at Purfleet and viewed from Trinity Wharf at Blackhall – was exhibited on the night of 31 May 1830 to a distinguished group of observers, including Hall. On the following day – on behalf of this group – Hall wrote a very detailed report on the result to Drummond, concluding that the whole company had 'but one opinion of the immense superiority of your light over all the others brought into comparison with it.'[43] If nothing else, it says something for Hall's reputation as a meticulous observer to be charged with recording this important assessment (Hall's comments on the experiment above were extensively reported in the *United Services Journal*).[44]

Notes

80 In an article in the *United Services Journal* of 1839 Hall used his accurate drawing of the capstan to promote the use of the *camera lucida* for such purposes.

81 Thomas Drummond (1797–1840). A Scottish engineer who invented the 'Drummond Light' using burning lime. He eventually became Under-Secretary of State for Ireland.

Hall was especially concerned to develop a more continuous light and proposed one which revolved. He wanted to see some experiments carried out using the island of Inchkeith in the Firth of Forth[45] (Hall was sufficiently accredited to obtain the use of the 350-foot-long room at the Board of Ordnance for some of his experiments, having recommenced his lighthouse research in that year).[46] However, Alan Stevenson claimed that his proposed 'whirling light' would not work – but revolving lights not dissimilar to Hall's design, became standard in later years.[47] An odd coda was added to these experiments when the proprietors of the vast Colosseum in Regent's Park (Note 82) asked if his 'experimental lighthouse' could be exhibited to the public as part of their display. Hall – while not ruling this out – was obliged to mention that his apparatus and facilities were partly the property of the Commissioners for Northern Lights, and there is no evidence that the proposal came to anything.[48]

The *Scotsman* of 31 August 1831 reported that Captain Hall had suggested that for the prevention of accidents, steamboats should be steered from the bow rather than the stern (as previously). Although this seemed to the editors eminently sensible, they expressed surprise that it should come from Captain Hall – perhaps they felt that now retired and more noted for his literary works, he was not perhaps the most appropriate person to be offering technical advice. However, in their issue of 5 October of that year, they reported on a second letter by Hall in the *United Services Journal*, which they considered very worthy of attention, especially since the Comptroller of the Navy had already given directions that one of the Government ships should be fitted up with the apparatus recommended by Hall and that it was likely to be installed on all other vessels.

Hall was present at an experiment in Paris in 1836 – together with Richard Chevenix, a Mr Hamilton, and John Barrow (second Secretary at the Admiralty) – to make sea water fresh. The two phials were sent to Michael Faraday, but both were broken (although they had some ice crystals, which Faraday examined). He pronounced this fresh, but made the point that the distillation process used was well known – the problem being the amount of fuel required for this. The presence of Hall and Barrow indicates the Navy's interest in this perennial subject.[49]

Perhaps one of his more unusual interests was in promoting the practical inventions of a certain Thomas Grant, working for the Navy at Portsmouth. Grant had developed not only a very efficient biscuit-making machine, but also coal briquettes using coal dust and tar, which greatly reduced the fuel costs of the new steamships. In an extended correspondence in 1840 with the eminent geologist George Bellas Greenough (Note 83), Hall made a strong plea for Grant's candidacy of the very exclusive Athenæum Club, emphasising Grant's gentlemanly modesty and manners. Hall pulled out all the stops – even sending samples of Grant's productions to Greenough and detailing the considerable cost savings of these inventions – all to no avail. Hall was mortified by this

Notes

82   The Colosseum in Regent's Park, London, was designed in 1824 with its architecture based on the Parthenon. It had a diameter of 126 feet and three-foot thick walls. It displayed the wonders of the world as models, and its centrepiece was a panorama of London occupying more than an acre of canvas, first exhibited in 1829.

83   George Bellas Greenough (1778–1855) was a noted geographer and geologist who founded the Geological Society of London in 1811. He produced large-scale maps of England, Wales and India and had many other interests including architecture, archaeology and ethnology.

failure, and there is a suspicion that the club did not look too kindly on men whose main achievements were practical – or perhaps to the sheer persistence of Hall's advocacy.[50]

Although more interested in geology than biological natural history, Hall has the distinction of being the first recorded collector of both one of the smallest animals and one of the largest: he obtained specimens of the rove beetle *Philonthus politus* from an owl nest in Nova Scotia[51] and in 1831 presented to the Geological Society of London a collection of mastodon bones received from the Philadelphia Museum (Hall sat on the Council of the Society from 1831 to 1833). He was closely in touch with its president – the renowned Sir Roderick Murchison – and in a letter to him in 1830, stated that he disagreed with him on the decline of science in England and that 'on the contrary … I am satisfied … that it is still flourishing more than in any other Country on Earth'.[52]

Even in the midst of his naval and diplomatic duties during his eventful stay in South America, Hall found time to give a detailed description of the activities of an exotic bee and its hive.[53] Furthermore, referring to flying fish, 'No familiarity' says Captain Hall, 'with the sight, can ever render us indifferent to the graceful flight of these most graceful of the finny, or, rather, winged tribe'. Hall describes the behaviour of the fish in considerable detail before reminding his readers: 'we may excuse the old Scottish wife, who said to her son, when he was relating what he had seen abroad: "You may hae seen rivers of milk, and mountains o' sugar, but you'll ne'er gar [make] me believe ye hae seen as fish that could flee!"'[54]

Hall was prepared to go to some lengths to prove a scientific point. When Audubon – the celebrated American ornithologist and bird painter – was castigated by his detractors in Philadelphia for his apparent mistake in depicting a rattlesnake climbing a tree to get at the nest of a mocking bird, Hall attempted to prove his friend's point.

Hall's interest in science and innovation was nothing if not eclectic: in 1840 he wrote to the post office reformer Rowland Hill, suggesting that all post office clocks show London time, but it was not until 1880 that Greenwich Mean Time was adopted as the standard for UK by statute. One of the vehicles that Hall used for the publication of letters and occasional articles – especially on technical or military subjects – was the *United Services Journal*. His substantial article on civil engineering in America (commenting on an earlier work by David Stevenson) – a discourse on the importance of learning from the American experience of major construction works from canals to dry docks – enjoined British military officers to take an interest in these topics (in the same article, he presciently forecasts a war between States, probably over slavery).[55] Elsewhere, he commends the achievements of British naval surveyors and their importance for navigation across the globe,[56] while his lengthy article on the Austrian Army ranges over the particulars of their various regiments, not excluding their pay, conditions, and discipline – although it is not clear why this should be a subject of interest.[57] Hall's wide knowledge of seamanship and navigation prompted Adam Black – proprietor of the *Encyclopaedia Britannica* – to ask him to revise the original 1797 section on this topic. While Hall demurred initially (on the basis that he could not improve on Black's earlier scientific and philosophical treatment), he did contribute an appendix on the subject. In his last book *Patchwork*, Hall comments authoritatively on the recent innovations of iron cables (replacing hemp ropes) together with iron tanks for water and other storage, as well as improvements in instruments, charts, introduction of tinned meats to replace carriage of domestic animals, and the modern education of seamen and officers.[58]

By the end of his life, Hall had made connections with many of the eminent figures of British science of his time – although his own achievements in the several fields he involved himself in were modest, partly due the demands of naval life but largely because of his lack of a scientific and mathematical education. Nevertheless, he appears to have been respected for the care and accuracy of his observations, and perhaps most of all, for his ingenuity in turning some of these – combined with his navigational experience – into practical effect in his various inventions. There can be little doubt that under other circumstances, his enquiring mind and endless curiosity might well have led him into the more productive scientific career that he certainly desired.

1. Basil Hall to Lady Londonderry, 11 June 1819, Kent Records
2. Hall, B. 1833
3. Basil Hall to Lady Londonderry, 11 June 1819, Kent Records
4. Basil Hall to Sir John Herschel, 29 November 1836
5. Letters from Basil Hall to J.D. Forbes, 1836, nos. 23, 51, & 62, December 1836– April 1837
6. Sir James Hall to Basil Hall, Forbes Autograph Collection, St. Andrews University, no. 33, 13 November 1815 & 6 February 1837
7. Forbes, 50
8. *Ibid.*, 83
9. *Ibid.*, 96
10. Mss JFOR/1/695 msdep7 – Incoming letters no.18, 20 June 1836, St. Andrews University
11. Sir James Hall to Marc-Auguste Pictet, 10 December 1809, Denton, E. (unpublished), 2003, 95–96
12. *Proc. Geol. Soc. of South Africa*, 49, xxxv-lxxii
13. Lyell, 158
14. Robert Fitzroy to Charles Darwin, Letter 403, 26 February 1838, University of Cambridge Darwin Correspondence
15. *Edinburgh Review*, Vol. 69, (1839), 467–93
16. Basil Hall to Macvey Napier, 26 April 1839
17. Charles Darwin to Basil Hall, Letter 550, 7 January 1840
18. Journal of J.D. Forbes, Journals no. I/10, 132–133, St. Andrews University
19. Basil Hall to William Whewell, 8 May 1830
20. Basil Hall to Dr. W.H. Wollaston, 6 March 1826, ref. RGS/CB2/551, Royal Geographical Society
21. Journal of J.D. Forbes, Journals no. I/10124-6, St. Andrews University
22. Basil Hall to Mary Somerville, 24 December 1831
23. *Ibid.*, 10 October 1823
24. *Ibid.*, 12 December 1824
25. *Ibid.*, nd
26. *Ibid.*, 13 February 1842
27. Basil Hall to Sir John Herschel, 19 May 1821
28. *Ibid.*, 11 September 1830
29. *Ibid.*, 23 January 1824, and 20 May 1834
30. Sir John Herschel to Basil Hall, 8 June 1831
31. Basil Hall to Sir John Herschel, 3 September 1832
32. Sir John Hershel to Basil Hall, 16 September 1832
33. Basil Hall to Sir John Herschel, 6 October 1832
34. *Ibid.*, 24 April 1833
35. *Ibid.*, 29 December, 1834 and 24 April 1835
36. *Ibid.*, Basil Hall to Sir John Herschel, 6 August 1835
37. *Ibid.*, 21 July 1836
38. *Ibid.*, 13 December 1839
39. *Chambers' Edinburgh Journal*, 18 September 1841, No.503
40. Sally Smith *pers. comm.*
41. *United Services Journal* 1831, Part 2, 538 and Part 3, 97
42. *Ibid.*, Part 3, 246–7
43. McLennan, 1867, 121–125
44. *United Services Journal* 1831, Part 2, 79
45. Basil Hall to J.D. Forbes, 30 November 1837 and 19 February 1838
46. *Ibid.*, 19 December 1839
47. *Ibid.*, Basil Hall to J.D. Forbes, 15 April 1841
48. Correspondence between Captain Basil Hall and Mr & Mrs Braham, Somerset Archive and Record Service
49. Correspondence of Michael Faraday, Vol I, 1811–31, Letter 424
50. Basil Hall to G.B.Greenough, 1840
51. Majika, C. J., Klimaszewski J. & Lauff, 1194:33–47
52. Basil Hall to Sir Roderick Murchison, 1830
53. The Hive and the Honeybee: Selections from the E. F. Philips Beekeeping Collection, 211–212
54. Hall, quoted in Goldsmith, Vol II, 304
55. *United Services Journal* 1839, Part I, 40–47
56. *Ibid.*, 433–449
57. *Ibid.*, 1835, 18–30 and 168–180
58. Hall, 1841, 205 *et seq.*

'As a Captain, Happiest!...'

Some time in 1842, Hall (who was then living at 6 Queen's Terrace, Southsea near Portsmouth) began to show signs of mental instability, characterised by violent fits. At the request of Margaret, James Hall wrote to the Royal Geographical Society on 21 December 1842 asking to remove Hall's name from list of members, 'in consequence of his severe, and it is now apprehended, hopeless illness'. His wife had poured out her heart to her husband's 'oldest and kindest and much valued friend', Lady Jean Hunter in the autumn of that year:

> My hand will scarcely move – at times it seemed my mind was as blank as his is always now – worse, he is no longer at home but at Haslar – you will believe the struggle we made to avoid this last move – it was so detrimental to himself, so utterly subversive of every chance or probability of amendment – humanly speaking – on the 12th of this month he was removed there. Many were the plans and places talked of but there seemed none so eligible as Haslar – as close to myself, among his own people – under the management of Dr Anderson, who is of first rate reputation in his melancholy case – besides being one of the best, kindest, and most benevolent of men, who watches over him night and day and is assisted by another excellent man, Dr Richardson, an intimate and valued personal friend who feels for him as a brother and whose wife is no less devoted to our service – all those alleviations to our deep sorrow, which we could not have elsewhere. With it all, the misery is great.[1]

Haslar Hospital, Gosport, near Portsmouth was established as a hospital for the British Navy in 1794 and today is still the largest of all service hospitals in the United Kingdom. In its time, it was the largest brick building in the world. Until the mid-19th Century, it was notorious for its conditions (baths were not available until the early part of that century) – being regarded almost as a prison with many of its inmates having been press-ganged into the Navy. It was seen by impressed men as a convenient jumping-off point for escape from the Navy, often using its sewage tunnels leading to the open estuary – which was also the route for import of illegal alcohol.[2]

In a letter to Dickens in the previous year, with some prescience, Hall makes a telling reference to Haslar which he intended to include in a work on the naval dockyards at Portsmouth, without dwelling unduly on the horrors: 'I have seen things in Haslar which, handled improperly, would make people's hair stand on end – but which, properly handled, may kindle their gentlest sympathies. I saw 2,700 wounded men carried into

*A patient at Haslar Naval Hospital where Hall was incarcerated
for the last years of his life.* Illustrated London News.

that great brick building in one week'[3] (enormous numbers of soldiers were received after the retreat from Corunna, many thousands dying of typhus[4]).

An inspection in 1838 – some 4 years before Hall was incarcerated there – revealed that there was 118 in the lunatic asylum, 'labouring under mania in different forms'. The medical officers of the time held the view that mental disease could be controlled by the administration of strict disciplinary measures and some of the men were severely and brutally treated – including excessive purging and bleeding, while others were placed in solitary confinement or put in strait-jackets if violent.[5] It was not until the appointment of Dr Anderson and the Scottish surgeon-naturalist Dr John Richardson, that more humane conditions were instituted under his more benign regime (it is ironic that on his last visit to North America, Hall had spent some time looking at the conditions in lunatic asylums and the treatment of the inmates).

Dr (later Sir) John Richardson from Dumfries was a renowned explorer in the Canadian Arctic and fine naturalist who accompanied Captain John Franklin on several expeditions – by a strange coincidence Hall had met him (and Captain Franklin) in Canada on his return from his first expedition. He was appointed physician at Haslar in 1838 and subsequently became Inspector of Hospitals for the Admiralty (he was later to influence the career of Florence Nightingale). He and Dr Anderson introduced a new regime at Haslar, emphasising cleanliness, fresh air and humane treatment in more congenial surroundings.

The Halls experienced a very short respite over the Christmas period 1842–3, after Basil had left Haslar on 23 December for a spell in a lodging at Anglesea, near Gosport – as Margaret describes:

> There was no improvement in the language, but in other respects the mind revived wonderfully itself and we were really comfortable and happy but alas all our hopes were dashed on 22nd January when he was attacked by his father's old complaint and had four fits in the course of seven hours. Bleeding, blistering and strong medicine were naturally had recourse to, which weakened him considerably in body and in mind … all too plain that the dire disease is there.

She expressed the hope that 'there is sufficient quietness to keep him under his own roof '.[6]

The reference to his father's old complaint is interesting. Sir James Hall experienced many years of illness before his death. In a letter to Lady Helen Hall from her brother, Thomas, 5th Earl of Selkirk, it was said that Sir James (then aged 50) had been ill for the last 12 months with 'alarming epileptic fits … three in one day [so that it was] necessary to bleed him'. By 1819, Sir James' daughter Magdalene thinks him very ill – possibly fatally so (which delayed her marriage to Captain Harvey). Sir James apparently lived in dread of losing his mind before his death, but died in June 1831.[7] In a letter to Mary Somerville in 1824, Hall revealed that his 'father's mind was demolished at a blow, or rather his memory, for in other respects he is alive'.[8]

In early March, Margaret reported to Lady Hunter that Hall had suffered a record number of fits in the last month, and that she was again obliged to have him removed to Haslar. She herself felt 'more hopeless than ever' but was comforted by the health of her girls and 'my darling Baby'.[9]

In June, Margaret reports that there had been occasional little changes in Basil in the last three months: 'nothing at all materially better, though on the whole there is the absence of the power of giving way to his restlessness – not much hope, nor how long his sad existence (and mine) will last.' She feels sometimes like lying down and dying, with so much worse suffering than death: 'the longer the endurance, the worse it is – a month ago, he lost much of the power of his left arm – and side but that has almost entirely returned – but Doctor thinks only temporary – I have seen him only three times in the last weary three months – but thought it did him more harm than good – it only excited a wish to get away from where he was which seems at other times to lie dormant.' Margaret often dreads seeing him. The fits occured at regular intervals of four weeks since the first attack in January, and had not ceased. It appears that Mrs Hunter's daughters had been staying with Margaret and she looked after her son – their places to be taken by Captain and Mrs Francis Scott. She ends her letter with sympathy for Mrs Hunter's own illness.[10]

On 18 October Margaret announces the passing of her husband:

> Some days before he was seized with an attack of paralysis, which from the first deprived him of consciousness and he sank gradually, without the least apparent suffering – Eliza and I witnessed his departure. James was in Cumberland with his cousin, Mrs Francis Scott (Note 84) but could not remain after hearing of his Father's illness and travelled upwards of 300 miles quite alone. I have had my boy brought from school to assist to lay his Father in his last earthly house, to which we shall attend him on the 17th next Tuesday.[11]

Her next letter to Anne Hunter, daughter of Lady Jean Hunter, reports hearing of Lady Hunter's death on the very day she herself had written to Anne intimating Hall's death. She 'who had so often welcomed him when alive' had survived Hall by only nine hours. Margaret lets Anne know that after Easter she hopes to go to Paris for six months to ensure her son gets into the habit of speaking French before he goes to sea.[12]

It is not clear exactly what contributed to Hall's death, but some clues may be had from a typescript document without attribution, entitled *Traditions of Dunglass* (Note 85):

> It was the medical treatment available at Dunglass that ruined Captain Basil Hall's health; that is to say injured it so that he was never really well afterwards; he had come back from Italy with ague, which he attributed at least to eating fruit when overheated; probably he overdid things in every way, for somebody said, who had been with him abroad, that it tired him to *see* Captain Hall doing the sights. Unfortunately for him, it was just when Arsenic was coming into use as a medicine; and though I do not know where his medical advisor lived, he gave it in the old laudamy [laudanum] and calamy style, and naturally the corroding effects of the new medicine, so given, destroyed his digestion beyond remedy. He employed the country doctor because he was anxious to be well, so as to be employed again, but it certainly would have been wiser to have gone to the Edinburgh faculty, with the family house available (Note 86).

Certainly in the 19th Century, 'ague' and malaria were often treated with Fowler's Solution – a form of potassium arsenite, considered a useful alternative to quinine. It

---

Notes

84   Frances Harvey, daughter of Captain Harvey was married to Rear-Admiral Francis Scott who was the son of Agnes Scott Johnston.

85   I am indebted to Mr David Miller for a copy of this document.

86   The author then goes on to relate how, falling from a horse, Hall had very badly twisted his ankle and reset it himself by hitting it with both fists.

Margaret Hall wife of Basil Hall by Sir Francis Heggat Chantrey circa 1820–40. National Portrait Gallery.

can be fatal at high dosage. Ague is the term previously used for alternating chills and fevers, such as malaria. Laudanum was widely used in Hall's time for a variety of medical conditions, as an alcohol-based tincture of opium – excessive use can cause insanity and death. Calomel ('calomy') was a mercury-based purgative.

A post mortem was carried out and following the technical and medical report, this statement is recorded:

Some days ago we mentioned the death of the lamented Captain Basil Hall. His funeral took place at Kingston near Southsea on Tuesday last. It was strictly private. For two years Captn. Basil Hall has been lost to his friends, & to the world. A post-mortem examination of the brain was made proving that the cause of illness, & death arose from a softening of the brain, producing in the first place paralysis. There can be little reason to doubt that this disorder was brought on by severe mental exertion & by arduous application to the duties of his profession, especially in tropical climates. We add for the benefit of our professional friends the technical account of the examination of the brain, copied from the original statement of Dr. Jas. Anderson of Portsmouth.[13]

Given the primitive neurological knowledge of the time and the advances that have been made since, this diagnosis must be treated with considerable caution. Nevertheless, from what we know of Hall from his childhood onwards, his apparent hyperactivity and prodigious mental energy, coupled with certain obsessional traits, it is perhaps hardly surprising that he suffered a complete mental breakdown in his last years.

According to his Testament dated 1846, he left significant sums to his children and to his wife. His manuscripts, apparatus, and letters were to be given to his eldest son Basil Sidmouth de Ros, or on the latter's early death, to his second son Frederick Richard (the will indicates that he had four children at the time of writing in 1840). The last will and testament seems to have been completed in the presence of the Archbishop of Canterbury and Sir Herbert James, Master Keeper or Promissory of the Prerogative Court of Canterbury. The administration of the will was granted to his wife Margaret and the Honourable John Frederick Filygrald de Ros.

Perhaps the best epitaph for Captain Basil Hall's life – which he himself might have wished – were the words he wrote ten years before his death while he was at Schloss Hainfeld:

> I have enjoyed to the full each successive period of my life, as it has rolled over me; and just as I began to feel that I had had nearly enough of any one period, new circumstances, more or less fortunate and agreeable, began to start up, and to give me fresher, and, generally speaking, more lively interest in the coming period than in that which had just elapsed. As a middy, I was happy—as a lieutenant, happier—as a captain, happiest! I remember thinking that the period from 1815 to 1823, during which I commanded different ships of war, could not by any possibility be exceeded in enjoyment; and yet I have found the dozen years which succeeded greatly happier, though in a very different way. It is upon this that the whole matter turns. Different seasons of life, like different seasons of the year, require different dresses; and if these be misplaced, there is no comfort. Were I asked to review my happy life, and to say what stage of it I enjoyed most, I think I should pitch upon that during which I passed my days in the scientific, literary, and political society of London, and my nights in dancing and flirting till sunrise, in the delicious paradise of Almacks (Note 87), or the still more bewitching ball-rooms of Edinburgh![14]

References

1. Margaret Hall to Lady Hunter, 22 October 1842, NLS MS 14196 ff.184–187
2. Revell, 41
3. Basil Hall to Charles Dickens, 19 March 1841, Huntington Library, MS 18504
4. Revel, 27
5. *Ibid.*, 42
6. Margaret Hall to Lady Hunter, 2 February 1843, NLS MS 14196 ff.188–91
7. Sally Smith, *pers. comm.*
8. Basil Hall to Mary Somerville, 12 December 1824
9. Margaret Hall to Lady Hunter, 11 March 1843, NLS MS 14196 ff.192–197
10. *Ibid.*, 10 June 1843, ff.198–203
11. *Ibid.*, Margaret Hall to 'Anne', n.d. ff.204–205
12. *Ibid.*, 18 October 1844, ff.206–209
13. Examination of Capt. Basil Hall's head on September 12 1844, General Register Office, GD206/2/321/3
14. Hall, 1836, 161

Notes

87 The exclusive Almacks Assembly Rooms in St. James's London was where fashionable society met on Wednesday nights for supper, dancing and gambling during the London season – the city's place to see and be seen.

Appendix 1

The *Quarterly Review*, Vol. 57, September–December 1836, pp.130–132

The reviewer includes a long letter from Sir Walter Scott in 1820 (no other date) to the Countess Purgstall – when he was at the height of his fame (he had breakfasted with her brother Henry the previous day). The letter includes acknowledgement of receipt of a book (probably *Denkmahl* – the memorial to the Countess' son) – and says that Scott often thinks of spending some time in Graz. He is very sympathetic to her tragedies, 'we who once saw each other daily'. He tells about having giving up poetry in favour of Byron, explains poor health from what sounds like an ulcer (spasms in the stomach alleviated by copious calomel) and philosophises about late life and loss of romance, etc.

My Dear and much-valued Friend,

You cannot imagine how much I was interested and affected by receiving your token of your kind recollection, after the interval of so many years. Your brother Henry breakfasted with me yesterday, and gave me the letter and the book, which served me as a matter of much melancholy reflection for many hours.

Hardly anything makes the mind recoil so much upon itself, as the being suddenly and strongly recalled to times long passed, and that by the voice of one we have so much loved and respected. Do not think I have ever forgotten you, or the many happy days I spent in Frederick Street, in society which fate as separated so far, and for so many years.

The little volume was particularly acceptable to me, as it acquainted me with many circumstances, of which distance and imperfect communication has left me entirely ignorant, or had transmitted only inaccurate information.

Alas! My dear friend, what can the utmost efforts of friendship offer you, beyond the sympathy which, however sincere, must sound like an empty compliment in the ear of affliction? God knows with what willingness I would undertake anything which might afford you the melancholy consolation of knowing how much you old and early friend interests himself in the sad event which has so deeply wounded your peace of mind. The verses, therefore, which conclude this letter, must not be weighed against their intrinsic value, for the more inadequate they are to express the feelings they would fain convey, the more they show the author's anxious wish to do what may be grateful to you.

In truth, I have long given up poetry. I have had my day with the public; and being no great believer in poetical immortality, I was very well pleased to rise a winner, without continuing the game, till I was beggared of any credit I had acquired. Besides, I felt the prudence of giving way before the more forcible and powerful genius of Byron.

If I were greedy, or jealous of poetical fame – and both are strangers to my nature – I might comfort myself with the thought, that I would hesitate to strip myself to the contest so fearlessly as Byron does; or to command the wonder and terror of the public, by exhibiting, in my own person, the sublime attitude of the dying gladiator. But with the old frankness of twenty years since, I will fairly own, that this same delicacy of mine may arise from more conscious want of vigour and inferiority, than from a delicate dislike to the nature of the conflict. At any rate, there is time for everything, and without swearing oaths to it, I think my time for poetry has gone by.

My health suffered horridly last year, I think from over labour and excitation; and though it is now apparently restored to its usual tone, yet during the long and painful disorder (spasms in the stomach) and the frightful process of cure, by a prolonged use of calomel, I learned that my frame was made of flesh, and not of iron, a conviction which I will long keep in remembrance, and avoid any occupation so laborious and agitating, as poetry must be, to be worth anything.

In this humour, I often think of passing a few weeks on the continent – a summer vacation if I can – and of course my attraction to Graz would be very strong. I fear this is the only chance of our meeting in this world, we, who once saw each other daily! For I understand from George and Henry, that there is little chance of your coming here. And when I look around me, and consider how many changes you will see in feature, form, and fashion, amongst all you know and loved; and how much, no sudden squall, or violent tempest, but the slow and gradual progress of life's long voyage, has served all the gallant fellowships whom you left spreading their sails in the morning breeze, I really am not sure that you would have much pleasure.

The gay and wild romance of life is over with all of us. The real, dull, and stern history of humanity has made a far greater progress over our heads; and age, dark and unlovely, has laid his crutch over the stoutest fellow's shoulders. One thing your old society may boast, that they have all run their courses with honour, and almost all with distinction; and the brother suppers of Frederick Street have certainly made a very considerable figure in the world, as was to be expected, from her talents under whose auspices they were assembled.

One of the most pleasant sights which you would see in Scotland, as it now stands, would be your brother George in possession of the most beautiful and romantic place in Clydesdale – Corehouse. I have promised often to go out with him, and assist him with my deep experience as a planter and landscape gardener. I promise you my oaks will outlast my laurels; and I pique myself more upon my compositions for manure than on any other compositions whatsoever to which I was every accessory. But so much does business of one sort or other engage us both, that we never have been able to fix a time which suited us both; and with the utmost wish to make out a party, perhaps we never may.

This is a melancholy letter, but it is chiefly so from the sad tone of yours – who have had such real disasters to lament – while mine is only the humorous sadness, which a retrospect on human life is sure to produce on the most prosperous. For my own course of life, I have only to be ashamed of its prosperity, and afraid of its termination; for I have little reason, arguing on the doctrine of chances, to hope that the same good fortune will attend me for ever. I have had an affectionate and promising family, many friends, few unfriends, and I think, no enemies – and more of fame and fortune than mere literature ever procured for a man before.

I dwell among my own people, and have many whose happiness is dependent on me, and which I study to the best of my power. I trust my temper, which, you know, is by nature good and easy, has not been spoiled by flattery or prosperity; and, therefore, I have escaped entirely that irritability of disposition which I think is planted, like the slave in the poet's chariot, to prevent him from enjoying his triumph.

Should things, therefore, change with me – and in these times, or indeed any times, such change is to be apprehended – I trust I shall be able to surrender these adventitious advantages, as I would my upper dress, as something extremely comfortable, but which I can make shift do without.

Bibliography

Unpublished

American Papers of Sir Charles Richard Vaughan, MSS NLS

Correspondence between Basil Hall and Charles Dickens – Huntington Library, California, USA

Correspondence between Capt. Basil Hall and Capt. Francis Beaufort, 1839 Huntington Library, California, USA

Correspondence between J.D. Forbes, Basil Hall and others – St. Andrews University Library

Correspondence between Sir John Frederick William Herschel and Capt. Basil Hall, Cat. Ref JH/A, The Royal Society, London

Correspondence between Capt. Basil Hall and Mary Somerville, Dep.c.370, Bodleian Library Special Collections and Manuscripts, Oxford

Correspondence between Capt. Basil Hall and Mr & Mrs Braham, Somerset Archive and Record Service, ref. B/B4/49-51, February 1840

Correspondence of Wilmot Horton of Osmaston & Catton, D3155/WH 2741– D3155/7919, Derbyshire Record Office

Correspondence between Capt. Basil Hall and G.B. Greenough, Collection No. 45, Greenough ref. 104, University College London Special Collections

Correspondence between Capt. Basil Hall and William Whelwell, Add. Ms.a. 205, Trinity College Library, Cambridge

Correspondence between Capt. Basil Hall and Macvey Napier, Add. MSS.34614, 34619-21 passim, British Library Manuscript Collections

Notes on an Interview with Bonaparte at St. Helena, 13 August 1813, National Army Museum, London, ref. 6087-391

Denton, E. (2003), *Sir James Hall, Un Homme de Science dans la Revolution*,

Edition critique et commentaire de son journal de voyage en France avril-aôut 1791, thèse pour le diplome d'archiviste paleographe, 2003, Diplôme d'Etudes Approfondées École Nationale des Chartres

Letter to Lady Londonderry 11 June 1819, Centre for Kentish Studies, U840 C574

Letter to Dr Hyde Wollaston, LMS H1, 6 March 1826, ref. RGS/CB2/551, Royal Geographical Society

Letter from Robert Fitzroy to Charles Darwin, Letter 403, 26 February 1838, University of Cambridge Darwin Correspondence Project, 2007

A Memoir of Maria Edgeworth: 1867, *A Selection from her Letters* (unpublished), Frances Anne Beaufort Edgeworth, Vol. 3

Murchison Correspondence – Basil Hall Letters, ref. LDGSL 838/h4/1–4, The Geological Society, London

Papers of the Addington Family, Viscounts Sidmouth, (152 M C1812/OF – 152M/ C1824/OC), Devon Record Office

Edinburgh University Special Collections

National Library of Scotland:

    MS 14196 Letters from Basil Hall to Mrs (later Lady) Hunter

    MS 10453 Letter from Lord Grenville to Basil Hall

    MS 2553 Letter from Jane Cranstoun to Walter Scott, 18 November 1796, f.74

MS 2553 Letter from Countess Purgstall to Walter Scott, 26 July 1799

MS 932 Letters of Lockhart, Vol. 10

MS 1752 fn.383/384, Letter from Walter Scott to Roberyt Cadell, 15 September 1831

MS 3242 Letter from Robert Cadell to Walter Scott n.d.

MS 792 Constable Letter-Book, 1829–36

MS 39152 M/C1816/OF4 Letter from Basil Hall to Admiralty

Lilly Library, Bloomington, Indiana, Letter from Basil Hall to Sir Evan Nepean, 1 April 1817

Public Records Office ADM 51/2324

Private Collections

Published

Works by Captain Basil Hall

Hall, B., 1815, 'Account of the Structure of Table Mountain, and other parts of the Peninsula of the Cape', *Trans. Royal Society Edinburgh*, vii: 269

_____., 1818, *Account of a Voyage of Discovery to the West Coast of Corea and the Great Loo-choo Island, with an Appendix Containing Charts, and Various Hydrographical and Scientific Notices and a Vocabulary of the Loo-Choo Language by H. J. Clifford*, London & Edinburgh, John Murray

_____., 1818, *Account of a Voyage of Discovery to the West Coast of Corea and the Great Loo-choo Island*, Edinburgh, A Constable & Co

_____., 1818, 'Account of a Voyage of Discovery to the West Coast of Corea and the Great Loo-choo Island', *Edinburgh Review*, 29: 475–97

_____., 1826 a., *A Voyage to Loo Choo and other Places in the Eastern Seas in the Year 1816, including an Account of Captain Maxwell's Attack on the Batteries at Canton: and Notes of an Interview with Buonaparte at St. Helena, in August 1817*, Edinburgh, Archibald Constable & Co

_____., 1826 b., *Extracts from a Journal written on the Coasts of Chili, Peru and Mexico in the Years 1829, 1821, 1822*, Edinburgh, A. Constable & Co

_____., 1829, *Forty Etchings from Sketches made with the camera lucida, in North America in 1827 and 1828*, Edinburgh, Cadell & Co and London, Simpkin & Marshall, and Moon, Boys, & Graves

_____., 1830, *Travels in North America in the Years 1827 and 1828,* 3 vols., Third ed., Edinburgh, Robert Cadell

_____., 1831–1840, Various articles in the *United Services Journal*, London, Henry Colburn

_____., 1832, *Fragments of Voyages and Travels.* Second Series. Robert Cadell, Edinburgh

Hall, B., 1833. *Fragments of Voyages and Travels.* Third Series. Robert Cadell, Edinburgh & Whittaker, Treacher & Co., London,

_____., 1835, 'Notice of a Machine for regulating High Temperature, invented by the late Sir James Hall', *Transactions of the Geological Society*, Series 2, no 3, 489–490, London

_____., 1836, *Skimmings; or A Winter at Schloss Hainfeld in Lower Styria*, Philadelphia, Carey, Lea and Blanchard

_____., (trans.), 1837, *Napoleon in Council, or the Opinions delivered by Bonaparte in the council of State*, Edinburgh, Robert Cadell

_____.,1841, *Patchwork*, 3 vols, London, Edward Moxon

_____., 1841, 'The Diving Bell: An Account of a dive in the waters of Plymouth, England undertaken by Captain Hall and his naval companion, Captain Robert Elliot. Stray Chapters from My Journal', *Chambers' Edinburgh Journal*, 18 September 1841, No.503

_____., 1852, Fragments *of Voyages and Travels*, Series 1, 2, & 3, Edinburgh, Edward Moxon, London

_____., 1931 & 2005, *Travels in India, Ceylon and Borneo*, ed. Prof H.G. Rawlinson, London, G. Routledge & Son

Other Published Works

Alison, Lady (ed.), 1883, *Some Account of My Life and Writings: An Autobiography of Sir Archibald Alison*, 2 vols, Edinburgh, Wm. Blackwood & Sons

Allibone, S.A., 1859–1871, *A Critical Dictionary of English Literature, and British and American Authors*, Philadelphia & London

Anderson, W.E.K. (ed.), 1972, *The Journal of Sir Walter Scott*, Oxford, Clarendon Press

Ashworth, J.H., 1935, 'Charles Darwin as a Student in Edinburgh 1825–1827' in *Proceedings of the Royal Society of Edinburgh*, 55: 97–113

Audubon, M. R., 1900, *Audubon and his Journals*, New York, Charles Scribner's and Sons

Bethel, L. (ed.), 1985, Vol. III, 'From Independence to *c*.1870', *The Cambridge History of Latin America*, CUP

Biddle, R., 1830, *Captain Hall in America*, Carey and Lea, Philadelphia

Blackwood's Edinburgh Magazine, London, Blackwood & Sons & T. Cadell

Brennan, E.N. (ed.), 1997, *The Old Curiosity Shop*, Oxford, Clarendon Press

Brenton, E.P., 1837, *The Naval History of Great Britain*, 2 vols, 2nd ed, London, C. Rice

Carlyle, T., 1909–14, *Sir Walter Scott*, Boston, The Harvard Classics

'A Week at Waterloo', Vol. LXXI, April 1906, No.6, 821–45, New York, *The Century Magazine*

Chalmers, J., 1993, 'Audubon in Edinburgh', in *Archives of Natural History*, 20:15–66, London

Chalmers, J., 2003, *Audubon in Edinburgh and his Scottish Associates*, Edinburgh,

NMS Publishing

Cockburn, H., 1874, *Journal of Henry Cockburn being a continuation of the Memorials of his Time*, Edinburgh, Edmonston & Douglas

Cockburn, H., 1909, *Memorials of his time*, Edinburgh, T.N. Foulis

Conlin, J., 'Buffalo's Original Canal Terminus Building: Cantilevered Architecture on the Canal Basin', *Western New Heritage*, Vol. 4, No.1

Constable, T., 1873, *Archibald Constable and his Literary Correspondents: A Memorial by his son Thomas Constable*, 3 vols, Edinburgh, Edmonston & Douglas

Corning, H. (ed.), 1940, *Letters of John James Audubon 1826–1840*, Boston, The Club of Odd Volumes

Crockett, W. S., 1912, *Scott originals: An account of notables and worthies, the originals of characters in the Waverley Novels*, Crombie, B.W., 1882, *Modern Athenians*, Edinburgh, Adam and Charles Black

Dalgairn, Mrs., 1829, The Practice of Cookery adapted to the Business of Everyday Life, Edinburgh, Robert Cadell

Donghi, T.H., 1993, *The Contemporary History of South America*, Durham, North Carolina, Duke University Press

Douglas, D.D., 1894, *Familiar Letters of Sir Walter Scott*, 2 vols., Edinburg, D. Douglas

Erskine, W., 1819, 'Account of the Cave Systems of Elephanta' in *Bombay Literary Society Transactions*, 214–270

Forbes, J. D., 1859, *Preparatory Note on the Present Progress and Present Aspects of the Theory of Glaciers*, Edinburgh, Adam Charles, and Black

Ford, A., 1967, *The 1826 Journal of John James Audubon*, New York, Abbeyville Press

Fleming, F., 1998, *Barrow's Boys*, London, Granta Books

Frank, A.J.L.J. (ed.), 1991, Correspondence of Michael Faraday, Vol I, 1811–31, London, Institute of Electrical Engineers

Gibson, M., *Jane Cranstoun, Countess Purgstall: A Possible Inspiration for Le Fanu's 'Carmilla'* in Le Fanu Studies, Nov. 2007

Goldsmith, O., 1859, *A History of the Earth and Animated Nature*, 2 vols., London Edinburgh & Glasgow, Blackie & Son

Grant, J.P. (ed.), 1845, *Memoir and Correspondence of Mrs. Grant of Laggan*, vol. III, London, Longman, Brown, Green & Longman

Grant, E., 1911, *Memoirs of a Highland Lady: The Autobiography of Elizabeth Grant of Rothiemurchus 1797–1830*, London, John Murray

Grayson, J.H., 2007, 'Basil Hall's Account of a Voyage of Discovery: The Value of a British Naval Officer's Account of Travels in the Seas of Eastern Asia in 1816', *Sungkyun Journal of East Asian Studies*, Vol. 7, No.1, Academy of East Asian Studies, Sungkyun Kwan University, April 2007

Grierson, Sir H.J.C., 1938, *Sir Walter Scott, Bart. A New Life Supplementary to and Corrective of, Lockhart's Biography*, London, Constable & Co

_____., (ed.), 1932–37, *The Letters of Sir Walter Scott*, 12 vols., London, Constable & Co

Griffis, W.E., 1882, *Corea, The Hermit Nation*, New York, Scribner's

Hammer-Purgstall, J., 1821, *Denkmahl auf das grab der beyden Letzen Grafen von Purgstall*, Vienna

Hannah I.C., 1913, *The Berwick and East Lothian Coasts*, London, T. Fisher Unwin

Hare, A.J.C. (ed.), 1895, *Life and Letters of Maria Edgeworth*, 2 vols., London, Edward Arnold

Hart Davis, Duff., 2003, *Audubon's Elephant: The Story of John James Audubon's epic struggle to publish The Birds of America*, London, Weidenfeld & Nicolson

Hogg, J. & Maryat, F. (eds.), *London Society*, 1878

Holmes, R., 2008, *The Age of Wonder*, London, Harper Press

Hook, A., 1975, *Scotland and America 1750–1835*, Glasgow, Blackie

House, M., Tillotson, K., & Storey, G. (eds.), 1969, *The Letters of Charles Dickens*, 12 vols., Oxford, Clarendon Press

Humboldt, Alexander von., 1858, *Cosmos: A Sketch of a Physical Description of the Universe*, London, Henry G Bohn

Innes, Cosmo, 1854, *Memoir of Thomas Thomson*, Edinburgh, Bannatyne Club

James, F.A.J.L. (ed.), 1991, 'Correspondence of Michael Faraday', Vol. I, 1811–31, (Letter 424), *Institute of Electrical Engineers*, London

James, W., 1902, *The Naval History of Great Britain*, 6 vols., 8th ed., London, Macmillan

Johnson, E., 1970, *Sir Walter Scott: The Great Unknown*, 2 vols., London, Hamish Hamilton

Joyce, M., 1951, *Edinburgh, The Golden Age 1769–1832*, London, Longmans Green & Co

Kauffmann, J-P, 1999, *The Dark Room at Longwood; A voyage to St. Helena*, London, Harvill Press

Koebel, W.H., 1917, *British Exploits in South America*, New York, The Century Co

Koh, G., 2006, 'British perceptions of Joseon Korea as reflected in travel literature of the late eighteenth and early nineteenth century', *The Review of Korean Studies*, vol. 9, no.4, December 2006

Lemaistre, J.G., 1806, *Travels after the peace of Amiens, through parts of France, Switzerland, Italy, and Germany, etc.*, London, J. Johnston

Lockhart, J.G., 1882, *Memoirs of Sir Walter Scott*, 8 vols., Edinburgh, T. & A. Constable

_____., 1898, *The Life of Sir Walter Scott*, London, Adam & Charles Black

_____., 1914, *The Life of Sir Walter Scott*, 5 vols., London, Macmillan & Co

Lyell, Mrs. (ed.), 1881, *Life, Letters & Journals of Sir Charles Lyell*, 2 vols., London, John Murray

Macintyre, G., 2003, *Dugald Stewart: The Pride and Ornament of Scotland*, Brighton & Portland, (n.d.) Sussex Academic Press

McLennan, J.F., 1867, *Memoir of Thomas Drummond*, Edinburgh, Edmonston & Douglas

McLeod J., 1818, *Narrative of a voyage in His majesty's late ship Alceste to the Yellow Sea, along the coast of Corea and through its numerous hitherto islands to the Island of Lewchew; with an account of her shipwreck in the Straits of Gaspar*, Philadelphia, M. Carey & Son

Majka, C.G., Klimaszewski, J. & Lauff, W., 2006, A. 'New Coleoptera Records from Owl Nests in Nova Scotia, Canada', *Zootaxa*, 1194:33–47

Marshall, J., 1823–1830, *Royal Navy Biography*, 12 vols., London, Longman, Rees, Orme, Brown, and Green

McCunn F., 1909, *Sir Walter Scott's Friends*, Edinburgh, Blackwood & Sons

McLeod, J., 1817, *Narrative of a Voyage, in His Majesty's Late Ship Alceste, to the Yellow Sea, along the Coast of Corea, and through its Numerous Hitherto Undiscovered Islands, to the Islands of Lewchew*, London, John Murray

Miller, D., 2001, 'The Black Bottle Affair and its Family Background', *Journal of the Society for Army Historical Research* 79, 209–218

_____., 2008, *Lady de Lancey at Waterloo: A Story of Duty and Devotion*, Chalford, Stroud, Spellmount

Moore, T., 1834, *The Works of Lord Byron with his Letters and Journals, and his Life*, 17 vols., London, John Murray

'The Navy and South America', 1962, 807–23, Aldershot *Navy Records Society*, 104

'The Naval Chronicle', 1904, 40 vols., London, 1799–1818, Aldershot *Navy Records Society*

O'Byrne, W., 1849, *A Naval Biographical Dictionary*, London, John Murray

Paik, L.G., 1935, 'The Korean record on Captain Basil Hall's Voyages of Discovery to the West Coast of Korea', *Transactions of the Royal Asiatic Society*, Korea branch edition, 24, 15–19, London

Paroissien, D.H., 1971, 'Dickens's *Pictures from Italy*: Stages of the Work's Development and Dickens's Method of Composition' in *An English Miscellany*, Vol. 22, 260, Rome, The British Council

Partington, W., 1932, Sir Walter's Post-bag, London, John Murray

Philips E.F., 2009, *The Hive and the Honeybee: Selections from the Beekeeping Collection*, Albert R Mann Library, Cornell University

Pope-Hennessey, U. (ed.), 1931, *The Aristocratic Journey: Being the outspoken letters of Mrs. Basil Hall written during a fourteen months' Sojourn in America 1827–1828*, New York & London, G.P. Putnam's and Sons

'Account of a Voyage of Discovery to the West Coast of Corea and the great Loo-choo Island by Basil Hall and a Vocabulary of the Loo-choo language by H.I. Clifford', 1818, *Quarterly Review*, vol. 18, No.36 (January 1818), 308–24, London, John Murray

Ralfe, J., 1828, *Naval Biography of Great Britain*, 4 vols., London, Whitmore & Fenn

Rankine, E., 1981, *Cockburnspath: A Documentary History of a Border Parish*, Edinburgh, T. & T. Clark

Revell, A.L., 1979, *Haslar the Royal Hospital*, Gosport, The Gosport Society

Roskil, S.W., 1980, 'A Visit to the Lu-Chu Islands and Napoleon at St.Helena, 1816', *Mariner's Mirror*, 351–357

Russell, Lord John (ed.), 1856, *Memoirs, Journal and Correspondence of Thomas Moore*, vol. IV, London, Longman, Brown, Green, and Longmans

Smalley, D. (ed) 1949, *Domestic Manners of the Americans* by Frances Trollope, New York, Alfred A. Knopf

Smiles, S., 1911, *A Publisher and His Friends: Memoir and Correspondence of John Murray*, John Murray, London

Smith, A., 1925, *Carlyle's Essay on Sir Walter Scott*, London & Toronto, J.M. Dent

Smith, S., 1999, *Cockburnspath: History of a People and a Place*, Dunglass Mill Press

Sultana, D., 1986, *The Journey of Sir Walter Scott to Malta*, Gloucester, Alan Sutton and New York, St. Martin's Press

Syret, D. & Dinardo R. L., 1994, *Commissioned Sea Officers of the Royal Navy, 1660 –1815*, Scholar Press for the Navy Records Society, University of Michigan

Tait, J.G. (ed.), 1950, *The Journal of Sir Walter Scott*, Edinburgh, Oliver & Boyd

Todd, W.B. & Bowden, A., 1998, *Sir Walter Scott: 1796–1832 A Bibliographical History*, Newcastle, USA, Oak Knoll Press

Trollope, F., *Domestic manners of the Americans*, Frances (ed.), Donald Smalley, 1949, New York, Alfred A. Knopf

Tucker, S.C. and Reuter, F.T., 1996, *Injured Honor: The Chesapeake–Leopard Affair, June 22 1807*, Annapolis, Naval Institute Press

Twain, M., 1883, *Life on the Mississippi*, Boston, J.R. Osgood; and London, Chatto & Windus

Wareham, T., 2001, *The Star Captains: Frigate Command in the Napoleonic Wars*, Rochester Chatham, Chatham Publishing

Index

Abbotsford 59, 61, 62, 67–9, 98, 127, 159
Abercorn, Marchioness of (Anne Jean) 67
Adams, John Quincy 84–5
Admiralty 96, 99, 124, 137, 139, 161–62, 166, 168–70, 175
Alceste, HMS 29–31, 35
Alison, Sir Archibald 102–106
America 115, 127–28, 133–35, 140, 144, 146, 150, 155, 168, 171, 175
American War of Independence
Amherst, Lord 30–31, 35, 48
Anderson, Dr. James 173, 175, 177
Arbuthnott, Lady 79
Arbuthnott, Sir William 79
Archduke John of Styria 114, 116, 118–9
Argentina xii, 54
Athenaeum Club xiv, 50, 170
Audubon, John James 75–82, 93, 171, 175
Austria 111–5, 118–121, 171

Balzac, Honore de 114, 141
Banks, Sir Joseph 103, 137
Barham, HMS 98–100
Battle of Waterloo xi, 17, 43–7, 151
Beaufort, Sir Francis xv, 99, 126–8, 162, 168, 169
Berkeley, Admiral George 14–16
Bermuda 13–16
Bertrand, Count 37,42
Biddle, Richard 74
Blackwood's Magazine 102, 138, 141
Board of Longitude 158, 161–2
Board of Ordnance 170
Bolivar, Simon 54, 57, 59
Bombay 23–7
Boston 90
Brienne 4, 38, 42
British Empire xii, 13
Broughton, Captain William Robert 32

Buffalo 85
Burns, Robert 2, 138
Byron, Lord 64, 102–4, 126, 131, 134, 144, 151, 179–80

Calbeck. Miss 16
California ix, xiv, 52, 57, 83
Callao 55–8, 60
Camperdown, Battle of 9
Canada 105, 175
Canova, Antonio 102–3, 114
Canton 30–1
Cape Horn 55, 77
Capel, The Honourable Thomas Blayden 18
Cardigan, Lord 52
Carlyle, Thomas 67
Catania 109–10
Catermole, George 149
Cato Street Conspiracy 147
Ceylon 24–5, 27–8
Chamberlain, Basil Hall 34
Chambers Edinburgh Journal 154, 169
Channing, William Ellery 89
Chatham 18
Cheltenham 153, 155
Chesapeake, USS 14–5
Chile 54–6, 58–9
Church of England 90
Clark, General William 93
Clark, Lady Mary 79
Clifford, Herbert John 34, 37, 42
Clinton, John de Witt 85, 87
Cochrane, Admiral Thomas 54, 56, 59
Cockburn, Lord Henry 4, 8
Cockburnspath Tower 2
Cockerell, Charles Robert 77
Coleridge, Samuel Taylor 103
Colosseum, Regent's Park 170
Columbus, Ohio 91–2
Commissioners for Northern Lights 170

Conrad, Joseph xv
Constable, Archibald 131–2, 134–8
Constable, George 99, 100
Constable, Thomas 48
Constable's Miscellany 36, 47, 67–70, 135–8
Conway, HMS 55–7, 136, 162
Cook, Capt. James 14, 136–7
Cooper, Fennimore 84
Copiapó 58
Corcubion 21
Corunna 18–21, 24, 44–5, 148, 151, 174
Cownie, Mrs. 85, 90–3, 114
Cranstoun, Henry 141
Cranstoun, Lord (George Cranstoun) 112
Creek Indians 92
Crimean War 52
Cuidad Rodrigo 139

D'Arcy, Helen 112
Daer, Lord (Basil William Douglas Hamilton) 2, 4
Dalgairn, Mrs 132–3, 136
Dalrymple, Grant 162
Davy, Sir Humphry 103, 106, 126
Davy, Lady 103, 118, 142
De Lancey, Lady (neé Magdalene Hall, Sir William Howe's wife) 42, 46–8, 79
De Lancey, Sir William Howe (first husband of Magdalene Hall) 21, 43, 45–7, 79, 139, 148, 156, 173
de Ros, Capt. The Hon Frederick Filygrald 10, 177
Dessera 25
Dickens, Charles 44, 46–7, 48, 51, 144–156, 173
Dove, Heinrich Wilhelm 159
Drummond, Thomas 169
Duke of Wellington 6, 17, 43, 45–7,120, 139

Duncan, Admiral Adam 8, 9
Dundee 99–100, 132–3, 169
Dunglass vii, 1–5, 9, 13, 44, 51–2, 71, 102, 126, 148, 157, 160, 176
    Wemyss, Earl of 102

Edgeworth, Fanny (Maria's sister) 127
Edgeworth, Anna (Maria's sister) 126
Edgeworth, Honora (Maria's sister) 129
Edgeworth, Maria viii, xiv, 126–30, 1501, 161
Edinburgh xiv, 2, 4–6, 8–10, 36, 46, 48–50, 62, 65, 71–82, 87, 99, 102, 108, 112, 114, 126, 131–135, 141–2, 159–60, 164–5, 169, 178
Edinburgh Literary Journal, The 135, 143
Edinburgh Review, The 36, 72–3, 80, 127, 131, 134, 161
Edinburgh University 5, 76, 80, 112, 142, 158
Elephanta Caves 26
Elliot, Captain 169
Ellis, Henry 36
Endymion, HMS 18, 21–2, 44–5
Erie Canal 83, 87
Erskine, William 26–7
Essex, Earl of 18
Europe 5, 25, 31, 35, 39, 61, 73–4, 76, 84, 86–7, 102, 104, 106–110, 113, 115, 118, 121, 129, 154, 158, 166

Faraday, Michael 170
Fast Castle 1, 2, 5, 9
Ferguson, Sir Adam 64–5, 126
Firth of Forth 1, 9
Fitzroy, Captain Robert 106, 161
Florence 29, 102–3, 106
Forbes, James David 110, 144, 158–9, 162–3
Foster, Henry 161–2
Fragments of Voyages and Travels vii, 21, 25, 97, 134–5, 143, 164
France 4, 42, 80, 121, 130
Franklin, Sir John 89, 131, 175
French Revolution xi, 54, 103, 128

Galapagos Islands 57–8, 161–2, 165
Galignani, Giovanni Antonio 134
Gallatin, Albert 128
Gemallaro, Mario 110
General Hewitt, HMS 29–30
Goethe, Johann Wolfgang von 118
Graham, Sir James 96–7, 166
Grand Tour 4, 49, 102, 108
Grant, Elizabeth 36

Grant, Mrs. Anne of Laggan 142
Graz 15–6, 121, 124, 179–80
Greenhill, Alexander 169
Greenough, George Bellas 170
Greenwich Mean Time 171
Grenville, Baron William Wyndham 15
Gurwood, Col. John 139

Hainfeld 115–7, 119–23, 125, 130, 140, 142, 146, 166, 178
Halifax, Nova Scotia xiii, 8, 10, 12–4, 16
Hall, Basil
    Artist 85,133
    Assessment of 35–6, 59–60, 78, 105–6, 126, 130, 143, 161
    Character xi, xiv–xv, 10, 12–3, 15–6, 31–33, 36, 49, 50–52, 55, 57, 60, 77, 81, 85, 96, 98, 105–7, 124–7, 129, 132–138, 141, 143–144, 147–153
    Death 107, 176–7
    Death of son 152–4
    Early life xi, 6, 8–9
    Family 71, 73, 77–80, 83, 91, 107–8, 114, 118–123, 148, 151, 154, 155
    Insanity 173, 175–7
    Writer 17, 30–1, 34–6, 39, 50, 60–7, 78, 84–6, 89, 91, 93–95, 101, 103–4, 107–8, 110, 115, 125–144, 146, 148, 152–3, 155–6, 161–2, 164, 168–171, 173
    Locations named after Hall family 22, 32
    Naval Career xii, 9–13, 15, 17, 19, 44, 55
    Politics xiv, 59, 86–7, 89–90, 94, 106, 128–9, 134, 138–40
    Scientific interest xv, 5, 17, 35, 77, 87, 90, 93, 103–6, 109–10, 157–172
    Views on Scotland 72–73, 75, 77, 79
    Views on United States 85, 88–90, 94–5, 128, 133, 140
Hall, Basil Sidmouth de Ros (eldest surviving son of Basil Hall) 114, 146, 177
Hall, Eliza (first daughter of Basil Hall) 74, 83, 87–8, 91–3, 105, 108, 114, 176
Hall, Fanny Emily (second daughter of Basil Hall) 114
Hall, Frances ('Fanny'– sister to Basil Hall) 51–2, 65–6, 102, 164

Hall, Frederick (first son of Basil Hall, died aged 4 years) 107
Hall, Frederick Richard (second son of Basil Hall) 152, 177
Hall, James (Basil's brother) xii, 6, 43, 46, 50, 62, 65, 69, 76–7, 107–9, 139, 163, 173, 176, 112, 114, 159–161, 175
Hall, John (eldest son of Sir James) 126
Hall, Katherine (sister to Basil Hall) 52, 66, 74–5
Hall, Lady Helen (mother to Basil Hall) 1, 13, 43, 73
Hall, Magdalene (Lady De Lancey, sister of Basil) 21, 42–53, 79, 102, 148, 151, 175
Hall, Margaret (nee Hunter, Basil Hall's wife) 2, 36, 52, 65, 74–5, 88, 108, 114, 124, 133, 164, 173, 175–7
Hall, Sir James (father to Basil) vii, 2, 4–6, 9–10, 17, 29, 39, 76–7, 102
Hall, Sir John (1st Baronet) 1
Hall, William (son of Sir James) 6
Hamilton, Duchess of 73
Hamilton, William of Bangour 4
Hammer-Purgstall, Joseph von 123
Hardy, Sir Thomas 55, 166
Harvey, Major Henry xii, 48, 52–3, 151
Haslar Hospital 152, 173–5
Henderson, Thomas 165
Herschel, Lady 164–6
Herschel, Sir John Frederick William xi, 110, 158, 164–6, 168
Herschel, William 126, 167
Honourable East India Company 17, 24–5, 36, 48, 52
Hood, Sir Samuel 18, 20, 24–5
Humboldt, Alexander von 36, 135, 159
Hunter, Jane (sister to Margaret) 36
Hunter, Lady Elizabeth Barbara (second wife and widow of Sir John Hunter, father of Margaret Hall, (neé Hunter) 43, 74, 77, 79–80
Hunter, Lady Jean Dickson (wife of General Sir Martin Hunter) 13–6, 30, 73–4, 144, 173, 175–6
Hunter, Margaret (daughter of Sir John) 52, 65, 74
Hunter, Mary (daughter of Sir John and Lady Hunter) 52
Hunter, Sir John (father of Margaret,

Basil Hall's wife) 52, 74
Hunter, Sir Martin 13
Hunter, Sir William 80
Hutton, James 5, 9

Illustrious, HMS 24
India 6, 17, 20
Ingles, Henry Raeburn 81
Invincible, HMS 17
Ireland 88–9, 102, 169
Irving, Washington 144
Italy 103, 108–9, 114, 129, 176

Jackson, Andrew 84
Jameson, Robert 76, 78
Japan 34, 36, 39
Java 28, 30
Jefferson, President Thomas 93
Jeffrey, Francis 73, 80, 126
Johnston, Agnes Scott 176
Johnston, Alexander Keith (snr.) 8
Johnston, Catherine 50–1
Johnston, Charlotte 42

Kater, Captain Henry 57, 161–2
Kerr, Lord Robert 120, 126
Kerr, W.Raleigh 120
Kingston (Canada) 88–9
Kingston (England) 154, 177
Korea/ns xii, 32, 34–35, 39, 131

Lake Erie 85, 88
Lake George 89
Lake Ontario 88
Lake Geneva 106
Leander, HMS xiii, 10, 12, 14, 80
Leith 169
Leopard, HMS 14–5
Lewis, Meriwether 83, 93
Lima 55–7, 77
Linnean Society of London 78
Literary Gazette, The 135, 143
Liverpool 76–7, 83
Lockhart, John Gibson 61–2, 65, 67,
    69, 96, 98, 108, 126, 138–43
Lockhart, Sophia 98
London Geological Society xiv, 160,
    162, 170–1
Londonderry, Marchioness of 48,
    71, 157
Longwood 37–8
Loo-Choo 33, 39, 70, 102, 106, 135,
    161
Lowe, General Sir Hudson 42
Lowe, Lady Susan
Lucien, Charles 90
Lyell, Sir Charles 106, 109, 160–1
Lyons 104, 105

Lyra, HMS 29–31, 34–5, 37, 48

Mackenzie, Henry 73
Madras 25, 27, 37, 48
Madrid 74–5, 85
Maitland, Captain Frederick 42
Manchester 76
Manila 39
Mantua 114
Marquis of Wellesly, Richard 17
Martin, General Don José de
    San 54–60
Massachusetts 87
Maxwell, Sir Murray 29, 34–5
Maypo, Battle of 54
McCartney, Lord 30
McLeod, John 33, 36
Melville Island 161
Melville, Lord 35, 137
*Memoirs of the Life of Sir Walter
    Scott* 62, 69
Mexico 55, 58, 161
Milan 12, 102, 115
Miller, General 59
Minto, Lord 73
Mississippi 79, 83–4, 92–4
Mitchell, Sir Andrew 8, 10, 14
Monthly Review, The 143
Moore, Sir John 18, 20
Moore, Thomas 47, 103, 131, 134
Mount Etna 109–10, 155
Murchison, Sir Roderick 171
Murray, John 48, 102, 131–6, 138
Mysore 24–5,27

Napier, Lord 15–6
Napier, Macvey 136, 139, 161
Naples 102, 108, 114–5
Napoleon Bonaparte 4, 21, 37–43, 54,
    81, 90, 102, 114–5, 130–1, 138
Napoleonic Wars 18, 43, 52, 54, 77,
    102, 121
Nelson, Admiral Horatio 18, 24
Nepean, Sir Evan 23, 35
New Brunswick 131
New England 89
New Orleans 79, 83, 92
New York 79–80, 83, 85–7, 93
Niagara 79, 88
Niagara Falls 88, 128
Nile, Battle of 18, 24
Norfolk, USA 15, 91
North America 8, 14, 43, 74, 77,
    83–4, 89, 93–4, 127–8, 133, 135,
    140, 146, 168, 175
North Sea 1, 8, 148
Nova Scotia xiii, 8, 10, 12, 30, 74,
    132, 171

Nugent, Count 115

Ottawa River 89
Owen Glendower, HMS 56
Oxford University 144, 155

Padua 102, 114
Palermo 105, 110
Paris 4, 47, 51, 73–4, 103, 105, 108,
    128, 134, 140–41, 161, 170, 176
Pasley, Sir Charles 168
Patchwork xiv, 109–10, 146, 159, 171
Peace of Luneville 114
Pei Ho River 30–31
Peking 29–31
Pelet, Baron 130
Peninsular War xi, 18, 27, 43–45, 54,
    74, 139
Peru 54–60
Peterborough (Canada) 88
Petrarch 102
Philadelphia 71
Philosophical Transactions 57, 161
Pictet, Marc-August 159
Pierce, John 80
Platteklip Gorge 160
Playfair, John 5, 10, 131
Portsmouth 45, 52, 96, 98–100, 131,
    136, 149, 152, 170, 173, 177
Purdie, Tom 65
Purfleet 169
Purgstall, Count (Gottfried Friedrich
    Wenceslaus) 112–4
Purgstall, Countess (neé Jane Anne
    Cranstoun) xv, 110, 112–115,
    120, 130, 140–2, 179

Qing Dynasty 30
Quarterly Review, The 36, 65, 94, 108,
    138–41, 143, 179
Queen Victoria xi, 43, 50, 146

Raeburn, Sir Henry iv, 6, 81, 126
Rathbone, William 76–7
Rawlinson, H.G. 28
Reynolds, Captain John 52–3
Richardson, Sir John 89, 173, 175
Rideau Canal 88
Riegensburg 111
Rio de Janeiro 30, 161, 165
River Tweed 64, 158
Rochester 88
Rockhall 21-2
Roman Catholicism 59, 120, 123–5
Rome 49, 102, 106–7, 114, 125, 164,
    168
Rosa, Salvatore 104–5
Roseberry, Lord 38

Royal Academy 38, 149
Royal Astronomical Society xiv, 161–2, 164–5
Royal Geographical Society xiv, 162, 173
Royal George, HMS 99–100, 168
Royal Institution 80, 103
Royal Institution for the Encouragement of Fine Arts in Scotland 82
Royal Scottish Academy 80
Royal Society 5–6, 103, 160, 162, 164
Royal Society of Edinburgh xiv, 5, 10, 39, 77, 82, 123, 160
Russell, Sir James 158
Rzewuska, Countess (Evelinede Hanska) 114

Sabine, Captain Edward 161
Salisbury Crags (Arthur's Seat) 160
Samuel, Joseph 147, 149–50
Santiago 56
Santiago de Compostela 21
Savannah 92
Schiller, Friedrich 118
Scott, Jane 98
Scott, Mrs. Thomas 65
Scott. Sir Walter
    General 5, 6, 8, 69, 76, 112–3, 121, 129, 130, 159
    writer/storyteller 1, 9, 36, 42, 47–8, 61, 63–7, 72, 94, 98, 112–3, 116, 130–31, 134–5, 140–1, 179–80
    Interests 63, 65–6
    Character 64–69, 73, 98–100, 117, 129, 140, 180
    In Edinburgh 68–9, 73, 77, 81–2
    Relations with Basil Hall xii, xv, 8, 46-8, 61, 63, 65, 67-69, 77, 81, 94, 96, 98–100, 135–36
    En route to Malta 96, 98–9, 142
Scottish Enlightenment vii, xi, 2, 6, 8, 35, 71, 112
Selkirk, Earls of, 6, 175
Seringapatam 25, 48
Siccar Point, East Lothian 9
Sidney Smith 127

Simplon Pass 102, 106
Slough 24, 165–6
Smollett, Tobias George xii, xv, 71, 73, 108
Smyth, Captain W.H. 110
Somerville, Mary xi, 161, 163–4, 175
Soult, General 18
South Africa 158, 160, 164–6
South America xi, 50, 54–7, 59, 60, 70, 74, 78, 90, 103, 106, 129, 132, 135–8, 156, 161–5, 169, 171
South Chungcheong, Korea 32
Southey, Robert 103
Southsea 155, 173, 177
Spain 21, 27, 44, 52, 54, 85, 90, 148
Spithead 8, 29, 149, 168–9
St. Bernard 102
St. Blas, California 52, 57
San Blas, Mexico 58, 161
St. Helena 37–8, 42–3, 130–1
St. Kilda 22
St. Lawrence 88–9
St. Louis 79, 93
Staunton, Sir George 30
Steirmark 112
Stephenson, George 2
Stevenson, Alan 169–70
Stevenson, David 171
Stevenson, Robert 9, 169
Stewart de Rothesay, Lady 73
Stewart, Dugald 73, 112, 142
Story, Jude Joseph 85
Stuart, Gilbert 85
Styria 110–3, 115, 117–8, 124–5, 130, 142–3, 166
Sulphur Island 36
Switzerland 192

Table Mountain 159–60
Tacoo 31
Teide 169
Tenerrife 169
Tepic, Mexico 58
Thackery, William Makepeace 126
Thomson, Dr. 133
Thomson, Thomas 112
Ticknor, George 85
Tipoo Sultan 24

Trafalgar, Battle of 18
Transactions of the Bombay Literary Society 26
Trieste 115–6, 121
Trincomalee 24
Trollope, Frances 60, 94
Tuscany 102
Twain, Mark 86, 94
Tyrol 115

United Services Journal, The 10, 120, 143, 168–71
United States of America/USA 78–9, 85, 89, 94, 115, 128

Valparaiso 55–759, 164–5, 169
Vaughan, Sir Charles Richard 85
Venice 102–4, 131
Vesuvius 102, 104, 109, 159
Vienna ix, 114, 119–20
Vigo 18
Ville de Malan 12
Volage, HMS 23

Warren, Lady 16
Warren, Sir Borlase 14–6
Warriston House 112
Washington 85, 90–1
Waverley Novels 61, 67, 62, 98–9, 124, 126, 134–5, 149,
Webster, Daniel 84
Welland Canal 88
Wellesley Pole 17
Wellesley, General Arthur 24
Wernerian Society 76–8
West Indies 12, 24, 89–90, 106
Whampoa 35
White, Lydia 127
Whitney, Eli 84
Wilkinson, Sir John Gardner 155
Wilmot-Horton, Sir John 88
Wolf's Crag 9
Wollaston, Sir William Hyde 161–4
Worcester 49, 155
Wordsworth, Dorothy 98
Wordsworth, William 103